SERGEANT PEPPER

Covenant in the Jungle

STEPHEN PAUL CAMPOS

"He reached down from on high and took hold of
me: he drew me out of deep waters. He rescued me
from the powerful enemy". Psalm 18:16-17

authorHOUSE'

AuthorHouse™
1663 Liberty Drive
Bloomington, IN 47403
www.authorhouse.com
Phone: 833-262-8899

Published by AuthorHouse 02/08/2021

ISBN: 978-1-4817-2347-3 (sc)
ISBN: 978-1-4817-2348-0 (hc)
ISBN: 978-1-4817-2349-7 (e)

Library of Congress Control Number: 2013904129

★　★　★　★

"Because of my Marine brothers I lost in Vietnam, I was very angry with the people here in the U.S. This book is so raw with the truth that it will make you laugh, cry and hate what was done to the Vietnam Veteran. We never lost this war but the public was told a lie by the media and the Vietnam Veteran is still paying the price. Let the healing begin and the demons die with this book." *CPL J.C. Corella, Delta Company, 9th Engineers, USMC 1966*

"I didn't have any problem when I came home from either tour—I was in a supportive environment, both at home and at 'work.' Then about 2004, I had an emotional breakdown. First, I curled up in bed and cried for about a week, and then I sat in church for about a week, begging God to help me to open my heart. Then, I went to the VA. Both the church and the VA gave me the help I needed. I'm pretty much OK now, but I remain on medication.'

"My problems were due to survivor guilt and leader's guilt. I am bothered that so many better men than I died when I was allowed to live. I am hugely bothered that men were killed while doing something I told them to do. My only 'anger' has to do with not being allowed to win that war. LT. Col. Hugh Foster United States Army Retired served two tours in Vietnam with a combat infantry division." *1968-1969: First LT. 5th/12th/199th. Light Infantry Division-3rd. Platoon Leader 1970-1971 Hugh Foster served as a rifle company commander captain for the 1st Cav. Div. (B/1-5 Cav.) He retired in 1990 as a LT. Col.*

"I enjoyed each of the stories that I read from your book. Amazing when you look back over a long winding road and see the faithful hand of God.—Isn't it?" *Dr. David Seifert - Senior Pastor- Shelter Cove Community Church, Modesto, California*

"I also personally identified with the struggles of coming

home and not being able to find a decent job and being rejected to the point of having to work in the fruit and vegetable fields until God put me on the right path. I too put my faith in our Lord and learned to cope with the many obstacles that were placed in front of me…I know that your personal story is not just of your struggles returning home. It identifies with thousands of what other returning Warriors have gone through and many that are returning will go through. Thank you for touching my life and the lives of many others with your written word." *Jess Quintero, National Secretary Hispanic War Veterans of America, Washington, DC*

"Steve, my personal problems from Vietnam stem from when I came home. It is not the government that I have problems with but rather the American public. It was not the fact of being treated with open hostility or behavior from a few idiots, but rather the quiet snickers behind my back when people learned I had served. The questioning looks your friends gave you when they asked you why you didn't get out of serving, of people not letting you explain or talk of Vietnam, telling you they did not want to hear of your experiences. I can't tell you how many people told me to forget that silliness in Asia and get on with my life.'

"I became an isolationist, a functioning alcoholic, and a hard hearted S.O.B. when people got too close. As I get older I guess I have mellowed to an extent with the exception of one thing: I will never forget how America treated her Warriors who came home from an unpopular war and I can never truly forgive them. The irony is that knowing what I know now, I would have still served in Vietnam. It was the right thing to do. Take care and God Bless my old comrade in arms." *Sgt. Huel Dale Attaway Co. C 5th Battalion 12th Infantry 199th Light Infantry Brigade, Republic of Vietnam*

★ ★ ★ ★

PREFACE

There is a battle that goes on inside the human spirit. The battlefield is our very life, in our mind and spirit. There is also another battle that is fought in times of war, death, and tragedy. After such tragedy we dare to find some kind of inner peace. We struggle in search of new birth, serenity, and love.

Since, returning home from Vietnam as a combat infantry soldier, I have been fighting other battles that go on deep inside my soul. I am like many others who have faced war, death, and the fears of the unknown. I have found something that gives me hope each day as I try to find my life's purpose, and as I reflect on what happened to me through all the tragedies of my life.

There is a particular Bible passage that I have read over and over again in an effort to make sense of my madness. It is said to have been written by one of the wisest men who ever lived. This is what King Solomon wrote in Ecclesiastes 3:1-8:

There is a time for everything,

And a season for every activity under heaven:
A time to be born and a time to die,
A time to plant and a time to uproot, A
time to kill and a time to heal,

A time to tear down and a time to build, A
time to weep and a time to laugh,
A time to mourn and a time to dance, A time to
scatter stones and a time to gather them,
A time to embrace and a time to refrain, A
time to search and a time to give up,
A time to keep and a time to throw away,
A time to tear and a time to mend,
A time to be silent and a time to speak, A time to love
and a time to hate, A time for war and a time for peace.

After my combat experiences I have faced many challenges,
I have succeeded in overcoming some of my fears and anxieties
to some degree. Yet, each challenge has its own obstacles. It is
during these transitions that I find it most difficult to adapt. I
try not to fail, so I become an introvert and dysfunctional. I try
too hard and I become proud or arrogant. Sometimes I think
I'm more powerful and stronger than my enemies, so I distance
myself. I think, maybe the dead are better off, for they no longer
have to endure these struggles.

I experienced many dysfunctions after my combat experiences.
I believe we are all born dysfunctional in one form or another. It
shows up in our relationships, our attitudes our tendency to self-
destruct, and in the way we deal with the stresses and pressures
of life.

I believe our short life on earth is to be able to find our God
given purpose and to find a better way to live and to overcome
our dysfunctions.

This is what my story is about: Surviving the turmoil and
uncertainties of life and trying to heal and make sense of them
afterward. This is my personal journey from my "in-sanity" in
my addictions and dysfunctions to new birth, hope, peace and
serenity.

I found it impossible to fit back into society after experiencing combat. In Vietnam, I had real camaraderie with those whom I fought beside. My buddies and I took care of one another in the jungles, and we took care of ourselves — we had our M-16's always at the ready to take care of any threat. We felt secure among ourselves. We trusted one other. We loved one another.

When I came home from Vietnam, all of that was gone. I had no one to trust, because the kind of trust we earned in combat does not translate to society in general. I had no comrades to care for and no comrades to care for me.

Finding it difficult to handle my own emotions, I denied even having them. I denied that anything was wrong with me. Yet, it was obvious to others whenever they would see me jump or hit the deck whenever a car backfired. I often found myself scanning my surroundings, still looking and waiting to hear an explosion or automatic-weapon fire coming my way. I kept guarded as I watched and listened for signs of the enemy. Those combat instincts and fears do not go away easily. The fear and trembling inside never go away.

The fear of the unknown I experienced from combat led to nightmares about returning to Vietnam tour after tour. In my dreams I would tell the Army that I had already been to Vietnam, but they kept sending me back to fight anyway. I would wakeup time and again with those thoughts fresh in my mind.

During the down times off the battlefield, some of us used alcohol and marijuana to have a good time and to forget about our surroundings and our fears. Booze and drugs hid the panic attacks I was experiencing then and would still experience years later.

Confronted by the fear of death and the unknown, I felt myself enveloped in a gray cloud, virtually paralyzed by a deep sense of anxiety. I noticed that in combat many of my fellow brothers reacted to stress differently on the battlefield than off. There were a few men who went crazy with fear and had to be taken off the field. There were others who put a bullet in their foot and were taken home.

Then there were those men who loved war, who relished the challenges of facing down danger as they would hunt and kill the enemy. They became apart of the land and the elements. They loved the rush of fear and were valiant in battle.

Most of us internalized and withheld our fears. We played the part of the soldier that goes against a man's nature. Character, values, and upbringing may determine how we react to the pressures in life, but our training and education as soldiers taught us how to survive, how to react quickly and instinctively to any threat. We were trained to go above and beyond the normal call of duty.

In the Army, we were taught to react under fire. We were trained over and over on what to do when fired upon. We were trained how to use our weapons and to become skilled in battle. Teamwork was essential; following orders was crucial. Soldiers could lose their lives or be taken prisoner if they failed to follow orders.

In training, it was easy to follow orders, because there was no fear involved. There are no real bullets flying at your head, no one getting wounded or killed alongside you. There is not the confusion that sometimes happens in real combat. After the training exercises were over we could sleep in comfortable barracks, safe and secure.

The Army was very good in training us to follow orders and not to surrender. Our drill sergeants and officers were the best. They instilled discipline and made us tough.

When it was time to be sent to Vietnam, I felt I was ready. I was ready to fight. I was ready to kill the enemy. I was ready to win on the battlefield. I was skilled, I was trained, and I was determined to follow orders that would save my life.

Then the day came when everything was real. I woke up in the mud with my feet in ankle-deep water. At times I would be in a river with water up to my chest filled with leaches and dysentery. Or sleeping in the bush with the rain pounding on my helmet, soaked to the bone. I was wet from head to toe and my feet had jungle rot.

All the training in the world and all the education will not help with the mental aspects of dealing with the elements or killing your fellow man. In combat, it's easy to become disoriented. Adrenaline rushes throughout your body, and you get tunnel vision. There is confusion and chaos. The best you can do is to tremble with fear inside while letting your instincts from training take over and control you're every move.

Gunfire and explosions disorient you even more. There is smoke all around, and it can become hard to see. All around you weapons are firing, and the thick smoky air takes on the smell of burning rubber.

People are yelling at each other trying to make sense of the situation. You have officers and sergeants telling you what to do. When someone is wounded, there is screaming and moaning. It feels like you're in hell after everything stops.

Sometimes, I would feel extreme anxiety. My breathing and heart rate would increase. My heart would feel like it was moving up into my throat. It would be hard to catch my breath. My body and hands would sweat; my mouth would go dry, and it would become hard to swallow. I would fear I was dying.

The anxiety would paralyze me. I would want to run from the fear and trembling I felt inside. I would do anything to get out of that feeling. My mind would focus on what terrible things might happen to me.

In battle, soldiers do things in order to stay alive that they would never do otherwise. They react to the situation. They become a different person. They become hardened to death. They learn to kill without emotion. Survival is all that matters — no matter who or what is in the way.

Combat is filled with uncertainty and in-sanity. There is an evil presence that is noticeable and acts like a sixth sense. You can feel it, for it surrounds you and speaks to your mind. The only remedy to ease the pain and suffering is prayer.

Many times in combat you have no choice, but to react out of instinct. Sometimes you will try to save yourself and save those you love. Other times all you can do is watch helplessly and powerlessly as soldiers die around you.

Then there is the guilt you feel when you let your buddies down or freeze from fear in combat. You feel like a failure, less than a man. When someone dies, you blame yourself. Combat may come to an end, but the war goes on deep inside, never to go away completely. Years may pass, and you may for a time forget about the trauma you experienced — until some event ignites the memory and the insanity returns.

When I got out of the Army in 1970 I used marijuana and alcohol, not knowing the side effects it would have on me later in life. I didn't realize then that it helped me avoid facing my emotions and my problems. It altered my perception of reality and stole my self-worth. It possessed me and fed my rebellious nature. The demons that haunted me after Vietnam seemed fresh, horrible, and unmanageable.

I was so eager to get on with my life after the Army that I tried everything in order to gain acceptance by my peers. I tried to fit in as though I was normal, but deep inside the war had changed me. I didn't realize it until it was almost too late. For you who have been in combat **PLEASE take heed and get help**. War does change a person. But, we can overcome it and make something beautiful out of our lives.

Most of all, I wanted to tell everyone about my Vietnam experiences, but they all shut me out. They all opposed the war and talked only about the terrible things they saw on television. I tried to be positive and tell them the truth, but they would not listen. I wanted to tell them that our soldiers were great warriors and that we were winning the battles daily on the battlefield. I wanted to tell them how our military was helping the Vietnamese to win their freedom and that they were being deceived by the media.

No one listened. No one wanted to hear the truth. No one

wanted to understand how our young men were fighting with courage and dignity.

I was one of the few who had come home from the battlefield with honors from my combat unit. I was proud of my service to my country and my duty. Yet, I was soon to be silenced by the negative reactions from the American public and even my own friends.

So, I became angry and felt numbed by the rejection. I tried to forget all about my military service, my experiences in Vietnam. Along with most everyone who served in this unpopular war, I became silent.

I withdrew into my own world of self-destruction and hardened my heart. I distanced myself from everyone over the way Vietnam veterans were treated with disrespect and indignity. I became a cold hearted, self-centered person.

Yet, despite everything I have been through, something sustained me. I was on the brink of suicide. The powerful dark forces called out for me to kill myself.

In my anguish and pain I cried out for help. I was going insane. My addictions had captured my soul.

Later that morning I saw a light of hope that captured my heart and soul. I was given a second chance. I was changed by a power greater than myself. It set me free and broke the chains of my addiction.

So, here I am, ready to say it, now, after many years of denial; "I am FINALLY ready to face the demons of my past."

Stephen Paul Campos 1968

Chaplain Lickey- Medal of Honor recipient

★ ★ ★ ★

DEDICATION

I wrote this book because of my profound love for fellow combat brothers James L. ("Dyckes") Dyckhoff and Eric ("Tiger") Yingst, and my love for God and country. I dedicate this book to their courage and companionship that helped me stay alive. We share a common bond of brotherhood and a love that unites us against the forces of good and evil.

I also want to acknowledge the men and women who fought in Vietnam, to all those who suffered and those who gave their lives. I especially dedicate this to the men I fought side by side with in Vietnam during the years in April 1968 to April 1969, my fellow combat brothers of the 199th. Light Infantry Brigade, Charlie Company 5th, 12th Infantry Division and Charlie Company 4th of the12th.Infantry. Our combat experiences changed us, and we changed America's future!

I dedicate this book also to my wife Kathy, who has allowed me to dream once again and encouraged me to write this book; and to my sons — Christian, Matthew, Nicholas and Kelly — who are the crowns of my life and the joy in my heart.

I am thankful for the opportunity to have served in the U.S. Armed Forces and to fight in Vietnam. It taught me to value life, to appreciate our military forces, and to finally accept my role in this war, even though it is years later.

To all those people who have influenced my life for better or for worse, to all of those who have traveled with me on my road in life. God has placed them in my life at certain times to help me overcome rejection, failure, and resentment. I hold all of them in my mind and heart forever. I thank you for sharing your life with me.

And, of course, I dedicate this book to God, who intervened at the right time and gave me a new life and second chance when I was deep into my addictions.

★ ★ ★ ★

FOREWORD

The **peace sign** was very popular in my day. It was designed and used first in Britain in the **Campaign for Nuclear Disarmament** and became a major symbol of the 1960s counterculture. In the US and Canada, it became synonymous with opposition to the Vietnam War.

The counterculture **of the 1960s** was a cultural phenomenon that developed first in the United States and United Kingdom and spread throughout much of the Western world between the early 1960s and the early 1970s. The movement gained momentum during the U.S. government's extensive military intervention in Vietnam.

As the 1960s progressed, widespread tensions developed in American society that tended to flow along generational lines regarding the war in Vietnam, race relations, human sexuality, women's rights, traditional modes of authority, experimentation with psychoactive drugs, and differing interpretations of the American Dream.

New cultural forms emerged, including the pop music of the British band the Beatles and the concurrent rise of hippie culture, which led to the rapid evolution of a youth subculture that emphasized change and experimentation. In addition to the Beatles, many song writers, singers and musical groups from the

United Kingdom and America came to impact the counterculture movement.

1960-1969 was more than just a decade; it was a state of mind. The SIXTIES were an exciting, revolutionary, turbulent time of great social and technological change: assassination, unforgettable fashion, new musical styles, civil rights, women's liberation, a controversial and divisive war in Vietnam, the first man landing on the moon, peace marches, World's Fairs, flower power, great TV & film, and sexual freedom.

Due to the baby boom between 1945 and 1955, over half the population was under 30 years old. To say these young people had a strong desire to change the world, would be an understatement. They began to revolt against society to make their statement to do away with the conservative beliefs of the adult world.

Most of their demonstrations were peaceful; they merely wanted to be an example that they could live in their own society, and create their own social system. The most famous demonstration that was held was Woodstock. It took place in 1969, and lasted for 3 days. It was a living example that a large number of people could stay together for an extended period of time with peace and love in their hearts. The hippies, as they were called, were frequently known as the lost generation. They rejected traditional family values in order to have other arrangements based on love.

The styles of music were drastically different than past eras. Now that teenagers had money to spend on music, much of the music produced was directed towards them. The music reflected the new sexual permissiveness and drug trends. There was no ONE style of music that was most popular. There was a revival of folk music, African American artists were beginning to be played more, rock and roll continued to be mainstream, and Motown was born. The most popular music was by the Beach Boys, Bob Dylan, the Beatles, the Supremes, the Everly Brothers, the Rolling Stones, Jimi Hendrix, Janis Joplin, Sonny and Cher, the Who, and The Doors.

Unfortunately, when our soldiers came home after serving their country they were caught up in the turmoil and confusion of this society. They were looked down upon by the media and the public. So, they became silent and withdrew. Internalizing their anger and not being accepted by society many veterans turned to drugs and alcohol in order to cope and fit in.

TABLE OF CONTENTS

★ ★ ★ ★

$\bigstar$ $\bigstar$ $\bigstar$ $\bigstar$

I: THE AGE OF AQUARIUS

✯ ✯ ✯ ✯

CHAPTER 1: RESPECT – ARETHA FRANKLIN

The Assignment Editor for a large newspaper was sitting behind his desk with a letter in his hand.

Across from him sat a reporter, named Jonathan. He had a notepad in his lap. His head was down and he was taking notes, as fast as he could.

The editor spoke, "Jonathan, I received a letter from the editor from our affiliate newspaper in Northern California. They want to do a story on their hometown war veteran. They didn't say much, except that three combat men were meeting to honor a vow "unto death" made after a firefight in 1968". Jonathan stands. The editor hands him a note.

The editor continued, "They're meeting together for the first time in forty years. Here's the phone number for one of the vets who lives in Baltimore. Find out why it's taken them so long to meet".

Jonathan takes the note and places it on his notepad and heads back to his seat. He takes out his notepad and places it out in front of him. Then he takes the note and dials. The telephone on the other side rings a few times and someone finally answers.

"Hello". "Hello, I'm calling for Stephen Campos, the Vietnam veteran. My name is Jonathan Miller. I'm from your home town newspaper.

"Yes, this is he", I answered.

"Mr. Campos. The newspaper would like to do a story on you and your two combat buddies.

I smiled and took a deep breath. Next, to my phone was a framed photograph on the table. It was a picture of three twenty year- old Army soldiers.

Jonathan spoke, "Mr. Campos, uh, Mr. Campos"?

Tears filled my eyes. "Yes". I said.

"I understand you haven't seen each other since you were together in combat".

"That's correct, I said.

"That was in 1968?

"Yes, that's correct".

"Well, we're going to run your story on the front page this coming Memorial Day. So, we need to meet, but first I want to ask you a few questions".

I was suddenly angry. "Questions"? "Look, I served in combat and risked my life. And then when I came home I was called a "baby killer and loser". We veterans were looked down upon like dirt and scum".

"That's why we're talking, Mr. Campos. America is ready to hear the rest of the story. We know now that you soldiers were mistreated and we want to make things right. I just need the truth".

"Okay, I understand. Excuse me for my anger. I guess I still have a lot of deep rooted feelings inside. Please, call me Stephen".

Jonathan starts to write, "Ah, Mr. Campos, I mean, Stephen, are you from an Army family?

"No, I said. But, I always played soldier when I was a kid".

It was 1958. I was 10-years-old. I was walking down the street near my grandfather's house by Baldwin Street and I had to take a leak. So, I looked around, nobody was watching. I dashed behind a home. You know, when you got to go, you got to go!

I had to pee so bad that I didn't realize what was before me. When I finally looked up my eyes widen. It was a bright forest, colorful with big trees. It looked like a jungle. I was amazed. Hurriedly, I tried to zip up my pants. Halfway, I gave up. I turned and started running back towards my grandparent's house. In the front yard all my cousins were playing. I turned the corner and jumped over the hedges onto the grass.

My whole family was there. We were celebrating Easter. All my aunts and uncles and cousins attended during the holidays. We always had a turkey dinner with all the trimmings. My grandmother always made sweet-tasty tamales and Pumpkin pie, yum!

I was so excited I had found my jungle, that I yelled, "Hey, you guys! You gotta see this! Come on". I waved my arm. "Follow me! And, I sprinted back down the street. I turned and yelled, "See what I've found".

Most of my cousins followed after me. "There was Ronnie, the oldest, then Wayne, Roger, my brother, Mike and Pat, Rennie and Joann, Chris and Jeff.

A few minutes later we reached the spot.

"Look, over there". I pointed

"It's amazing". "Wow", said Pat.

"Yah, double wow, said Mike. It's, it's a jungle".

Ronnie, 15, the oldest, took charge. 'This is a great place to play Army".

"Yah, I'll be the captain", said Chris.

"Well, I wanna be da captain, too", said Jeff.

"No, you can't" said Chris.

"Yes, I can", said Jeff,

"Shut it, all of you", said Ronnie. "I'm the oldest and I'm in charge. Get in single file from oldest to youngest. We're all going in, Army style".

Everyone took our places, as we slowly entered no man's land.

We were all frightened. We walked a few hundred yards, past two signs that read, "No Trespassing" and "Keep Out".

Boy was I scared we might get caught and get put in jail.

"Keep on the alert men. Look out for signs of the enemy men and watch your step".

Wayne, who was the second oldest at 14 years old, said, "keep your weapons in a ready position, men".

Well, we didn't have any weapons. So, we pretended with our hands like they are holding rifles.

Roger, my brother, was in front of me. He turned and said, "You heard what he said, Butt Head, be on the alert. I don't want to be killed, because of you".

Ronnie, in the front, signaled with his hand in the air, "QUIET! We're deep in enemy territory. The enemy is all around us, so be quiet".

"I'm getting hungry, said Jeff. I want to go back".

A few minutes later Ronnie stopped." Let's go back to Grandpa's work shop and make some weapons and get some grub. Men, we can't fight on an empty stomach."

Personally, I think Ronnie was scared too. Relieved, we all turned around and headed back to grandpa's house.

Back at grandpa's we entered the garage where there was wood, nails and grandpas tools.

"I'll grab the grub", said Joann. She ran out of the garage and into the back door. Everyone else was busy making some kind of wooden gun, pistol, rifle or wooden block to use as a grenade.

Ronnie got finished with his rifle first and said. "Okay, men, five more minutes and we're heading out."

I hurried to find something that resembled a pistol or a rifle. I found a wooden stick. "That will have to do", I said to my.self.

Just then, Joann runs inside holding a small paper bag. "I got the grub, let's go".

Ronnie heads out the garage and we all follow.

Hey, wait for me", Jeff starts to cry. "Wait"!

"Catch up, kid or you can't come with us" said Wayne.

"Okay", said, Jeff, "I'm coming, I'm coming". He ran to catch up.

One hour later we're all walking deeper and deeper into the jungle, we called it.

During our search for the enemy, Chris and Jeff were eating everything in the paper bag. Joann gave it to them to keep them quiet.

"Where's the grub, asked Wayne, I'm hungry".

Joann put her hand down the bag. "Ah, well, it's all gone", said Joann.

"What do you mean, gone, said Wayne? He was angry. "That's all the food we got"? Well, I'll take some water then".

"Ah, I didn't bring water, Wayne. All I got was a few pieces of candy, a pack of bubble gun and some graham crackers. Chris and Jeff ate it all".

A few minutes later, Ronnie dives for cover and yells. "Enemy fire! Bam, Bam, Ka-Bam! You're dead, Chris". You too Jeff, you're dead". The enemy killed you".

Chris, screams, grabs his chest, and falls to the ground. So, does Jeff, both casualties of war.

"Gather round them men. Wayne, you be the Chaplin. Say a few words for the dead, said Ronnie.

We all gathered around Chris and Jeff, who were still lying on the ground. Wayne, folds his hands together. "Ah, we're gathered here.

"Just say the dang words, so they'll go straight to heaven!" yelled Ronnie.

Wayne continues "Ah, in the name of the Father and of the Son"; he makes the sign of the cross.

I close my eyes.

1968 South Vietnam

It was 1968. I was in South Vietnam with my company deep in the jungles, somewhere close to the Cambodian border. Our whole company was assembled together. We are wearing our full Army combat gear and standing in rows, each squad next to each other.

In the front were there are two M-16 rifles jammed into the ground. On top are a steel helmet and an empty pair of combat boots below. This was our first taste of death in Vietnam style.

That day I was surrounded by my best friends, Eric "Tiger" Yingst and James L. Dyckhoff "Dyckes". Our whole brigade had trained together at Fort Lewis, Washington. We all flew over together on April 3, 1968. No one had seen combat before except our company commander and one sergeant. We were all "green" and un-experienced. We had only been in country for two weeks. Our new company commander stepped forward to address the troops.

FLASHBACK – JUNGLE – NIGHT BEFORE

Our company is on search and destroy mission at night. The dark is so dense; each man had to touch the pack of the man in front of him to keep from getting lost. We slowly made our way thought the jungle, not knowing where we are headed.

A FLARE lights up the night and all Hell breaks loose. Tracer rounds and bullets fill the night air. You can smell the smoke. It smells like burning rubber. Soldiers hit the deck or run for cover, returning fire. One soldier takes a sniper bullet to the head. He's flung against a tree like a rag doll. Another soldier takes a barrage of bullets. His body dances as he takes bullet after bullet into his side, opening his body like a can opener. He falls down in the damp jungle.

The night air is filled with the spray of machine-gun bullets and grenade explosions. And then comes the sounds of fear over the company radio, "Captains been hit, Captains been hit, hold your fire! You're firing on your own company. Stop firing on us".

L.T. and I move forward. "Let's go Campos" came the frantic words from my Lieutenant.

Someone yells "We're over here, captains been hit, hurry".

L.T. and I find him. L.T. shines his light on him. Captain is riddled with bullets in both legs. blood is pouring everywhere. He's griming in pain. "Medic", yells L.T, "Medic, give me a damn medic, right now".

It was a bizarre evening. We had gotten separated from the rest of our company. It was pitch dark, so dark; you couldn't see a foot in front of your face. We were on our way back to find the rest of our company.

The darkness led to the confusion. We were lost, so captain sent out a man to find us. Someone freaked out and yelled, "Open fire". We were all on line like a firing squad. Our company was only fifty feet away on the side of the gully.

Two hours later we had the dead and wounded air lifted. We gathered together in small groups of men. The entire company is in shock. Guilt was etched into each face and the fear of "death" hit was like a thick fog that covered the entire company.

All I could do was think about the situation that just occurred. I kept thinking about it, over and over again, replaying the whole scenario in my mind. We could have killed our entire company. Man, we were lucky.

If it wasn't for someone who yelled, cease fire, over the radio there may have been more killed, perhaps the entire company.

My mind was racing uncontrollably. I was in deep depression and anxious. My hands sweat and my mouth felt dry. My heart rate was extremely high and pounding out of my chest. I couldn't stop thinking; my head was numb and pounding with my heart rate.

Then, I started thinking, what if I had gotten killed or wounded? What about Tiger or Dyckes? They were my best friends. How would I feel then?

I couldn't wait any longer. I wandered over to find Dyckes or Tiger. I found Dyckes, first. I needed to tell him he was my best friend and that his friendship meant more to me than just words. I loved these guys and if anything ever happened to them I wouldn't want to live.

"Listen, Dyckes, I need to say something I've been thinking about, where's Tiger?

"I'm right here, man. I can't believe all this shit. We killed a man and wounded our captain. I fired on my own company, man. I can't believe I did it"! I could have been the one who shot the captains legs off".

"Listen up, both of you. I need to talk, in case we don't make it. You guys are my BEST friends. I trust you with my life. If, anything ever happened to either one of you I wouldn't want to live. I love you more than brothers. "I mean it"

"Me, too, Stone Pony". I feel the same way, Bro", said Tiger.

"Man, I love you both. I would die for either of you", said Dyckes.

Tiger extends his arm and hand, "Put it here brothers"!

Tiger leads. "I agree to die for you, Stone Pony and you too. Man, I will protect you guys so one of us gets back home safely.

Dyckes extends his arm and I extend mine. "Stone Pony" and Tiger, let's make a pack to keep each other alive.

"I'm in. I said.

I make this vow to die for you Dyckes and you Tiger. SO, help me. I look up to the heavens.

"Let God and the stars be our witness"!

"I got one more thing to say", said Tiger." When we get back to the world we'll Re-unite!

Dyckes followed, To the World men".

"One for all and one for all", exclaimed Tiger!

We all looked up into the bright stars.

Still in shock and disbelief over what happened that night, I started to numb out the pain. That's the way I handled death. I hardened myself to reality. I didn't want to feel that emotion ever again. I wouldn't allow myself to be vulnerable or I might lose it. It wasn't until forty years later that I would wake up from my denial and face my fears.

Part of my healing today has come from looking back into my life and allowing me to grieve. My healing has come in different time periods during the hardest times of my life. And when I think I don't have the courage to face my problems I sometimes look back and say "I can endure anything with God's help."

When I got back from Vietnam I was hardened. Over the years I started to hate the person I had become. The booze, hangovers and relationships was making me captive to addiction. I always practiced the things that I hated. I could not free myself from the addictions or my mind on my own.

CHAPTER 2: ANOTHER BRICK IN THE WALL – PINK FLOYD

I grew up in Modesto, a small agricultural town in central California rich in produce including various fruits, vegetables, almonds, and dairy products. The agriculture supported a lot of seasonal farm workers from Mexico, and there was much prejudice toward Mexicans in those days.

My heritage is part Mexican, part English, and part Albanian. My father was born in Los Mochias, Mexico, where my grandfather owned a cattle ranch. When my father was a baby, my grandparents had to hide with him during the Mexican revolution in the early 1900s for fear that Pancho Villa and his men might kill the family. The family survived, but Villa and his gang confiscated my grandfather's property and cattle during a pillaging raid.

My grandparents fled across the border to Nogales, Arizona, around 1918. My grandfather found part-time work on the railroads in Utah. He later moved the family to Westwood, high in the mountains of Northern California, where he found full-time work in a lumber mill.

My father started working at the lumber mill when he was fifteen years old to help support the family. They lived in a two-room cabin with neither heat nor air conditioning. The winters were cold and harsh, and the summers reached 105 degrees.

My father was ambitious and wanted something better

for himself. After high school, he attended Sacramento State University, and then went on to earn a teaching credential at the University of California at Berkeley in 1944.

Out of duty to his country, he enlisted in the Navy during World War II and served as a chief petty officer. He met my mother at a dance in New York City after the war had ended. They were married several months later and moved to Houston, Texas, where my father partnered with a Navy buddy in the business of making corn chips.

After a year, the partnership dissolved and my father, mother, and newborn brother moved to Modesto, where my father found work as a Spanish teacher at Modesto High School.

A year later, my father received from his former business partner in Texas a large crate of manufacturing equipment — a conveyor and a corn grinder. So in 1947, he and his brother Ray started a company called Campos Foods and signed a contract to make corn chips for Frito-Lay. Only a year later, however, Frito-Lay moved its manufacturing headquarters to Southern California. The corn chip business couldn't survive, so my father and uncle dissolved it.

My dad went back to teaching Spanish at Modesto High School and tried to sell his equipment. By coincidence, a lady who came to see the equipment stopped by and advised my father to use the equipment to make tortillas.

"I don't know how to make tortillas," my father told her.

"I can show you how to make them," she answered. "You use the same equipment. No one makes them around here. They would be a big hit."

The next weekend, she showed my father how to make the tortillas. He made fifteen dozen tortillas and packed them in plain clear bags. He took them all to the local grocery store and approached the store manager. "Can you sell these in your store?" he asked.

"Sure! We'll give it a try," the manager told him.

The very next day, my father stopped by to ask the store

manager how sales were going. "Just fine," he said, "All your tortillas were sold out just a few hours after you left them. Bring us some more tomorrow... By the way, you'll need a bag with a label to sell them here legally." That is how my father's tortilla-making business, Campos Foods, was established to serve the Central Valley of California.

I was born in 1948. At that time, we lived in a small two-bedroom house. We didn't have much money in those days, so my parents couldn't afford to buy me new clothes. I always got secondhand clothes or toys. As with most kids, Christmas was my favorite time of year.

I am told that when I was only a year old my three-year-old brother, Roger, out of sheer jealousy over the attention I received from our mother, pressed a hot iron against my face as I lay sleeping in my crib. My screams of pain echoed throughout the house.

Similar screams would echo throughout my teens as I often cried out to God in times of trouble.

By the time I was five, Roger and I were playing and fighting with the kids on our block. I learned how to protect myself at an early age. My brother seemed to enjoy watching me fight with the neighborhood bullies.

One day, as I rode my bike home from school, a few rocks sailed over my head from out of nowhere. When I looked back, I saw that it was Steve, a kid from school, who had been throwing them. I peddled my bike faster. When one rock barely missed the side of my head, I got angry.

That night I started plotting a way to get back at Steve. I decided I would make friends with him, win his trust, and then get back at him when he didn't expect it.

The next day, I pretended to be his friend. As we rode our bikes home together that afternoon, however, I let him know how I really felt.

"Hey, Steve, you almost killed me yesterday with that rock

you threw at me!" I told him angrily. "It sailed right past my head."

"Yeah," he laughed.

"Well, here's what I think about that," I told him as I rode alongside him and slugged him as hard as I could right in the middle of his chest. The blow knocked him off his bike. He got back up crying and peddled down the street in the opposite direction as fast as he could.

A couple hours later, I was riding my bike around the block when Steve's big brother, Ken, saw me and started chasing me. "I'm going to kill you!" he shouted. I was scared to death as I rode home, jumped off my bike, ran into the house, and slammed the door behind me.

"What's going on?" my brother asked as I ran into my bedroom.

"I was riding my bike home when this kid threw rocks at me yesterday. I paid him back today. He told his big brother, and now he's going to kill me!" I explained with fear in my voice.

My brother got visibly angry and went outside when the older brother came up to our house.

"Where's your brother?" Ken asked.

"Why?" Roger asked.

"Because I'm going to beat him up," said Ken.

"No you're not," yelled my brother. "You'll have to fight me."

"OK, then I guess I'll beat you up," answered Ken.

My mother ran outside after hearing the screaming, but she thought we were just playing. "If you boys are going to fight, then put on the boxing gloves," she said. We had just gotten some boxing gloves that Christmas. She handed them to my brother.

It seemed the whole neighborhood was gathering to watch the fight between my brother and Steve's brother. We all took a seat on top our 1956 station wagon and watched my brother beat the tar out of Ken, who finally gave up and ran away crying. My brother earned my respect that day. I started looking up to him as my hero.

When my little sister, Cecilia, was born, my father's attention turned to her. She was so cute and sweet, a princess and the apple of my father's eye. I felt my father favored her, but my brother was the one whom I idolized in our family.

Roger was very was popular in school. I always felt inferior to him. He was always at the top of his class and got straight A's. My own friends always got A's and B's while I struggled to get a C. I found it hard to retain information and remember things. I didn't care much about going to college because I figured I wasn't intelligent enough. I always searched for an easier road to travel whenever it came to school.

I always wanted to be with my brother's friends. I wanted them to like me just as they liked him. So wherever my brother went, I followed him. My brother was mean to me and didn't want me around him. He and his friends called me "T-Bone," a nickname I hated. My mother finally made them stop.

Although I had a hard time with grades, I loved sports. I excelled in baseball and was a star quarterback in football. Mickey Mantle was always my sports hero, so I always had his number 7 on my jersey in whatever sport I played.

Sports unlocked my frustrations. I got a lot of attention that way and made some friends, even among girls. There was always the risk of injury, but I didn't care. Sports made me feel like a man and made up for my poor self-esteem.

I wanted to earn one girl's approval mostly. Darlene and Susan were the best-looking girls in my school. Both were very popular and got good grades. All the boys wanted to be their girlfriend. Susan's father was a respected attorney, and they had a beautiful home with a swimming pool. Very few parents owned a swimming pool in those days.

But, I was just in second grade, when Darlene won my heart one day when she kissed me on the cheek. I wanted to kiss her back, so after school I walked her home and tried to kiss her. I was very shy when I was eight years old, but that kiss transferred me into a kissing maniac.

Throughout my elementary school years, I would try to impress Darlene with my sporting skills. She would always come to the football games and watch me play. When I noticed her on the sidelines, I would play harder.

I often dreamed of becoming a professional baseball player. I also fantasized about being in the Army, a soldier like John Wayne, and single-handedly winning the war.

Whenever Roger and I were together and he got hurt, I blamed myself. I remember one afternoon when my brother and I were walking up a long dirt driveway to visit one of his friends. Out of nowhere, a huge German shepherd came barking and racing straight toward us. My brother and I turned and ran.

As the dog got closer, my brother stopped and crouched to brace himself on a curb. His hands went down onto a board that had nails sticking out of it. Three nails went right though his hand and out the other side. He screamed as we ran home. There was blood all over his shirt and pants. As we entered the house, my mother quickly wrapped several cloths around his hand and rushed him in the car to the hospital. He was lucky: The doctors saved his hand and gave him twenty-two stitches. I felt guilty and blamed myself that he got hurt.

Another time we were playing tag in the house, and Roger got mad as he chased me. I knew he was going to hit me, so I went out our plate-glass back door and slammed it right behind me. There was a loud crash as Roger smacked into the door and shattered it into tiny pieces. My brother yelled, "I'll get you!" He was so mad; he didn't notice the blood spurting from his arms that had been badly cut by the broken glass. My parents rushed him to the hospital, and he got another forty stitches.

His words haunted me. Every day, he would tell me it was not the day for his revenge. Finally, after two months went by, he said, "Today is the day." I was anxious all day long, wondering when he would strike. At the end of the day, however, he told me he would forget about the accident and that he didn't have time to pay me back. I was relieved, but I was never sure whether he really meant it or not.

Whenever we fought, Roger always hit me in the face. My mother tried to stop him, but my father was the disciplinarian in our home. It was usually around evening time that he would discipline us if we got into trouble.

When I was twelve, my father came home one day to see me crying with my nose and lips bleeding. "What happened to you?" he asked.

"Roger hit me," I said, crying. My father walked around the corner and yelled. "Where's Roger?" I never saw my father so angry before. Ah, vengeance time, I thought. Finally my brother is going to get what he deserves.

My father walked briskly throughout the house looking for my brother. I could hear my brother running from room to room. "I'll catch you!" my father called out. "Come here!" My brother came out from hiding and walked toward him.

"What have you done?" my father yelled. "Didn't I tell you never to hit your brother ever again?" For the first time I saw my father's anger as he took his hand and held it out high to slap my brother's face. In response, my brother turned his face away quickly just before my father struck him. I could hear and see the impact as his hand slapped the side of Roger's head.

The impact caught the side of my brother's face and ear, causing him to scream out loud. He cried out immediately and then sobbed. I saw the panic look at my father's face when he heard my brother scream.

"My ear! My ear! I can't hear!" my brother yelled. My inner laughter turned to fear and guilt. That was the last time my father hit either of us. After that incident, my father was so afraid he was going to hurt us that he stopped disciplining us altogether.

I was introduced into the Catholic Church at an early age. My grandmother and my father's family was Catholic. My parents took us to church on Sundays, but my father and mother weren't allowed to receive Holy Communion. The Catholic Church didn't recognize their marriage because they weren't wed in the Catholic Church. When I asked my parents why, they just said that was the rule. I carried a bad taste in my mouth for the Catholic Church for a long time afterward. It didn't stop my parents from taking us to church, though. They wanted us to follow the Church's teachings. Every Monday after elementary school we had catechism where we learned about the Bible and Jesus Christ.

I remember receiving my first Holy Communion when I was eight years old. That was a big day for me. My whole family celebrated. My grandmother, aunts, uncles, and cousins all attended. It was almost like Christmas whenever the entire family got together. My grandmother's sisters, Aunt Chio and Aunt Concha, gave me a bright shiny dime for a gift. That dime would buy me a lot of candy at the candy store!

I dressed up that day in a new white shirt. My father even gave me his favorite tie to wear, and I felt honored. It was enormous on me but I didn't care. I was becoming a man.

When we arrived at Our Lady of Fatima Church, I made my way into the parish hall and sat down. There were forty of us there, boys and girls; all dressed up in our Sunday best clothes.

The nuns told us to get into our lines, boys on one side and girls on the other. We processed down the hallway and into the church, where we were met by hundreds of people. They were all taking pictures and waving. I think it was that day that I really sensed the meaning of God's love for me. I wanted to know more about God. I asked questions like, "Why am I here on earth?" "Why does God love me?"

In the center, at the front of the church on the altar was a huge wooden cross. There hung the life-size body of Jesus Christ. His body was slumped, presumably dead. His head was tilted down toward his chest. His hands stretched outward on each post. There was one nail hammered in each of his palms, pinning each hands to the wood. His feet were pinned by one nail through both of his feet. This was brutal, I thought. What a way to die. What a way to kill someone. There was blood dripping down from his head, from his hands, and from his feet. His face was swollen and beaten, and he had a deep wound in his side made from a soldier's spear. His body had been drained of all life. His face looked deeply tormented.

On his head, the soldiers had placed a crown of thorns. The thorns had pierced him so deeply that the blood had covered his entire face.

As I looked up at the cross, I couldn't imagine how much love it took for God to send his only son into the world to die this horrible death. I tried to imagine how grieved God the Father was to witness the torture of his son and the pain he had to endure. God must love me a lot, I thought, more than I could ever imagine. I prayed, "God, show me your love. I want to know you. I want to follow you." This kind of love made me feel good about myself, that I was worth something and that my life had meaning.

I couldn't understand it then but later in life I learned through the bible and church having salvation was a "Free" gift from God. I couldn't earn His love nor did I deserve His love. God sent His son Jesus, so we could be reconciled to himself. God loves us and wants us to know Him and Love Him in return.

As months went by, I tried to be as holy as Jesus. I tried to forgive my brother when he hit me and just turn the other cheek. It was hard to let go of my sins. I felt doomed. I couldn't be like Jesus, I thought, because I have sinned against God. I didn't want to be a priest, either, because I wanted to marry and raise a family.

When I prayed, I got no answers. I wanted a new bike and new clothes. I didn't get them. Little by little, I became angry with God because he did not give me what I asked Him for. I was frustrated because I was treating God like a genie in a bottle, someone who would give me what I wished for. I was jealous of my friends, who had more stuff. I always got used stuff. My father didn't seem to care about me enough to buy me anything. I wanted a new bike, and he always said yes, but it never happened, no matter how hard I tried to win his approval.

I felt a twinge of prejudice growing up. My father had been born in Mexico, but the word "Mexican" sounded dirty to me. At times I felt ashamed of my nationality. My mother was of Albanian descent and had grown up in the Italian section of Brooklyn, New York. I always told people that I was mixed Italian and Spanish, but mostly Italian. I didn't want them to know I was a Mexican because Mexicans were looked down upon. I didn't want to be called Mexican until my dad became successful in business.

In high school, I started going out with a girl, but after a couple of weeks she told me she couldn't see me anymore. I didn't know at the time, but her mother had made her break up with me because I was of Mexican descent. The girl confessed that to me at our twenty-fifth class reunion.

At fourteen, I began working for my father. That gave me confidence and made me feel like I was accomplishing something. I also got to work with my grandfather, making tortillas in the factory.

My father's business made a deep impression on me even when I was little. My father would take us to work with him on the weekends. I remember playing hide-and-seek among the hundred-pound bags of dry corn. We would watch the workers take a bag of dry corn and pour it into a huge, long tub with rollers. The corn was cooked for over eight hours, and then lime was used as a preservative. The corn would cool for another eight hours before it was put into a huge grinder and made into a corn dough called *masa*. When the *masa* was smooth, it was ready to be placed into the *masa* feeder. Next it would be cut into circles and rolled down into the hot tortilla oven and down the assembly line.

My grandfather would get up at four o'clock in the morning to open the factory doors. There would be three other Mexican men sleeping in their cars when he arrived. He would tap on their car window to wake them up, and then they would make tortillas all day long.

Everything was done by hand in those days. My grandfather and one of the workers, Dwayne, would count out twelve tortillas in his hands, then folded and shuffling them into a perfect column on the conveyor belt. Dwayne's brother, Dennis, would bag and seal the tortillas and place them in a box.

At the end of the work day, there were boxes and boxes of fresh warm tortillas ready for delivery. Early the next morning, another employee, Ray Ramirez, would put them in a van and drive them to the local distributor. They would repeat this cycle six days a week in order to stock the mom-and-pop shops and major grocery stores throughout the Central Valley.

I can still smell the fresh warm tortillas. The whole factory smelled like a bakery, and it made me hungry. The room where the tortillas were made was hot and humid, and when I worked there I would sweat profusely.

By the early 1960s, the tortillas business was booming. My father's warm and delicious tortillas were starting to change the eating habits of people who lived in the Central Valley and surrounding cities. Everyone was buying tortillas and liking Mexican food more and more.

I admired and respected my father as a role model. He was a gentle and kind man, and everyone loved him. He was an active member of the Elks Club and the Kiwanis Club, and he was directly responsible for changing the way people viewed Mexicans. He was one of the first producers to make corn tortillas, taco shells, tostada shells, and one-pound tortillas chips. He also pioneered the first Mexican fast-food franchise called Señor Campos Restaurants in 1964.

I struggled with self-confidence and self-esteem throughout my teenage years. I was searching for my identity. I wanted to be just like my father, to fit into his shoes and be a skilled and admired businessman. But I lacked the necessary patience, perseverance, and wisdom to become such a success.

In high school, all that mattered to me was being recognized as a jock and liking pretty women. Beyond that, I was not sure of anything. Most of my friends knew want they wanted to do with their lives, but I didn't have a clue. I just stopped thinking about it to avoid confusion.

My brother and I finally decided that I would be the one to run the family business when we got older. My brother had selected my career for me, and I listened to him because he was smarter than me. Now I didn't have to go through that confusion of choosing a career. All I knew was that I wanted to have a family a nice home and live the American dream.

Then I experienced another set of problems.

★ ★ ★ ★

CHAPTER 3: I GOT YOU BABE – SONNY & CHER

As my father's business grew in the 1960s, our family experienced a better quality of life. My parents bought a new house, and my father bought me my first car. It was a two-door black 1957 Chevy Bel Air. All my friends coveted my car. It made me popular, because not too many of my friends owned a car like that one. I was proud of it, so I polished and waxed my car every week.

My parents had their own problems. Before I turned seventeen, my mother and father divorced. I was hurt, angry, and bitter. By that time, I was so involved with sports and my girlfriend that I was nearly on my own. I tried to stop the divorce from affecting me, but it did anyway. During my teen years, I was always looking for appreciation and recognition. I never received it from my parents, so I looked for it elsewhere.

My Chevy would become my downfall. It helped me escape into another life with my girlfriends. We would go to the drive-in movies on the weekends, steaming up the windows with our kissing and necking.

I was around sixteen when I started experimenting with alcohol and getting drunk on two beers. That's about all it took back then. Alcohol helped me overcome my insecurity and shyness. I became a different person when I drank and would try things I normally would never do. The beer seemed to take away my inhibitions.

In the fall of 1964, I became serious about my girlfriend, Renee. We dated for several months and then started going out on dates in my car. The freedom of being alone with her brought many temptations. At first we would just drink sodas and eat popcorn at the drive-in movies. That all changed one weekend when I asked my friend Chuck, who was twenty-two, to buy me some beer. That was the beginning of a new direction in my life. Now Renee and I would drink beer at the movies. We both became less inhibited, and our level of physical intimacy went further and further.

One day at school, I heard one of my friends talk about a girl sneaking over to his friend's house and spending the night in his bedroom. Sex was on my mind a lot in those days. I didn't know anything about sex, but I wanted to find out.

One night at the movies, I jokingly asked Renee if she wanted to sneak out and meet me at my parents' home around midnight. "Sure," she said. I was only kidding, but in my mind I really wanted her to come over. That night, I was awakened around midnight by a tapping on my bedroom window. I opened the curtain, and there was Renee, standing in her coat outside my bedroom window. I was shocked. I didn't think she would actually do it, but there she was! I got out of bed and a slowly opened my bedroom door to peek down the hall toward my parents' bedroom. They were asleep. I could hear my father snoring. I walked slowly and deliberately down the hallway toward the back door and gingerly turned the door handle. I let her in, and we walked quietly to my bedroom.

We did that about every other weekend of my junior year of high school. Neither of our parents ever found out. She got pretty good at sneaking out of her house without being noticed. She would crawl out her bedroom window with her nightgown under her coat and walk eight blocks down the back alley to my home. We would kiss and touch each other for hours. I always had the radio playing so we wouldn't be heard, and I set the alarm in case we fell asleep — which we did many times. But she would always return to her home before her parents got up. It was a very romantic and sensual time for us.

Rene and I never had actual sexual intercourse, though, until my parents planned an overnight vacation in Santa Cruz and said that Roger and I could invite our girlfriends along. That weekend in Santa Cruz changed my life forever. My parents got a separate room for the girls, on the far side of the motel from the rooms where my parents, my brother, and I would stay. My parents felt pretty confident about letting the girls spent the weekend with us. My parents trusted us, but boy, were they wrong!

At midnight my brother and I switched rooms with the girls. My brother and his girlfriend and Renee and I would spend most of the night by ourselves. That night with Renee wasn't any different than all the others until just before four-thirty in the morning. She was almost asleep when we got carried away and we both lost our virginity.

After that weekend, we continued to have sex, and I prayed a lot that she would not get pregnant. Several times, her period would be late, and I would run to confession and pray that she wasn't pregnant. This happened several times over five months.

A few months later, it was no false alarm: Renee told me she was pregnant. My heart sank, and deep shame entered my soul. I felt depressed and guilty. I couldn't tell anyone about her being pregnant. I was scared to death. We both swore not to tell anyone, even our best friends at school. I often asked myself whether Renee and I should get married, but I was only sixteen and she was fifteen. What about my future? I wanted to make everything right, but it never was right.

I'll never forget the day in March 1965 her parents found out. Renee's mother was taking her to school one morning when Renee threw up in the car. That was the final clue: By then, Renee was four months pregnant and her clothes didn't fit her. She finally confessed to her mother that she was pregnant.

That night, Renee's parents called my parents, and we held a family meeting at her parents' house. I remember sitting in her parent's home next to Renee. Renee's father started the conversation: "Art, do you and Marian know why you are here tonight?" Her father looked directly at me with anger on his face.

"No," my father replied.

Her father looked back at me and then looked at my father. "Well, it appears that your son got my daughter pregnant," her father boldly blurted out. "And we are all here to talk about what to do next."

Renee and I sat there, not saying a word. Our parents would make the decisions for our future. I would have no say in the conversation. Both our parents would make the decision for us.

Renee's father controlled the conversation. He was a commander in the Navy Reserves who worked for the city of Modesto as second in command to the city manager. He was very well respected in the community. He had an attitude of stern confidence, and I felt I had to walk on eggshells whenever I was around him. He asked my father if I was college material, and whether I could take care of his daughter if we got married.

"I plan to go to junior college, and then work for my father," I told the group, true to the career decision my brother and I had made. Renee's father looked back at me with that anger in his eyes. I looked at Renee and whispered, "It'll be OK."

Her father took control of the meeting and ruled out abortion. Abortion was too risky during those days, and some women had died after abortions. The Catholic Church is opposed to abortion, and Renee's parents knew we were Catholic.

"Is your son prepared to pay for the baby after it is born?" Renee's father asked my dad. That was a question that had never entered my mind. How would I pay for the baby when I had no money and was only a junior in high school? I was in shock. I'll be paying for this baby for the rest of my life, I thought. I was too scared to say a word.

Finally, her father decided that Renee would give up the baby for adoption. It was the only sane option. We were too young to get married, and they didn't want to raise a baby in their home. He wanted Renee to go to college and to marry someone he could be proud of, not just some tortilla maker. There was a touch of that prejudice against Mexicans in the decision.

A plan was designed: Renee would live at her grandmother's home in Oakland. Renee and her parents would tell everyone that she was leaving for boarding school. The pregnancy would be kept secret, and her father would not have to be shamed by it.

He also decided that I would never see his daughter again. He had all the details worked out, and I wouldn't have to pay for the baby. But that just made us more defiant. We vowed that nothing would tear us apart, and we found ways to meet on the sly.

In September 1965, Renee's mother called me one Friday night and told me Renee had given birth to a baby girl.

During my senior year, the country changed in a big way. Students on every campus protested against the Vietnam War, and smoking pot became more common. The hippie movement was gaining attention and was becoming a revolution.

It was a confusing time for me as a teenager. I didn't want to be like my parents, and yet I wanted the American Dream. I started to question what I wanted to do with my life and what would make me happy.

We were living in the Age of Aquarius. On the television screens were Sonny and Cher, "Laugh-In," the Beatles and the influential music of our day. People were trading their good clothes for jeans and tie-dyed t-shirts. Women took off their bras. Our generation was experimenting with Marijuana and LSD. There were "love-ins" on the college campuses. Everyone was talking about "free love."

After I graduated from high school, I felt so guilty about the pregnancy that I asked Renee to marry me. I felt so ashamed of myself that I wanted to make everything right. Her parents said yes, and so we got married. They were glad to get her out of their home. Besides, Renee had a younger sister whom they wanted to raise without her influence.

It was kind of ironic that I was beginning my marriage just my mom and dad was ending theirs. After their divorce, my dad stayed at home with my sister and me until the house was sold. My mother left town and moved to Reno, Nevada. Within about a year, they would both find new partners and remarry. Just like that.

Our generation used terms like "Love is cool," "Love is in the air," and "Make love, not war." We were searching for love, but we ended up equating it with sex, drugs, and rock 'n' roll. Renee and I spent plenty of time getting stoned and listening to music with our friends.

The hippie lifestyle appealed to my insecure nature. I threw away all my nice clothes and wore jeans and t-shirts instead. We experimented with promiscuous sex. Our generation had no goals or priorities and soon descended into chaos, as all rebellion does.

The popular music of the day expressed this rebellion. Our parents listened to Perry Como, and we had rock 'n' roll. The Beatles, the Doors, Jimi Hendrix, Jefferson Airplane, the Rolling Stones, and even the musical "Hair" were part of the music revolution.

We became a generation of hair. I began to grow my hair long. I wore a peace sign around my neck, bought posters and incense, and decorated my place with colorful designs and pillows. I bought a small pipe to smoke hash and pot. I wanted to be called a "hippie" and a "flower child." That, I thought, would finally give me an identity.

At junior college, my grades suffered terribly because I never went to class. Later that summer, I received my grade report from junior college and was placed on academic probation. I was failing my studies and was suspended for a semester.

Renee and I enjoyed our adult "freedom." But somewhere during our first year of marriage, I began to feel that I really didn't want to be married. I felt trapped. All my friends were having fun and dating girls, and I wasn't. I was married. Our partying got worse and worse. By the summer of 1967, Renee and I were constantly fighting. Our fights kept getting worse until, Renee finally gave me an ultimatum: "Go into the service, or we'll get divorced."

I was in a lot of trouble that summer. I had gotten picked up by the police several times for being drunk. Maybe the service wasn't a bad idea. If I joined the Army, then I wouldn't have to worry about getting drafted and being sent out in the infantry.

The television news often showed men burning their draft cards. Some students even burned the American flag. It made me angry that someone could burn our flag. There was even talk that one of my friends was going to move to Canada to avoid the draft. What was wrong with this nation? How could someone do that and not feel like a coward? In my eyes, those people weren't Americans. They were traitors to our country. They didn't respect the rights and privileges we have in America. Why a person would not want to fight for his country, especially after living in a free society?

America isn't perfect, but we have freedom of worship, freedom of speech, and freedom to pursue our own destiny. I believe many people don't appreciate or respect our rights as citizens in these United States. We have so much more than other people in our world. How dare we turn our backs to those countries in need? I felt those people who desecrated our flag or wanted to burn their draft cards should be the ones who get drafted first and sent to Vietnam. That would fix their disloyalty! If I was drafted, I thought to myself, there would be no doubt I would fight for my country.

All my friends opposed the war. The whole country was in

rebellion in some form. The media constantly portrayed the war protesters as the real American heroes. Television zoomed in on campuses all over the country showing students opposing the war. American was in turmoil. It felt like our government and President Lyndon B. Johnson were not to be trusted. American citizens didn't know whom to trust. President Johnson tried to stop the war by bombing Hanoi. That didn't work. The North Vietnamese kept on fighting. We had the Paris peace talks, but they never got anywhere. Ever since President John F. Kennedy was assassinated in 1963, the whole country had seemed confused.

We heard of how Communism was lurking in all corners of our world. Was the United States just to sit back and let communism spread? I think everyone questioned the future of our country. We were fighting in a distant land that most Americans couldn't find on a map, fighting a war that lacked the support of the majority of Americans.

The United States had all kinds of problems. Communist Russia was a threat to freedom and had the military strength and missiles to exert its influence. The Soviet-American arms race was in full stride. Fear of nuclear attack hung over the world, and U.S. newspapers fed this fear. Life magazine even published a cover story on how to build a fallout shelter for your family.

The war was not the only major protest on campuses in the 1960s. Segregation policies were being dismantled, and the integration of black and white schools also drew angry protests. Our country seemed to be coming apart at the seams.

When Renee told me it was OK to go into the Army, my mind was made up. I would enlist in the Army. I was so confused about life that the Army sounded good to me. It would give me time to get my life in order.

I had often asked myself what I would want to do if I were in the Army. I thought flying helicopters would be cool, but that probably wasn't realistic since I was such a daydreamer who had a tough time academically in school. Once again, I couldn't make a career decision. I finally figured that I would just join the Army and see where it led. The Army would put me through evaluations during boot camp, and they would decide what duties would best fit my skills.

Thousands of men were being drafted at that time. A government lottery assigned a number to each day and month of the year, and the number that matched your birthday was your draft number. The government was calling up men with draft numbers 80 and lower. Mine was 79. The government was especially drafting men who had dropped out of school, had poor grades, or were not enrolled in college. They would come for me sooner or later, and I wouldn't have any options. By voluntarily enlisting, I reasoned, there was a good chance that I would not be sent to Vietnam to fight in the infantry. I would have a nice easy job back in the States. Maybe they would even assign me to Hawaii!

The following Monday, August 19, I headed to the local Army recruiter to begin my new career. The recruiter told me that if I was interested in flying planes, I would be evaluated and then sent to flight-training school. I trusted his words and signed away three years of my life.

That very night, I said my goodbyes to family and friends. I was to board a Greyhound bus the next day and leave for Fresno, where I would be sworn into the United States Army. Then I would be flown to Fort Lewis, Wash., where I would do my basic training. Everything sounded so wonderful!

The next morning, I said goodbye to Renee. My father drove me to the bus station. I waved goodbye to him, and then I waited for my mother to arrive. She had told me she would meet me at the bus depot to see me off. I waited and waited, but she never came. The bus driver waited about twenty more minutes, but then he couldn't wait any longer. I boarded the bus and took a seat next to the window. There were about eight of us enlistees on the bus that day.

Finally, the Army recruiter told the bus driver to pull away. Just as the bus was turning the corner, I saw my mother. She was running and yelling, waving her arms. I could see the tears in her eyes, "Stephen, Stephen!" she yelled. I blew her a kiss and waved as the bus sped away. I didn't know where or whether I would ever see her again. All I knew was to trust the Army and put my faith in God. I hoped everything would work out fine.

After we arrived at the Army Recruiting Station in Fresno, we got off the bus and entered a large hall. There were two hundred to three hundred men and one woman standing there. On a podium in the middle of the room stood an American flag and Army flag, side by side. A few minutes later, several Army men entered in front of us. One of the Army men who had stripes on his sleeves stepped forward and shouted, "Atten-Hutt!"

Then another man entered. He looked like an officer because he had two gold bars on his hat. He stepped to a podium and commanded in a loud voice, "Raise your right hand and repeat after me." I held my right hand and gave my allegiance to the United States of America and to the United States Army. I vowed to defend and honor my country, to obey the Constitution of the United States, and to protect the President of the United States, "so help me God."

"I will," I said along with the hundreds of others in one loud voice.

"Welcome men," the officer shouted. "You're now in the United States Army!"

PART II: YOU'RE IN
THE ARMY NOW

★ ★ ★ ★

CHAPTER 4: PEOPLE ARE STRANGE – THE DOORS

So I had just raised my arm and pledged allegiance to the United States Army for three years. Was I crazy? I soon found out that I was one of only four men in that room who had volunteered. The other 280 had been drafted.

We boarded a plane that day bound for Seattle. From there we boarded a bus to Fort Lewis, a bus that seemed to pull up at every bus stop known to man. Around three o'clock in the morning, the bus driver said, "This is the last stop, men." The doors opened, and we filed out. The trip had taken five hours.

Fort Lewis was where I would get my basic training for six weeks. When that was over, I would get another six-week assignment to learn my specific career position, whatever that might be. I thought to myself, how rough could this be anyway? Nothing on earth was as tough as "Hell Week," the intense conditioning drills the football team went through at Davis High School. Coach Dan Gonzales made sure that we suffered as much as possible before we even began our season. I got through that all right.

The post at Fort Lewis was surrounded by a twenty-foot fence. At the entrance was a sign that read, "You are entering hell." As we left the bus, we were met by a man in uniform who wore what looked like a "Smokey the Bear" hat. He seemed wide awake compared to those of us who were half asleep from the long drive. I was barely awake myself and somewhat in a state of shock.

"Get in line men!" he shouted. "About face, forward march!" We all turned and started following him. It was four o'clock by the time our group reached our barracks. The sergeant told us to take a bunk. "The latrine is down the hall. Get some shut-eye. We'll be getting you up in an hour and a half," he shouted.

The barracks was a huge room with about forty Army cots in it, set up like bunk beds. I walked over and lay down on one of the cots. Some men undressed and then got into their beds. I wasn't comfortable taking my clothes off in front of strangers, so I just lay on top of the blankets fully dressed and closed my eyes. I was too exhausted, overwhelmed, and excited to sleep. Within minutes, I could hear someone snoring. I just lay there with my eyes wide open, thinking about my family and my wife, what I had been through with Renee and what our future held. It was a leap of faith that I had enlisted and given my life to the U.S. Army for the next three years.

Just as I was dozing off, I heard a voice yelling at the top of his lungs, "Wake up, you stupid maggots. It's time to get up. This isn't your mama speaking." I looked at my watch. It was five-thirty in the morning "You have just fifteen minutes to shit, shower, and shave, and be in formation for reveille at oh-five-forty-five," our drill sergeant shouted. "You hear me, you bunch of crunchies? Do you hear me?"

"Yes, drill sergeant," a few men sputtered out. He turned around and walked back into his office. I remember saying to myself, "What in the heck is reveille?" I soon found out that reveille is how the Army begins each day, standing at attention and saluting the American flag as it was raised. I really liked that part of our day. It made me feel proud to be a soldier and to serve my country. It felt good to wake up and watch the sun come up while remembering my allegiance to the United States.

After reveille we would march over to the mess hall and stand in another line for breakfast. We were instructed to eat "chow" in fifteen minutes and be back into our formation at oh-six-forty-five. Next we would get into formation for an hour of exercise in our t-shirts. I can't understand why we needed exercise because we were always marching or running to our next assignment.

We had a new training assignment every hour of the day, in every phase of military instruction. Every class was highly structured. The Army made sure we were fully trained and capable of confronting any enemy. We stood in line and our drill sergeant would yell out command: "Attention," "at ease," "right face," "left face," "about face," "forward march," "your left, your left, your left, right, left ... all together!" yelled the drill sergeant.

In the first two days, we learned to march, run, and walk in cadence. We learned all the commands our drill sergeant taught, and we learned to do it all together in sync. We also learned several cadence songs. One of them went like this: *"They say that in the Army / the coffee's mighty fine / It looks like muddy water / and tastes like turpentine / Oh Lord, I wanna go / but they won't let me go / Oh Lord, I wanna go home. Hey!"*

I began respecting my drill sergeant and the Army during basic training. Our drill sergeant had a tremendous responsibility because he was the one who would be credited with changing us from civilians into fighting men. Later I realized how important those first few weeks were. The drill sergeant had to change us from the inside out. We lost all our individual rights and learned about teamwork and authority. When our platoon did our drills wrong or someone was not paying attention, we were all ordered to drop and give ten push-ups. It was often the same person who kept screwing up, but we all had to pay for his mistakes. It seemed unfair, but the Army was teaching us to depend on each other. The Army was all about training as a unit, as a team. What a change from growing up and learning to become independent with so many choices to make! In the Army, you had no choices. You just did what you were told.

It was really hard for me to adapt because I was so rebellious in spirit. I guess there were a lot of men like me. We grew up believing in individuality and questioning authority. The Army hated people who thought independently. It also hated conscientious objectors, cowboys, queers, and anyone from California. There was only one type of person the Army loved, and that was its enlisted men and officers. If you were a fighter or had a bad attitude, the Army found a way to break your spirit and punish you. The Army changed boys into men, and men into fighting men.

The drill sergeant tried to degrade us and make us feel worthless. "Get in line, you bunch of sissies," he would scream over and over until we got our cadence right. Slowly, we all made the adjustments.

Some men didn't want to take a shower with the rest of the men. Our drill sergeant told us we had free rein to take that person and scrub the hell out of him with a Brillo pad or take a pillowcase over his head and take him into the shower. Believe it or not, there were several men who defied the sergeant's orders and were scrubbed until they were almost bleeding to death. That changed their hygiene habits.

At every opportunity, the drill sergeant would tell us, "You're in the Army now, you slugs. Your mommy's not here to kiss you and tuck you into bed, so listen up or you're going to die in combat. It's my duty to make you soldiers so when you go to Vietnam you won't come back home in a body bag."

Early in the morning on the second day, our drill sergeant had a smirk on his face and told us we had a surprise coming. We marched for what seemed like forever until we started noticing other platoons marching back from where we were going. They looked different than before. In fact, they all looked the same. They all had bald heads.

Our sergeant was laughing because we were all headed to get our first haircut, Army style. We were being changed into non-persons, robots, non-thinkers who had no will other than to do the will of the Army. We kept marching toward the barbers' quarters.

I had this feeling that I was going to be in trouble. My freedom was important to me. Just yesterday, it meant letting my hair grow, drinking beer, and doing what I wanted in life. Now the Army is telling me what to wear and where to go. Why would I allow anyone to treat me this way?

It reminded me of when I was six years old. I had just gotten a doctor's kit that Christmas and decided to play doctor. You might say I was inquisitive about the female anatomy. I invited the beautiful blonde girl from next door to walk with me out along the bank of the canal. I found the perfect place to test my doctor's kit. Just before I asked her to pull up her skirt, however, I heard this loud voice from out of nowhere: "Mr. Campos, what the hell are you doing to my daughter?"

I was shocked out of my shoes. "Ah, nothing, sir," I told the girl's father unconvincingly.

"You're in deep trouble son" he said. "I am going to call your father and tell him exactly what you have done, and he is going to whip your ass."

After I returned home, I waited all day next to the telephone. I knew her father was going to call my father and tell him that I was planning to rape his daughter or something. I planned to intercept the phone call and then hang up. I waited all the next day, too, but still no phone call. That call never did come, but the anticipation of what might happen was probably more painful than if he had actually called.

I had the same feeling as we marched to the barbers' quarters. I was in deep trouble. My emotions were in turmoil until we would reach our destination. Finally, just before noon on my second day in the Army, my life, my freedom, and my long-haired hippie identity changed.

The drill sergeant yelled, "Platoon, halt!" and we came to a screeching halt. We all stood there not moving a muscle until he shouted again. "At ease, you maggots," he said with a smile.

"What does that mean," I whispered to the guy next to me. "I think we can stand without being at attention." he whispered back.

"What did I hear?" shouted the drill sergeant. "Did I hear someone say something?" "No, drill sergeant," the whole platoon shouted back. I didn't say a word. I hoped he didn't know it was me. I didn't want to do any push-ups.

We all stood there not knowing what to do next until he said, "Wait here men, I'm see what's taking so long." There were other men waiting before we got here. I watched as men entered in one door with hair and out the other door with a smooth bald head. These haircuts were the fastest I had ever seen.

My heart started beating when I realized my turn was coming soon. I thought the barber would treat me different because all the other grunts were drafted and I had volunteered in the Army. Maybe I didn't have to lose my long hair. I took a seat when the barber told me in a nice way, "Son, you're next." Laughing, I told him, "I just want a trim." I sat down. "Sure, son," he replied.

It took the barber precisely thirty-five seconds for his shears to cut down one side of my head and up the next. I couldn't believe it as I watched my long hair hit the floor. When he was finished, I walked out the door a new person. It was like someone waved a magic wand over me. I was changed instantly. I looked around at the other men and couldn't believe what I noticed: We all looked alike.

After we got back into formation, the drill sergeant told us, "You belong to the Army now, and you're mine." Then he smiled.

Day after day of basic training, we all grew stronger and more proficient in our training. In just one week, we learned how to work together as a team, or we would do countless push-ups. I remember one day we had so many push-ups that it seemed the day would never end. We even did push-ups in inclement weather, no matter if it rained, snowed, or was windy. It was always at least one of those. I remember thinking: What kind of training was this in cold weather? It seemed that we were getting trained for Germany, not Vietnam. I didn't know where they trained for Vietnam, but it surely was not here.

Throughout basic training, we were required to run everywhere. When we weren't running, we were standing in line somewhere. Sometimes we ran in full gear with our rifles over our heads. Basic training started to remind me of "Hell Week." I would get this burning sensation all over my body, and I would feel like I was going to throw up all the time. Basic training was ten times worse than "Hell Week." After the day had ended at nine in the evening, we would return to our barracks exhausted. We would shine our boots and get our gear ready to grind out another day before going to sleep.

Every morning, our drill sergeant would wake us up at four-thirty to get showered and ready for reveille. We had to have our bunks made, our barracks cleaned, our floor polished, and the latrines cleaned. We had to stand at attention next to our beds for inspection each morning. Our drill sergeant wanted us to win the competition for the best platoon in the company. He pushed us because he wanted recognition from the company commander and respect from the other drill sergeants.

When I arrived at boot camp, I weighed one-hundred and ninety pounds. In just three weeks, I lost thirty pounds from all the running. For the next four weeks, I turned my beer fat into lean, hard muscle that would help give me an edge during combat.

The Army also tested how proficient we were at completing specific tasks. We were scored twice during my time at boot camp. In order to graduate, I had to have a score of 450 out of 500 points or I wouldn't pass. Everyone who didn't make it would have to take boot camp over. That motivated everyone to try for the best possible score.

In my second week of training, I took the proficiency test. It consisted of a grenade toss within five meters of the target, a mile run, hanging and crossing monkey bars, hanging as long as you could hang a live fire crawl while machine-gun bullets flew past your head, and several other endurance tests. On our first proficiency test, I scored 451 points out of 500. I barely passed, but there were other men in my company who scored below 450. Our drill sergeant had his work cut out for him to make sure that everyone in our company passed.

When it came to brainwashing, the Army was good at that, too. I think the Army trained the drill sergeants to use every possible form of humiliation in boot camp. The drill sergeant's command style was to put men down, especially if you were from a particular state they didn't like. They would make you feel worthless. I always thought it was humorous when the drill sergeants would call people from California "queers" or "fruits." Everyone had a stereotype. We were called "grunts," "candies," and "crunchies," which was the lowest form of human being possible. It worked: It made me feel like I was under the Army's complete control and that I would do whatever the Army asked of me.

Accomplishments were important, especially when it came to shooting a rifle. I learned how to shoot an M-14, an M-16, fifty- and sixty-caliber machine guns, and a forty-five pistol. I earned sharpshooter and expert medals. No matter what the Army threw at me, I excelled. I think my athletic abilities and competitive spirit helped me. It made me feel good about myself, and I actually started to like being in the Army. I was gaining pride in myself for the first time in my life, and I was developing a deeper love for my country and for authority. I took pride in wearing my uniform, in being a soldier, and in being rewarded by the Army for my efforts.

My accomplishments accumulated until right before graduation from boot camp. I was ready for my proficiency test. After I completed the course, I was amazed. So was my drill sergeant, who kept counting and recounting my score. I had scored 497 points out of 500. What an accomplishment!

I felt really proud of my accomplishment. The company

commander shook my hand and congratulated me as he announced my score in front of the whole company. I was one of three soldiers who came close to achieving the maximum score. I found out later I was tied for second place. Few men ever earned a perfect score at boot camp.

That was also the day I would find out where my calling in the Army would take me for the next few years. The company commander started to read a list of names and assignments in alphabetical order. I waited in anticipation to hear my own name. I still thought I would get a non-combat assignment because I enlisted. He finally called out my name: "Campos, Stephen Paul, AIT, Fort Lewis," he shouted.

"AIT? What is that?" I whispered to the guy next to me. "It's Advanced Infantry Training," he said.

Advanced Infantry Training? Oh, my God. I could get killed, I thought. The Army had made a big mistake. I couldn't be going into the infantry, I told myself in disbelief. What a minute, this couldn't be true. I enlisted!

Suddenly, reality hit me like a ton of bricks. I was scared. I soon became angry, too. I felt paralyzed and panicked for a several hours. I walked around outside the barracks in circles, wondering what went wrong. I had enlisted to avoid combat! I should be rewarded!

That was the first time in my life that I thought about death. Life and death was constantly on my mind from that point on. I'd be going to Vietnam. I might die. I might have to kill someone. I might get my arms or legs blown off. I might not be able to have children. I'd become an outcast among my friends. Those voices played over and over in my head. My happiness at graduating with honors from basic training was gone.

So it was Advanced Infantry Training. I'd be taking another six weeks of combat training while other men were being trained in clerical work, supply duties, or mechanics. My new career would be 11B20 (military occupational service). I would learn to fight, to kill, and to stay alive.

Later that night, I called my father. "Dad, I'm going into the infantry," I told him. "The Army had decided my fate. Pray for me, and don't tell Renee or Mom. I'll tell them later."

I was so afraid that day that I found the first sergeant and asked him if I could see the captain. "Why do you want to see the captain, son?" replied the first sergeant. "Ah, it's personal," I said. I was so scared, I wanted out of the Army. I figured that if I told the captain I used drugs in the past, maybe they would find me unfit and send me home. I would ask to be released from the Army.

I mustered all the nerve I had and entered the officers' quarters. "Okay, son, I'll see if he will see you," the first sergeant said. He came back and told me I could see the captain, and then walked me into the captain's room. I entered his office, and the first sergeant closed the door behind me. I stood at attention and saluted. "At ease," the captain said.

"Captain, sir, I enlisted in the Army to attend flight school. I wasn't drafted, I volunteered. I think the Army has made a mistake. Are you sure the Army has put me into the infantry to attend AIT?"

"Yes, son that's correct," the captain said. "Do you have a problem with that?"

"Well, yes, I do, sir. You see, I may be affected by drugs."

"What do you mean, son?" answered the captain.

"Well, before I came into the Army, I used drugs, even LSD a couple of times, and I smoked marijuana. I may be unfit for military service. I'm having flashbacks. I don't think I would be good for the Army. I think it would be best if the Army just let me go home."

I was sure he would tell me I was right and send me home. I didn't want to tell him that I was terrified of dying.

Captain looked back at me and said, "Private, you just scored one of the highest test scores on your final PIT test, and I am proud of you. You'll be a fine soldier. You'll be OK. Now," he continued, "would you like to see the chaplain?"

"Ah, I guess so, sir," I said.

"Well, then you may go and talk to him. That's all, Private," he ordered, and I turned around and left his office. I headed toward the chaplain's office. How is the chaplain going to help me? I asked myself. Maybe the chaplain will talk the captain into letting me out of the Army.

I entered the chaplain's office and stood at attention. "Ah, Father, I had a drug problem before I enlisted, and I am having hallucinations," I told him. "I am not fit for duty in the military. Besides, the Army made a mistake by putting me in the infantry. You see, I enlisted, sir, I wasn't drafted. I don't want to be in the infantry. I volunteered for flight school. I think the army needs to send me home."

"What's the real problem, son?" he asked me. I suddenly felt I could tell him what I was really feeling. "Ah, Father I'm scared. I'm sacred I 'm going to die."

"Son, trust in God," the chaplain said. "Do you want me to pray for you?"

"Yes, Father."

After he prayed for me, he sent me back to the barracks. I realized no one could help me now. I couldn't run, I couldn't hide. I was stuck in the infantry. I was in a state of deep depression. Because of my confusion and indecision, the Army had decided my future, just like my brother once did.

CHAPTER 5: AND IT'S 1, 2, 3 WHAT ARE WE FIGHTING FOR – COUNTRY JOE AND THE FISH

I made up my mind to accept my role in the Army. What choice did I have? I told myself I would become the best-trained soldier I could be. I would learn everything I could, and I would volunteer to advance my opportunities. Fear can do one of two things to you: It can cripple you, or it can make you do the impossible. I resolved to be diligent from that day forward. I would train hard and did my best.

After my six weeks of AIT, it was graduation day. Once again, I stood in formation with the other graduates to hear my call of duty and my next assignment. Finally, it came. "Private Campos, Richard, Korea; Private Campos, Stephen P., Fort Lewis, 199th."

The soldier next to me had the same last name as me, but his name came before mine because his first name began with an R and mine began with S. If that guy was a Thomas Campos or Victor Campos, maybe I would have been the one sent to Korea and he would be joining the 199th. Such was my fate. I sensed that I was headed to Vietnam.

That afternoon, I packed my bags and got ready for my new assignment with the 199th Light Infantry Brigade. Some of the men around me had expressions of fear or doubt on their faces. I wondered if my face had the same fear.

That night, the barracks were completely silent. It was a time for solitude and reflection about what would happen next. No one knew anything about the 199th. There were rumors that the unit was training for Vietnam, but no one knew for sure.

My mind told me to accept my circumstances, even if I had enlisted. I had no control of where the Army was going to send me anyway. My dream of being stationed in Hawaii and relaxing on the beach was a fantasy. I was no different than any of those other men who were drafted. The Army had the right to put where they needed me. There was nothing I could do but accept my fate and put myself in God's hands.

The next morning, I stood in line with about fifty others and boarded the bus that took us to the 199th headquarters. When it was my turn, I entered and stopped at attention in front of the sergeant major. "Sergeant Major, Private Stephen P. Campos reporting for duty," I said. He didn't say a word. He had his head down and grabbed my paperwork. My next question was my hardest. I cleared my throat. "Ah, Sergeant Major, where is this company training for"?

"We're training for Vietnam," he told me. "We are replacing the 101st Airborne Division in South Vietnam. We'll, be leaving around April." My heart sank. I couldn't say a word. I immediately remembered my drill sergeant's words at boot camp: "You belong to the Army. You have no choices. The Army owns you now, soldier. My job is to train you so you don't come back home in a body bag and a pine box."

It was now November, just before Thanksgiving, and I hadn't been home since August. I had no time to think about my family now. All I could think about was that I had several months of training to fight in Vietnam. My career was that of a highly trained professional killer.

The sergeant major gave me some papers. I was assigned to

Charlie Company, 2nd Platoon. He handed me back my other papers and told me a jeep would take me to my next stop.

When I arrived at Charlie Company headquarters, I was immediately greeted by my platoon sergeant — that is, if you call "What do you want?" a greeting.

"Private Campos reporting for duty, Sergeant," I shouted with pride.

"Campos, where are you from, soldier?" the sergeant asked.

"I'm from California, Sergeant," I shouted.

"Well, son I'm from Georgia. Welcome to the 2nd Platoon. You can call me Sergeant Turner." Sergeant Turner assigned me to second squad as a rifleman. I liked rifles, especially M-16 rifles with ammunition.

The following week, I trained like it was Hell Week. I wanted to impress my leaders and let them know I could handle any job.

I never knew many of my combat buddies' first names. The Army always called us by our last names. It was written on everything we were issued, even our underwear, so most of us called each other by nicknames.

It was during that first week that I met the first of my two new best friends. Sergeant James L. Dyckhoff was a squad leader. I started calling him "Dyckes" because it was easier to remember. He called me Campos. We became friends fast. When you are training to go into battle, you become close. You trust your buddy with your life.

Several months later, I would ask Dyckes to call me "Stone Pony." Later, that week I met my other best friend, my forever combat buddy, Eric "Tiger" Yingst from Pennsylvania. At first I called him Yingst, but later we'd call him Tiger. He was also a rifleman. He started calling me "Stone Pony". Mainly, because Linda Rodstadt was from Sacramento California. She grew up only a hundred miles away from my hometown. She was a very popular singer in the 1960's and her group was called the "Stone Pony". The name stuck.

When we were assembled by our company commander one

morning, we were all asked to volunteer. No one knew what we were volunteering for, but I raised my hand, and Yingst lifted his. We were the only ones who had volunteered. It was early January 1968. We had no idea what we were getting into.

Just like when I enlisted, I figured I would be better off if I volunteered. In all the Great War movies and Westerns, the guys who volunteered were the heroes. It was Audie Murphy, John Wayne, and James Stewart who would do the volunteering. They all won respect, they got all the good-looking women, and they were all sent somewhere special. After the war, they would be reunited and live happily ever after. It was so simple: You volunteer, you win the war, you'd get better duty, and you get promoted. It made perfect sense!

Yingst and I soon learned what we had volunteered for: We were to carry the radio and be trained as radio operators, or RTOs. We became the best of friends. So while our whole brigade trained for the next four months, Tiger and I trained with the radio and received our security clearance. I thought volunteering into something like the radio operator would help me stay alive.

I was in charge of most of the communications to the whole company and to the brigade. I heard everything that was going on from the artillery support to the fighter pilots and the C-130 "Snoopy" gunships. I also heard everything that happened on our missions and ambush patrols.

I carried the radio for the Lieutenant, and Yingst carried the radio for the platoon sergeant. We formed an alliance of friendship and trust. We were brothers in combat and knew everything about the company and our missions. We heard all the radio talk about who was in trouble or who kicked some Viet Cong butt. We did a lot of that in Nam. We called in gunship support, Cobra helicopters, 155 Howitzer artillery rounds, air support, jets with bombs, and other firepower. We knew everything that was going on and happening to our unit and to other companies.

Dyckes and I also became close friends. We talked about our

families, my father's business, his twelve brothers and sisters. He respected his parents and deeply loved them. We lived not too far from each other in California. Since the drill sergeant was always calling men from California queers, we resolved to prove differently. We decided we were "Comanche Commandos," and we called each other "warriors."

Dyckes entered the Army with a handful of pride from his father. His father had flow as a Navy flyer in the South Pacific, around the time we evaded Guadalcanal. His father saw lots of action. There were lots of pictures hanging on the walls in his home as he grew up, reminders of his father's heroic treats.

Before he enlisted, he attended college, but his grades were on the slide. He also was partying too much with the hippies, drinking and smoking pot. I guess he needed a change, and the Army was his choice. He had enlisted and attended Officer Candidate Training School and could easily have commanded our platoon, but he got discouraged when the Army told him that as an officer he would be enlisted for four years instead of three. So he was sent to the 199th as a squad leader.

Dyckes was different from anyone else I had ever known. He was one our best squad leaders. He didn't seem to be afraid of anyone or anything. I liked his personality and his confidence. He had excellent leadership skills, and always looked out for the welfare of his men. He trained with a passion, without fear. I knew he was a survivalist and would help me stay alive in combat. I wanted to place myself with men like him who I could trust. I decided early on that I would stay close to him.

Yingst was a completely different person than Dyckes. He and I became the best of friends later in combat under extreme fighting conditions. He was compliant like me, but he was also a leader and was extremely well trained. He took it as his responsibility to learn everything there was to know about operating the radio. He memorized his entire security code book. He also had a friendly and warm personality that I admired. He could be funny and serious at the same time. He didn't question authority, and he followed orders by the book.

Tiger was courageous and modest, had a hero mentality, and opposed the war protesters. He was very patriotic and was willing to die for his county. He was drafted in 1967 and lived in Harrisburg, Pennsylvania. He loved cars and motorcycles, and he had a girlfriend named Joyce back home whom he would marry when he returned. He was fun to be around. You could tell he came from a good family. He was a leader with compassion, and he had a strong foundation of faith in God.

His great-grandfather had fought in the Civil War, his grandfather had fought in World War I, and his father had fought in World War Two. So when he was called to fight for his country in 1967, Yingst gladly accepted.

The unit we were to replace in Vietnam, the 101st Airborne Division, had been among the first divisions sent there. It had a long reputation of fighting skill and heroism, so it was an honor and a privilege to be placed in that same class with those heroic men. When it was first activated in 1942, its first commander, Maj. Gen. William C. Lee, promised his new recruits that the 101st had no history, but that it did have a "rendezvous with destiny."

As a division, the 101st never failed that prophecy. During World War II, the 101st Airborne Division led the way on D-Day in the night-drop prior to the invasion. When surrounded at Bastogne, Brigadier General Anthony McAuliffe answered "Nuts!" to a call for surrender, and the Screaming Eagles fought on until the siege was lifted. For their valiant efforts and heroic deeds during World War II, the 101st Airborne Division was awarded four campaign streamers and two Presidential Unit Citations.

There were hopes and rumors that the war would end soon. Even though the Tet Offensive was in full swing, the Hanoi and Paris peace talks were very much in the news. Presidential candidates were campaigning about ending the war. It seemed that all of America was screaming, "End the war!" The anti-war rallies and protests on our college campuses continued to grow stronger throughout the United States.

The United States was bombing the hell out of Hanoi hoping to force the Viet Cong into surrendering. It was not until much later that we realized that the North Vietnamese would never surrender. They had been fighting for decades in this land, and they would fight until the end. We had no concept of this kind of enemy.

Just before we left for Vietnam, we were all given a thirty-day pass. In March 1968, I flew back home. Those thirty days went by fast. I enjoyed the time I spent with Renee, my friends, and my family. I knew it might be the last time I would ever see them. I tried not to think about it, but that was in the back of my mind as I said goodbye. My company commander told us before we left that anyone who was even a day late in returning would be considered a deserter.

I will never forget the day my father drove me from Modesto to San Francisco International Airport. We didn't talk much. I didn't know what to say, and I could sense he was nervous. He didn't say much to me, either. I don't think he wanted to talk about Vietnam, so we just talked about what would happen after I was discharged from the Army. I agreed that I would work for my dad when my Army duty was over. My future was in God's hands. That's pretty much all we said.

Finally, we were crossing the Oakland-San Francisco Bay Bridge. We were going about 60 miles an hour when the car in front of us stopped suddenly and we smashed into its rear end. My father and I got out of the car and saw that the damage was minor. The other driver got out of his car, too, and noticed that I was in my Army uniform. He came over, looked at the damage, and said, "Don't worry about it." So we got back into the car and resumed our way to the airport. That incident gave my Dad and me something to talk about and broke the silence between us.

We laughed and talked more about working for him at Campos Foods.

When we finally arrived at the airport, I could see my father's eyes starting to well up with tears. I told him, "Dad, I'll be back, and when I get out, I'll work for you." Then I got out and walked away. I didn't turn to look back. I didn't want to think that this would be the last time I would ever see my father. I didn't know what my fate would be or if I would ever return home from Vietnam. I walked straight ahead into the airport and waited to board the flight to Seattle and back to Fort Lewis.

On the flight back, I felt proud. My unit had trained hard for months, and it was time to go fight for our country.

When I arrived at Fort Lewis, I sensed a different atmosphere among my combat buddies. There was an emotional distance, an eerie silence. No one was talking about Vietnam. No one wanted to talk about their time off, and no one was kidding around.

I saw Yingst and asked him about his leave. He said it was OK, and just walked away. "Did you do anything special?" I asked him. "No, I just spent time with my family and my girlfriend. What did you end up doing?"

"About the same," I answered. That was the way it was with everyone in my company. Everyone seemed in a state of depression. We kept to ourselves, and we were all very serious and edgy. I sensed the apprehension and uneasiness in leaving home and family. Guys who normally were outgoing and outspoken were now silenced by an inner fear — the fear of death.

I looked around me. Some of these men would not come back home except in a body bag, just like the drill sergeant warned. My last thirty-day leave could be the last time I would see my parents and wife. I was determined not to be one of the casualties of this war.

I had a future in my dad's business. I also had a wife I loved, and I wanted to have children and a nice home. I had my family and friends. I had a lot more to come home to than some of these men who had nothing. Some men had very bad relationships with their parents. Their girlfriends left them after they were drafted. Some had to go into the Army because they were too rebellious, and jail would be waiting for them when they came home.

On March 15, 1968, brigade headquarters sent an early arrival party to South Vietnam to get our camp ready for the entire brigade. My company commander had previously asked for volunteers and then selected a few qualified men that could do the job. Dyckes, of course, was one of the men chosen. Even though Jim had only been in the Army for eight months, he acted like a veteran. I was afraid for him and the other members of the team.

The rest of us left on April 2, 1968. We boarded buses that would take us to our plane, and from there we would fly to Vietnam.

At around seven o'clock in the morning, we all headed up the stairway up to the airplane in our combat-ready jungle fatigues and our steel pots (helmets). The only thing missing was our M-16 rifles, and we would be getting those when we landed. We would get five hundred rounds of ammunition and four grenades.

We boarded a civilian Pan American jetliner with a full crew and airline hostesses. Our officers took seats in the first-class section, and everyone else sat in coach. This is kind of cool, I thought. It's like taking a vacation. I closed my eyes and imagined I was flying to Hawaii. I will be sitting on the beach in just a couple of hours!

The captain's voice interrupted my dream. "Welcome, men. This is your captain speaking. Our first stop is in Hawaii to refuel. Next, we will be landing in Guam. Don't get too excited, though, as you will not be getting off this plane until we reach Vietnam." All the men groaned at that news. "By the way, the trip will take us twenty-one hours to get there. But, the best is yet to come. The weather in Saigon is clear, no clouds and a warm ninety-eight degrees!"

Wow, that will be great. We had been training in the cold weather where it had been 30 to 40 degrees every day. All I could think about for the rest of the flight was the nice weather.

As I looked around, I noticed that there was no expression on most faces. There was no joy, no laughter, no smiling. Just a vacant stare as they sat in silence.

The pilot was right. It took exactly twenty-one hours to fly to Vietnam, with one stop in Hawaii and another in Guam. Twenty-one hours came too soon when the captain's voice came over the loudspeaker: "We will soon be flying over Vietnam. Look out your left side of your window."

Everyone moved to the left side of the airplane and looked out the window. I saw the mountains, jungles, rice paddies, rivers, and trees. It was green everywhere. It looked like another world. It didn't appear to be so bad. I didn't see the enemy running around. I didn't see anyone shooting at each other. I didn't see any explosions, like I had imagined.

The captain's voice came over the loudspeaker again. "We will soon be landing. Fasten your seat belts." But instead of landing, we kept circling the runway for another forty-five minutes. Why aren't we landing? I thought. A few minutes later his voice came over the loudspeaker again: "Men, we won't be landing soon. The airstrip and runway are being rocketed."

Another forty-five minutes went by as we continued to circle. "I hope we don't run out of fuel," said the guy next to me. "Oh, right," I said. "It's just our luck. We are all going to be killed, and we haven't even landed!" I was kidding, but he didn't like my joke.

After several more minutes, we began our final descent to the airstrip at Bien Hoa. The anticipation of getting off the plane filled my mind. I looked over the side and out the window of the airplane to see if there were any bomb craters on the runway. Charlie—the name we gave to the Viet Cong forces, not to be confused with Charlie Company, the name for "C" company in any Army battalion—was bombing our airstrip. He knew we were coming. His intelligence knew about our "secret" brigade entry. Charlie was smart, smarter than we were led to believe.

Before we landed, our company commander stood and told

us to get off the plane as quickly as possible. We would be handed our M-16 rifles and ammo as we ran off the plane. We took his advice. When the plane landed, we all ran off as fast as we could. I looked back as the last man left the airplane. The stewardess quickly locked the airplane door and immediately the plane took off for the sky.

We all loaded onto trucks, about ten trucks that held forty men each. The sergeant handed us our M-16 rifles and ammo. It felt good to have a weapon in my hand. My M-16 rifle would become my best friend for the next 365 days. It would be beside me wherever I went or sleep or ate. It was in my hands, always, and I felt safer with it. I would never let anyone take it out of my hands, not for the rest of my tour until I was sent home.

The truck doors were shut, and we headed toward our base camp at Long Binh. It was hot, about 110 degrees that day. I kept watching the countryside and the barbed wire all around us. It looked like a concentration camp. There was also a foul smell, like a sewer treatment plant, or just foul garbage. "What is that smell?" I asked the guy next to me. "This is Vietnam," a guy sitting next to me said. "The whole country smells. The smell hits you right in the face when you breathe." Horrid!

Vietnam was filled with disease and filth. This was no vacation, I told myself. I jokingly said to the guy next to me, "Is this hell, or what?" "Yeah, bro, this is hell, all right," he answered.

In the next two weeks, we would all meet that hell's demon called fear. We would have to find the courage within us to stay focused on being soldiers and on playing this game of hide-and-seek with Charlie.

That was my first day in Vietnam. I had been in the country only two hours. I would serve 365 days there. From that moment onward, I counted the days I had left in my tour of duty. Everyone did.

I sat back and wrote 364 days left, on my steal pot, then closed my eyes and prayed, "God help me."

★ ★ ★ ★

CHAPTER 6: RUN THROUGH THE JUNGLE – JOHN FOGERY

We arrived in Vietnam on April 3, 1968. The following day, while we were out on a training mission, we heard over the USO radio that Martin Luther King Jr. had been shot. The news was broadcast on all the G.I. air stations and on television.

The 1960s were a time of extreme change for America. There was hatred and violence in the cities. There was mandatory desegregation in the schools for the first time in history. Back home, there was a silent war going on in the country between blacks and whites. It wasn't so evident in Vietnam, though. Black Americans accepted their role in this war, and they fought with heroism. They bonded with us, and we became brothers. We all helped each other stay alive.

In God's eyes, there is no racial distinction. God created all men equal — black, white, red, brown, and yellow. But almost since the fall of Adam and Eve, we haven't been able to get along. As a Mexican-American, I felt the effects of racism growing up. But I lived in a nice home and neighborhood. I don't think I felt the racial tension as much as many of our black citizens did, especially those who came from the poorer neighborhoods.

That day Martin Luther King died was a day of rebirth for our country. I remember watching the faces of my black brothers. Some men cried as if they had lost their only hope.

King's message was for harmony and fairness among all people. He died for that cause. He died for America, just like the men who died in Vietnam.

Some of the black soldiers started talking as if they hated all whites. They were sad for their friends and relatives back home. There was panic on some of their faces. Most of the men kept silent and withdrew to deal with their grief. Afterward, there was some fear of what might happen to some of the white soldiers. There was a silent, eerie mood that seemed to separate us along racial lines. That fear caused some to doubt the loyalty of our black soldiers.

Something happened later that day to change all of us. We got a call from brigade that afternoon that a visitor was coming. I remember hearing over the radio that "Big Dog/Alpha One" was flying to our location. Big Dog/Alpha One was the commander of our division, Brigadier General Frederick E. Davison. Why was the general coming to see us? What had we done wrong? Maybe the war had ended, we hoped.

We were ordered to get dressed and to stand tall that day. Our rifles needed to be clean and our boots polished. Our boots polished in Vietnam? That would be like combing your hair in the wind!

My lieutenant told me that the general had a special message and needed to speak to us directly. He had never done this before. General Davison was the first black officer to command a division in the U.S. Army. As our whole company stood in formation, an Army helicopter hovered over our heads. A few smoke grenades were popped, and then the helicopter came to a landing about one hundred feet way. Out of the helicopter climbed General Davison along with several of his advisors.

General Davison wasn't very tall. He stood about five-foot-ten and was lean in appearance. He was wearing highly starched jungle fatigues and polished boots. He carried a .45 pistol on his side and had a single shiny star on his steel pot. He was the first general I had ever met. I was proud that he was black, and I respected him for his courage and the obstacles he had to overcome. We all snapped to attention as he walked over to us. "At ease," he commanded.

"Today is a sad day for all Americans," the general told us. "Martin Luther King has been shot and killed in Memphis, Tennessee. I want you to understand the meaning of this. I want you to understand who you are in God's eyes.

"Take a look around you. Look to your left and look to your right. Look in front and look behind you. There is neither black nor white among you. God created you all equal. There is no color difference between us. We have all the same blood. Yet today is a sad day for America. It is a sad day for blacks in America. Martin Luther King fought for freedom, just like you are fighting for freedom.

"The enemy is not around you. Charlie is the enemy. I will not tolerate the kind of thinking that separates us as either black or white. You are professionals, all of you. You are soldiers in the United States Army. You have a duty to your country, to the president of the United States, and you have a mission, to find the enemy and destroy him. We are united by our cause. Anyone who is not with us is against us.

"You are all brothers in the United States Army. If anyone hurts his brother I will personally see to it that he is punished severely. You will be held accountable for your actions against your brother. You hold one another's lives in your hands. Let us fulfill our duty so we can all go home safely."

Then he turned and left. The helicopter flew away. His speech diffused any thoughts or fears of threats that might have triggered hatred between blacks and whites. From that time forward, blacks and whites respected each other in Nam. We fought side by side. There was no room for racism in Vietnam. We were all brothers, united by our common cause.

✮　✮　✮　✮

My first mission in Vietnam began on my ninth day there, April 11, 1968. On the previous night, our company commander had told us we would be picked up by helicopters and transported into the jungles the next morning.

Everyone was excited about going into combat. We were ready, and we wanted to show Charlie who was boss. We all were nervous, but we were prepared to do our job.

After chow the next morning, my platoon assembled. Our supply sergeant ordered us to carry three sets of fatigues, another pair of jungle boots, four pairs of socks, and C-rations for three days. That was already a heavy load — we needed a backpack in addition to our web gear pack. On top of that, we had our jungle hat, our steel pot, four percussion grenades, four smoke grenades, four flares, and over five hundred rounds of ammo. It seemed as though the Army was sending us into the jungles and we were never coming back. The web gear back would last us two weeks by itself, but now we had enough supplies to last a month!

Since I was a radio operator, I also had to carry extra smoke grenades, flares, and a thirty-pound radio. Then my lieutenant told me I also had to carry *his* grenades, *his* smoke grenades, and *his* flares. He told me he needed to carry just his maps and didn't want to feel weighed down. I carried two sets of his fatigues, extra socks, and two days' C-rations. My burden was so heavy, I could barely walk. Everyone was complaining about their heavy packs.

I was so pissed off at my lieutenant for making me carry his gear. I lost respect for him and hated him after that day. He was using me as his hired servant and mule. I held my anger and did what I was told to do, but only because I had to follow his orders. He was my superior.

Finally, I said, "Sir, I can't carry all this stuff." He looked at me and said, "OK, I guess I can take two flares and two grenades." He grabbed them out of my hands and then put them in his own backpack. Gee, what a relief. I could barely move another step. How in the heck could I walk in our patrol?

At seven o'clock in the morning, we could feel the heat. It was going to be the hottest day of the year in Vietnam, around 118 degrees. Our captain told us to carry all our gear. He didn't know when we would be returning to our base camp at Long Binh.

We had been trained at Fort Lewis to carry a lot of gear anyway. We wore cold-weather gear, and that was heavy. But this isn't Fort Lewis, and we're not in the cold forest. Captain was experienced as a Green Beret, so we trusted his judgment and leadership. He always played it by the book.

Our platoon got into formation and headed toward the helicopter pad. The weight on our packs was so heavy that we only made it about 100 feet before the 1st Platoon stopped. Finally, after what seemed like an hour of walking and resting, one of the squads in front of us started to take the clothes from their backpacks. They threw out their extra boots, socks, and t-shirts. Pretty soon, they threw down their entire backpacks.

Captain Kenny, who was leading the way, looked back and called out, "Drop your backpacks, men." The captain told supply to pick it up after we flew out, and so it was shipped into our base camp in the bush later that night. We still had our web gear packs, but leaving the backpacks behind made the hike far more tolerable. However, I still had my radio and most of L.T.'s things, so there was still a heavy burden for me to carry.

It would be my first flight in a helicopter. The chopper flew over the rivers and rice paddies and then over a thick "triple canopy" jungle. It seemed like a long flight to me.

I watched from our chopper as ten or twelve helicopters swooped in and dropped each squad off in open territory. Each Huey landed six men off the chopper and then lifted off into the sky. As our chopper approached the landing zone, we edged closer to the open helicopter door. When the pilot told us to jump out, we did.

The ground was firm as I landed, and all my gear was intact. I was nervous and scared that the enemy might be watching and waiting for a chance to shoot us. I ran swiftly but cautiously — no time to think about booby traps or AK-47 fire. I felt like a sitting duck in a wading pond. But there was no gunfire, and I made it to the edge of the jungle. I had never seen such foliage — it seemed like I was on another planet.

When I entered the batch of jungle, I was greeted by my lieutenant. Our point man was issued a machete, and he started to chop through the dense jungle. The brush and trees were the thickest and heaviest I have ever seen. We couldn't move an inch, so we all took turns chopping our way further and deeper into the unknown. Even the company commander took a turn. It was extremely hot that day.

About twenty minutes of chopping was all one person could handle. Men started to pass out from heat exhaustion. Two of our men had to be air evacuated due to heatstroke. It took our company six hours to travel five hundred feet that day, and it was getting dark. We weren't going to reach our base camp that way, and we didn't want to spend the night in that mess, either.

Suddenly, a voice came over the radio. "Alpha One, this is Alpha Papa One, over." It was our brigade commander asking about our position. "What was ETA [estimated time of arrival] to your base camp, over?"

Captain Kenny said, "We've encountered some heavy brush, over. It won't be until midnight until we reach our destination, over."

"We'll you'd better find another way out, Alpha One, over. You need to reach your destination by nightfall, over."

"Roger that, over," replied Captain Kenny. "Over and out."

"Are we there yet, Captain? This is Bravo Two, over?" one of our platoon leaders asked.

"Not yet, keep moving forward, over," Captain Kenny replied in frustration.

By this time, we were all hungry and tired and wondering

why it was taking us so long to get to our base camp. The dark night would soon be upon us. We needed to get to our location fast.

"Alpha One, this is Charlie One, over ... We need to find an alternate route, Cap." Captain Kenny knew we needed to secure a location and dig in before nightfall.

"I'm sending someone to find us an alternate route. This is Alpha One, over," came the reply.

Our company came to a halt, and we were able to take a rest stop while a squad from 1st Platoon searched for an alternate route.

"This is Alpha One, over," came the call a half-hour later. "We've found an alternate route, over, follow us, over."

"Men you've got to be careful, we'll be in the open," Captain Kenny told us. "Keep up and be swift." That meant it would be easy to get shot at by Charlie. We would be traveling in the open down a dirt road. In all the television movies I ever watched, I remembered that this was the most dangerous part of the movie. The Marines would be walking, and then all of a sudden, "Blam-Blam-Blam!" The whole squad was pinned down until John Wayne moved forward and killed everyone with his machine gun. Too bad this wasn't television, I thought. I could get killed right here after just a week in Nam.

As our platoon came to an opening in the jungle, I looked up and down the dirt road for the enemy. 1st Platoon was leading the way, and no shots were fired. I looked from side to side, waiting for all hell to break loose. It reminded me also of the movie "Bridge Over the River Kwai," when the commander was leading his troops through the jungles. Cinema had a way of reminding me of war scenes embedded within my brain since childhood. I would live out those scenes as though I had been there before, *déjà vu!*

The opening was filled with waist-high grass. I looked like the road hadn't been used in years. Lieutenant took off in front of me and started to call us forward. "Let's move, men," he said as he waved us forward. The lieutenant decided he would walk point — and I had to stay right behind him! This guy is crazy, I told myself. The lieutenant is supposed to walk in the middle of the platoon. Everyone learned that at basic training.

Every soldier was running as fast as he could. You could sense that the enemy was watching us as we scampered to safety. Charlie knew we were there in his jungle. We could tell because there weren't any birds chirping in the trees. In the jungle, we were told, when the birds stopped chirping, Charlie is close by... so watch out.

By the time we reached our command post, I was too exhausted to set my gear down. I didn't think I could hike one more step. What was the Army trying to do to us — kill us before we found Charlie?

me, German & Dyckes Hill 41

patrolling in the rice patties

No sooner had we reached our spot to rest than L.T. commanded us to "dig in." He must be kidding, I thought. I'm too tired to dig in, and I really don't give a shit if I dig in or not. If a mortar kills me, then too bad.

However, we did need to dig our foxholes while it was still light. We filled sandbag after sandbag. We dug deep into the ground for protection from mortar rounds and bullets. My lieutenant had me dig his foxhole, too. He was lazy and must have felt it wasn't his job because he was an officer. I had to not only do my own job, but his as well. I didn't think he treated me fairly. I was his radio operator, and so I had to be with him constantly. I would soon notice that had a hero mentality by day but was nowhere to be found at night. Maybe he was afraid of the dark.

I took out my shovel from atop my gear and started to dig two holes, one hole deeper for me and the other not as deep for him. I was just about ready to put my gear in my foxhole when I heard a thud beside me. In my foxhole was L.T.'s gear. He had just returned from the officers' meeting and had thrown his gear in my fox hole.

"Ah, L.T., that's my foxhole, sir," I said cautiously.

"What do you mean, Campos?" L.T. replied. "I don't see your name on it. It's mine now."

"Ah, yes, sir," I replied.

Then I was even more perturbed. I looked over at Yingst, who was standing several feet from me, and gave him a frown. He witnessed the whole event and was angry, too. "That S.O.B.," he said. We both were worn out from carrying all our gear and chopping through dense jungle only to be treated like a servant. It was still hot, and this day wasn't over by any means.

I sat next to L.T. while he put his head down on his steel pot and stretched out in his comfortable foxhole. I watched him until the sky grew dark, pitch dark, but I didn't say a word. I accepted my responsibility to be his aide, but I would not be his hired servant. I had to deal with my anger minute by minute. I prayed for my lieutenant to get transferred so that we could get another platoon leader. A good leader always thinks of his men first. This guy was selfish. It made me hate him more. I despised his authority.

The night became so dark that I couldn't see two feet in front of my face. I had never experienced that kind of darkness. It was as if God pulled the plug, and the sky turned black. There were no stars, no moon. This was going to be a long and scary night. Then I heard something that scared me to death.

"Bam-bam-bam!" came the sound from a long distance, and then "Kabam, kabam, kabam!" Incoming rounds of artillery were exploding outside our compound. I was sure it was from Charlie. I hadn't heard anyone call in artillery support. We never had experienced this before.

"Kabam, Kabam, Kabam!" The rounds kept hitting right outside our perimeter. "Are those rounds from us or the enemy?" I asked L.T. I didn't hear a word from him. He was silent.

"Sir," I spoke up a little louder. "Are those rounds coming from us, or is that incoming?" L.T. was nowhere to be found. "Where did L.T. go?" I asked Sergeant Turner. "I don't know," he replied. "Maybe he went to take a piss."

I dug my head deeper and deeper into the dirt. I thought it might be my last day on earth. I would surely die on this forbidden soil. I prayed, "Please, God, take care of my wife and my mother and father. I am going to die."

I could hear the artillery rounds whistling over our heads and exploding in front of us. The artillery kept coming one after the other for over an hour.

"I think it's our artillery, not from Charlie," a voice came from the dark. No one knew, and no one said a word. We just kept digging deeper and deeper into our foxholes.

A little later, L.T. returned and told Sergeant Turner to get our ambush patrol on the move and out of the compound. Second squad was told to set up an ambush.

I was happy it wasn't me going outside the perimeter. I wanted nothing to do with that ambush patrol that night. Besides, I was worn out and exhausted after digging two foxholes and walking with L.T.'s gear on my back.

It was about two o'clock in the morning when I heard some talking on the radio. "I can hear Charlie talking," came the whispering voice, "and he's ten feet away from me. He's all around us. There's a bunch of them, and I 'm coming in. I'm getting the hell outta here."

"You stay right where you are," ordered Captain Kenny on the radio. "Stay on ambush patrol, do you hear me?"

"I'm coming, I don't want to get killed," the frightened soldier replied. "We're coming in, don't shoot us."

A few minutes later, another ambush patrol started talking.

A soft voice reported, "I hear Charlie whispering. He's about fifteen feet away from us, over."

"Stay where you are," ordered Captain Kenny.

Suddenly there was loud scream. "Augh!! It's a snake, snake… We're coming in, too, don't shoot." A few minutes later, we heard the squad running back inside our compound.

Now there was only one squad left on ambush patrol. It took another five minutes before they called out over the radio, "We're coming in, too." It was our first night, and all our ambush patrols had returned to our company. We were all scared, and no one questioned them coming back into the compound.

Next, it was my lieutenant who started to see things. "I see Charlie over there!" he yelled. "I see him again over there!" he said, pointing in another direction.

"Where?" asked Sergeant Turner. "He's over there," said L.T., frightened. "Don't you see anything, Turner?"

"Ah. I don't see anything, sir," said Sergeant Turner. "It's so damn dark; I can't see a thing, Lieutenant."

L.T. freaked. He stood up, "I see someone over there!" he yelled as he started firing his AR-15 machine gun, blasting bullets into the bush in front of us.

I looked and looked, but I couldn't see anything. I think L.T.'s seeing things, I told myself. No one else sees anything except him. He's nuts!

"Do you see anything, Yingst?" I whispered. "No, I can't see a thing, it's too dark," he replied quietly.

"That's what I thought. Well, L.T. thinks he sees Charlie outside our perimeter," I whispered back.

By that time, everyone was really scared. Men were imagining Charlie outside the perimeter, and there was sporadic gunfire all night long. No one slept a wink during our first night in the bush. I kept praying for the sun or the moon to rise so we could see, but it remained dark. It would be one of the longest nights I ever spent in Nam.

At dawn, our commander called in the helicopters. They

picked us up an hour later and dropped us off at another part of the jungle for our next mission.

In our first week in the bush, we won our Combat Infantry Badges. The only way you get your C.I.B. badge is to get fired upon or to fire your weapon at the enemy. It was an award that all infantrymen wanted to get as soon as possible, a badge of courage and honor. While training at Fort Lewis, I was anxious to receive mine, and so was everyone else. After training for seven months, I couldn't wait to use my knowledge and training. I was very confident in my abilities and our teamwork.

It was our second day out in the bush, and we were searching for the enemy in the jungles. We were walking through a dense jungle area. We could sense Charlie was watching us. Over the radio, command informed us there was an intelligence report that Charlie had enemy troops in our area. I could hear Alpha One, our company commander, respond to brigade, telling our company to engage and make contact with the enemy.

While we walked through the jungles that day, it was hard to see more than ten feet in front of us. The jungle was extremely thick, with branches and bushes that tore right through my jungle fatigues. The branches scratched my arms, hands, and face as I tried the best I could to get through it.

Suddenly, the point man stopped and signaled for us to crouch down. I stooped and I listened for anything that made a sound. The birds had stopped chirping. All I could hear was the wind. It was an eerie feeling. My sixth sense told me something or someone was moving in front of us.

I watched as the man on our point started walking again. I watched him maneuver through the tree branches. He was about ten feet in front of me, and I could see the branches hitting him in the face and arms.

I saw him trip and lose his balance over a long branch on the ground. As he fell, he mistakenly fired his M-16. His finger was on the trigger, and his safety was set to fire. "Bam-bam-bam," the bullets sprayed the ground as he fell forward.

Everyone expected it was Charlie that was firing at us. The gunshots echoed throughout the whole jungle. It was only a single blast of our point man's M-16 rifle that I heard. The rest of our platoon behind me hit the ground. That's what we were trained to do whenever we heard gunfire.

A few seconds later, the point man, who tripped, started screaming his lungs out. Apparently, one of the bullet rounds had hit him in his leg. Lieutenant and I ran over to help him.

The guy had forgotten to put his M-16 on safety. We were always told by the Army never to have our M-16s on fire. The Army warned us about such accidents at Fort Lewis. An accident like that could wound or kill the guy in front or behind you. We wanted to shoot the enemy, not our combat buddies.

L.T. and I went to the fallen soldier as soon as he got hit. L.T. called out for a medic and asked me to call in a Medevac chopper. I called the chopper and waited while the medic bandaged up our point man.

Just after the gunshot sounded, a voice came over the radio. "Bravo One, this is Alpha One, over ... Did you make contact with the enemy, over?" He repeated the question several times before L.T. responded.

L.T. looked at me and ordered me to tell our commander we had made contact with the enemy. I hesitated, "Ah, sir," I answered, "Ah, I'm not good at lying, sir."

"Give me that damn phone," L.T. shouted, as he grabbed the phone off my backpack. He hesitated for several minutes before answering.

"Yes, sir, ah, Bravo One, this is Bravo Two, over. Yes, we made enemy contact, over. Our point man has been hit, over. We have called in a Medevac, over."

"Congratulations, Lieutenant," answered Captain Kenny.

"You men just earned your Combat Infantry Badges. How's your man doing, over?"

"He'll be fine, over. It was just a flesh wound, no one else is hurt, over," said L.T.

I was shocked when I heard L.T. tell our company commander we had engaged the enemy. He lied, I told myself. L.T. looked over to me and told me to keep my mouth shut. No one except the three of us would know the truth. L.T. ordered us not to tell anyone that he lied. He didn't want to tell headquarters that his point man had tripped over his own feet and shot himself. It would be too embarrassing.

L.T. told our point man while he was on the ground, "You got hit by a sniper. Charlie shot you, got it?"

"Yes sir, the point man answered back.

We cleared a landing zone site, and about twenty-five minutes later the chopper flew in and picked up the injured soldier. I helped put him into the Huey, and watched as the chopper flew into the air.

My whole platoon was awarded our Combat Infantry Badges because brigade headquarters believed we had engaged the enemy. I couldn't tell anyone. No one else knew about what took place. The whole company thought Charlie had fired at us and then ran away into the jungles. Later that day, I told Yingst and Dyckes what really happened. But I didn't tell anyone the rest of my tour. It's sad, but that's how I won my Combat Infantry Badge — by friendly fire.

A week later we all had our C.I.B. patch on our jungle fatigues. I still wore mine with pride. I felt honored, even though we had not really engaged the enemy that day. I knew in my heart I would earn it sooner or later anyway.

In Vietnam, every combat soldier deserved to wear his badge. A Combat Infantry Badge meant that you were a warrior. You had engaged the enemy, and you had survived. You were now ready to succeed in life. To some, it meant that you were a man.

At nineteen years old, I wanted to be recognized as being a man.

The wounded G.I. never told the truth, either. It was our first cover-up over friendly fire.

It would not be the last.

★ ★ ★ ★

PART III: JUNGLES, RICE PATTIES AND MORE RICE PATTIES

★ ★ ★ ★

CHAPTER 7: I-FEEL-LIKE-I'M-FIXIN'-TO-DIE – COUNTRY JOE & THE FISH

One week later, on April 18, we stood there in formation, lined up in our platoons and our squads. Stuck in the ground upside-down were two M-16 rifles. Atop each hung a helmet, and below each was a pair of boots. Our company commander read the names of two soldiers. Our chaplain led us in praying the Twenty-Third Psalm.

It was our first experience of death, Vietnam-style. In the dark of night the previous evening, two brother soldiers, David and Robert, had been killed in action.

Remembering that event brings tears to my eyes even today, but at the time, I couldn't cry. I didn't cry in Nam. I somehow shut off my emotions in war so as not to feel the pain. I did not allow myself to grieve. I had a job to do, and I had to stay alive.

I remember thinking to myself and asking the question: Why, God? Why did this have to happen? Why to these two men, in this country so far from home, so soon in their tour? Why was I spared? When would it be my time to die? Only God knows the answers.

The toughest job was left up to Lieutenant Hugh Foster, David's platoon leader. He had to call David's parents from Nam and tell them their son had died in combat. What a horrible

77

responsibility. I would not want to be the one who told the parents of the death of their son.

It's odd how meeting death can change your life.

My only previous experience of death was when my grandfather died in 1963, when I was fourteen years old. I was at school and in the middle of a class when I was paged over the loudspeaker to report to the dean's office. I figured I must be in some kind of trouble.

When I arrived, the dean said, "You have a phone call from your mother." He handed me the telephone and left the room.

It was my mother. "Stephen? You need to come home. Your grandfather died this morning," she told me. I put the phone down, gathered my things, and waited for her to pick me up.

My grandfather and grandmother had six children, and I had sixteen cousins. My grandfather was the pillar that held our family together during the holidays, because we would all gather at his home each Christmas and Easter.

I will never forget the funeral. Everyone was there, all our aunts, uncles, and cousins. The ushers wheeled a large black casket down the hall, placed it in the center, and propped open the lid. I was in the third row from the casket, so my grandfather's body lay fifteen feet away from me. I could barely see his body as we waited for Father Kennedy to celebrate the Mass.

It was a moving service. I remember it like it just had happened yesterday. There was much sadness, and everyone cried except me.

After the Mass, my father led the procession past my grandfather's body. When it was my turn, I looked at the body and realized my grandfather was gone forever. That was the first time that a person close to me had died.

I held in my emotions until later that afternoon. When I came home, I went into my room and immediately burst into tears. I couldn't hold it any longer. I never wanted to go through that emotion again.

Our whole family changed after that. My cousins and our

families stopped getting together at Christmas and Easter holidays. It wasn't the same anymore.

I thought of my grandfather's death as I stood there at the service for David and Robert. Why does God allow such suffering? One day, when I see my two combat brothers in heaven, I will know the answer, but for now I can only question.

My mind went back to what happened that previous evening.

It was the afternoon of April 17, and we had only been in Nam for fifteen days. I packed the radio for the Lieutenant as we walked point that day. The choppers had picked us up that morning as usual, but this day was different. Intelligence reported a North Vietnamese division heading toward Saigon to overrun the capital. Or job was to stop them and engage the enemy. The first North Vietnamese regulars were heavy armed, the scouts reported.

As we approached the landing zone, we anticipated engaging the enemy. We were told it would be a "hot" landing zone, which meant it was likely we would be fired upon before we even hit the ground. The helicopters weren't going to land in a hot landing zone, so we prepared to jump from five or six feet down to the ground. That's a long way down when you have thirty pounds on your back.

As we approached, our pilot said, "You're on your own, men, so get out fast." I was the first off that time because I was next to the open door. I hit the ground hard and bounced backward onto the radio. I needed to be helped up because I couldn't move, like a turtle rolled over on his back. L.T. was right behind me. He gave me a hand, and we were off to find cover.

This was the most remote place we had been so far. It appeared to have been bombed recently with some kind of spray. The trees and branches were vaguely orange in color. "It's an Agent Orange contamination area," our sergeant told us. "I've seen this before. We're not supposed to be in this area."

Agent Orange. Great! I told myself. Now I'll be killed by

some contaminant in Nam. The trees and bushed were completely dry. It was a leery and somber place, not like the jungles we were used to hiking in. The land was barren and lifeless.

I could hear on the radio that there was fighting all around us. It was the first and heaviest day of war for us. All the other companies, Alpha, Bravo, Delta, and Echo, had already engaged the enemy.

I think I was the first to hear the casualties list. Alpha Company had killed thirty N.V.A. (North Vietnamese regulars) and had two American soldiers killed and five wounded. Bravo Company killed eight N.V.A. and had one American killed and three wounded. Echo Company killed 10 N.V.A. and had three Americans killed and five wounded.

Everyone knew our turn was coming up soon. We were all edgy and tense. I scanned the trees and bushes everywhere and tried to listen to the birds. I didn't hear a thing. Charlie was following us. We could sense the tension in the air. Fear was stirring and night was coming fast. We needed to move quickly through the jungles and reach our base camp.

For the first time, it was evident that we would engage Charlie that day. There would be a huge firefight, and men would get killed.

I kept looking for signs of Charlie, the trees or perhaps the birds ruffling. I scanned the countryside up and down with my eyes in four-foot box sections. This was the way to spot the enemy. Our eyes focused on every branch. Charlie was smart: He could be hiding in the ground or up on a tree. He could pop out of nowhere and kill us with his AK-47 rifle. Our senses were tuned in everywhere. We had to become a part of the terrain or die.

Our company was at full strength with about 285 men that day. In Nam, most companies had fewer than a hundred men. Every man counted in a firefight. But, there was a lot of disease in Nam, such as jungle rot, which is like trench foot, only worse. Every morning we had sick call. The sick or diseased would be treated back at base camp or were airlifted or transported to a medical facility. When men would get sick or wounded, they weren't replaced for a few months. Consequently, most Army units functioned at about half strength.

Night was approaching fast, and tonight there would be no moonlight. Captain Kenny told the platoon leaders to take head counts to make sure we didn't leave anyone behind. All were accounted for just before dark.

When the thick night of darkness arrived, we still hadn't reached our destination. It was so dark that we had to travel one arm's length at a time. I held out my arm in front of me to touch the person in front of me. It was L.T. I couldn't see him, but my arm felt his backpack. We walked slowly in line, one man in front of the next.

One of the men from 3rd Platoon said he heard or saw something about twenty feet away from him. Immediately, there was silence.

When the point man stopped, both platoons quickly stopped. I crouched close to the ground in a kneeling position. I listened intently but heard nothing but the wind whistling in the trees. I looked up toward the horizon to see if I could catch a glimpse of a man, but saw nothing.

"I see something over there, Lieutenant," Sergeant whispered. "It looks like a man standing, but I'm not sure."

"Where is he?" Lieutenant Foster asked.

"Over there by the trees," Sergeant pointed. "Can't you see him?"

"No," said Lieutenant Foster. "Is it our flank man?"

I'm not sure," Sergeant replied.

"Did you take a head count, Sergeant?"

"Yes, sir," replied Sergeant. "We're all are accounted for, Lieutenant."

"Who is on right flank?" Lieutenant asked.

"David, sir."

"Well, call out his name, Sergeant, and make sure it isn't him."

"Roger," replied Sergeant. "David, is that you?"

We all listened for his reply. There was nothing but silence. No one uttered a word.

"I'm going to fire up a flare," whispered Lieutenant Foster. "Make sure you all are on the ground."

Lieutenant Foster shot a flare into the night air. The flare exploded in a white light that illuminated the sky and ground. We looked around, but all I could see were trees and bushes. There was not a shadow of a man anywhere.

"It might be Charlie," someone whispered. After the flare extinguished, it got real dark again.

My lieutenant and I were standing about twenty feet away from 3rd Platoon and Lieutenant Foster when all of this took place. In the night air, noise carries a long way. I was afraid Charlie might hear us.

"I still see someone standing over there," Sergeant said. "It looks like a man, but I can't tell, and it's so dark."

"David, is that you?" He whispered again, "David?" Still no reply, not a word.

"Well, fire a burst over his head, but make sure it's way over his head so you don't hit him," said Lieutenant Foster. "Yes, sir."

Sarge fired a burst of machine gun into the air. We all watched the tracer rounds but still didn't see or hear anything. Sarge called out David's name again. "David, is that you?" Still nothing.

Finally, Lieutenant Foster said, "We've got to move, men. Let's go."

Our platoons had gotten separated by this time. Two platoons and our company commander had continued to move forward while 2nd Platoon and 3rd Platoon was trying to figure out if there was a man in the bush.

Captain asked, "What's happening, Charlie three? Over."

"One of the men thought he saw something, Cap."

"Well, take a head count, over," came the orders from Captain Kenny. "We need to get to our C.P. (command post). It's late, and we're hungry."

Both platoons took head counts, and Captain Kenny asked for the results on the radio. "What's your answer, 2nd Platoon?" "All accounted for, sir," replied my L.T. "Third platoon how about you?" "We're one short, sir," replied Lieutenant Foster.

"Are you sure?" asked the captain. "Yes, sir," answered Lieutenant Foster. "We're short one. It may be David, sir, our flank. He never came back in after it got dark."

"Well, go back and find him," Captain Kenny replied angrily. "We're moving on. You and 2nd Platoon go back and get him, Lieutenant. That's an order. We're moving to our C.P. You'll have to catch up to us later, over."

"Let's go, men," ordered Lieutenant Foster. "We're headed back to where the gunshots were fired."

Both the 2nd and 3rd Platoons retraced our steps to find David while our other two platoons moved ahead to find the C.P.

Captain Kenny was a Green Beret who had been to Nam for a year already. Everyone in the brigade liked and respected him. There were rumors he was going to be promoted to major soon. Everyone knew he wouldn't be with us very long.

We moved back quickly to the area where the shots were fired. It took us about an hour to get back to the same spot. I didn't know what we would find. What had happened to David, anyway?

We came to the spot where Sergeant said he had seen something and fired his M-16 in the air. Sergeant led the way. Following closely behind were Lieutenant Foster, my own lieutenant, and me.

"I found him," said Sarge. "It's him. He's lying by a tree."

Lieutenant Foster knelt down by the tree where David's body lay and directed his flashlight at him. It indeed was David, and he was dead. He had a gunshot wound on his forehead. Charlie got him while he was traveling out on our flank. He was the first soldier in our company to be killed in action in Vietnam.

I knew David. He was in my basic training unit at Fort Lewis, Washington. We both had gone on to Advanced Infantry Training after just six weeks of basic training.

I remembered David sitting on the bleachers during basic training one day. The drill sergeant stopped the whole class and yelled at him because he was sound asleep during the drill sergeant's presentation.

I was curious to look at David, but all I saw was a swarm of red ants crawling all over his head and face. Sarge and others brushed off the ants and wrapped him in a poncho liner. The 3rd Platoon carried his body, and we resumed our hunt for the rest of our company.

By then we had been separated from the rest of our company for two hours. The great L.T., who for some reason liked walking point, was always in the lead, and I had to be with him. But I sensed that my Lieutenant was frightened that night. He was very silent, and he was very cautious. Now that David was dead, we were all becoming extra cautious. The darkness made matters worse, and the thought of someone else getting killed loomed in our minds. We hadn't eaten chow, and now we were lost and separated from our other two platoons. "This is just not our day," I told L.T.

I could hear the panic in L.T.'s voice when he talked to our company commander over the phone. He kept calling Captain Kenny about every fifteen minutes. "Alpha One, this is Bravo One, over… Where are you, Captain?" L.T. would ask over and over again. He seems to be scared, I told myself, and that's not good. But I could understand. We were all a bit scared.

"Bravo One, this is Alpha One," reported back the captain. "We've reached the C.P. and we're at coordinates Tango Mike 25 and Zebra Bravo 8, over."

L.T. took out his flashlight and looked at his map. "We're at Mike 22 and Zebra 4, over," said L.T.

"Then you're only about a thousand meters away, so keep moving forward, Bravo One, over."

"We found our man, over," said Lieutenant Foster. "He's dead, and we're bringing his body with us." There was silence on the other end.

Another half hour went by. My lieutenant was holding on to the radio as we walked slowly forward. He was almost dragging me with him.

"Alpha One, this is Bravo One, over. Where are you, over?" L.T. asked again.

This is Alpha One. We can hear you approaching, over. You're about eight hundred meters away. Keep moving forward, over."

I heard a frightened and questioning tone come out of my lieutenant's mouth. "Where are you?"

"Straight ahead," repeated Captain Kenny. "Keep moving forward. We all hear you."

Another five minutes went by. "Where are you?" L.T. asked again.

This is Alpha One. You're five hundred feet away. You're almost here, over."

"Where, and which direction, over?" asked L.T.

"I'm sending someone to get you," came Captain Kenny's reply.

A few minutes later, I watched as a man approached. He was headed straight toward Lieutenant and me.

By this time, Lieutenant had released his grip on the phone and let it go. I placed the phone back in place and knelt down to scan the horizon and see if I could recognize the figure that was coming toward us. I couldn't see who it was, but it appeared to be a G.I. He was wearing an Army helmet. L.T. saw him, too.

"Halt! who goes there?" yelled L.T.

At Fort Lewis, we had extensive training exercises for guard duty. The normal procedure while on guard duty was to call out "Halt!" if someone approached within fifty feet. This man who was moving toward us was unrecognizable, and my lieutenant responded in the appropriate way.

"Halt! Who goes there?" he yelled again, his voice trembling.

I watched as the man stopped walking and stooped down as if to see who was asking. I could see the reflection of his steel pot. He looked like a G.I., but no one knew for sure. Why wasn't he answering?

Lieutenant then called out, *"Chu hoy!"* — Vietnamese for "Who goes there?"

The man appeared to be stunned and surprised that someone would call to him in Vietnamese. The unidentified man was then about fifteen feet away from me. *"Chu hoy!"* repeated Lieutenant.

Another trembling voice finally responded: "Hey, it's Charlie Co–"

When my Lieutenant heard the word," Charlie," he freaked and immediately yelled out, "OPEN FIRE!"

Within one second, ALL HELL broke loose. Most of the firing zeroed in on the man in front of me while the rest of the platoon was firing all around. The night air was filled with the spray of bullets and machine-gun fire. The grenade launchers fired their weapons. Everyone to my right and my left had reacted to the lieutenant's order. Everyone was firing except me. When the shooting started, I hit the ground and buried my face in my steel pot. I didn't fire my M-16. I just knew it was an American.

To make matters worse, the rest of our company was to our right flank about one hundred feet away — and so was Captain Kenny's command post.

I watched as green tracer rounds began coming at us from the opposite side of the perimeter. Charlie used green tracer rounds! The tracer rounds came directly toward us, and there were explosions all around me. Had Charlie been planning to ambush us?

But my mind was focused on the body in front of me that had

fallen in a torrent of bullets. To me, he had looked like a G.I. It appeared to me that he was wearing a steel pot. Charlie wears a different kind of helmet than American soldiers. His is smaller, more like an African hunter's helmet.

I had watched the tracer rounds zero in on the man in front of me. It was like a firing range. The man had taken incoming bullets in his side just a few feet away from me. He had fallen after a few hits and never got up again.

Suddenly, over the radio, I could hear screaming and yelling. "Stop your firing! Stop your firing! You're firing on your own company! You're firing on your own company! Quit firing at us!"

Finally, Sergeant Turner yelled. "Stop your firing!" He yelled again and again. "Cease fire!" "Stop your firing!" Gradually, the shooting died down until I heard the last shot. It was too late, though. We had been engaged in a huge firefight with our own company for about ten minutes. If we had gone on much longer, I'm sure everyone would have been killed.

And now the air was filled with the screams and moans of American soldiers.

CHAPTER 8: I CAN'T GET NO SATISFACTION – THE ROLLING STONES

We were all in shock about what had just happened. It felt like we were in hell. In desperation to assess the situation, Lieutenant reached into my backpack and grabbed a red flare — the only red flare I carried, because red was used rarely and only for medical evacuations — and popped it into the air.

What happened next was like a scene out of "Apocalypse Now." As the flare exploded in the air, we were bathed in red light and smoke, just like hell. Red light, smoke, and the smells of burning rubber and gunpowder filled the night air.

After the firing stopped, L.T. and I moved forward to examine the man in front of us. I leaned down as L.T. shone his infrared flashlight on the victim's face.

It was Robert. He carried the radio for Captain Kenny. His face was contorted in a silent expression of shock and pain. L.T. immediately called for a medic. Robert lay there, barely breathing. There was nothing we could do. When the medic came, he gave Robert two shots of morphine.

Captain Kenny had sent Robert out to guide us in because we were lost, just as he said he would. Robert never knew what hit him. Everything happened so fast.

Robert had trained with Captain Kenny prior to coming to Nam. He was very smart and was extremely well liked by everyone in our company. He also had a brilliant sense of humor and was the company joker, always clowning around. To see him lying there in his last moments was horrifying for all of us. We all sensed that Robert would not make it through the night.

The screams and moans continued, and then someone on the radio yelled, "Captain's been hit! Captain's been hit!"

L.T. and I slowly moved forward to find the command post. We couldn't see much because of the smoke from the weapons, but we could follow the sound of the groans we heard until we reached the place where our company commander lay twitching in pain. Captain Kenny had multiple bullet wounds in both legs — eighteen in all, we would later learn. Blood was everywhere. L.T. sent up a white flare and called the medic over. The medic gave the captain two doses of morphine just as he had done for Robert.

The Army always told us never to give a wounded G.I. more than one shot of morphine, but this was different. Captain was in a lot of pain. We had essentially shot his air mattress out from under him, flattening it like a pancake. It may have saved his life.

Two other soldiers were lying near the captain, also wounded. A soldier named Bradbury was hit in the arm, as was Chu Rung, our Vietnamese scout. Both were in shock.

The command post happened to be directly in line with one of our machine guns. Captain Kenny got the worst of it. Thank God he was still breathing. But we had killed one of our own and wounded three others. What a nightmare.

Captain Kenny whispered in pain to my lieutenant. "Lieutenant, call in a medevac [medical evacuation] right away," he told L.T. "Tell them we were caught in an ambush with the enemy. Lieutenant, you saved us from the enemy. Do you understand?"

"Yes, sir," L.T. replied. I think he was in shock. We were all in shock.

"Campos, give me the horn," he commanded. I quickly handed him the phone.

"Hotel One, this is Charlie Bravo One, over," L.T. called to brigade headquarters. "This is Charlie Company's 2nd Platoon leader, over. We need a medevac pronto, over. Charlie One's been hit. I repeat, Charlie One's been hit, over. We have two killed and three wounded, over. Send us a medevac pronto, over."

"This is Hotel One, over," headquarters responded. "Where has he been hit?"

"He is hit in both legs. It's pretty bad, over. Get that chopper out, now, over."

"This is Hotel One; we're sending one to you now, over."

L.T. gave me the phone, and we waited for what seemed like hours. We tried to comfort Captain Kenny and figure out what went wrong. I wasn't angry at L.T. for ordering us to open fire, but I was sad for Robert, David, and Captain Kenny. The whole incident shouldn't have happened, but there was nothing anyone could do about it now. The damage was done.

As the chopper approached, I held out the strobe light and popped the smoke to give the chopper a target to land. I stood in view of the light to guide the chopper pilot onto the ground. We lifted Captain Kenny gently from the stretcher and placed him in the helicopter. Then we helped Robert, Bradbury and Chu Rung into the chopper. We placed David in last. The chopper flew away.

"Charlie Bravo One, this is Hotel One, over," over the radio. I gave the phone to L.T. "This is Charlie Bravo One, over."

"What's the status of Charlie One, over?"

"He's on his way, over."

Headquarters then gave us specific directions. "Lieutenant, listen to this: Tell your men to lay their weapons down. I am sending Alpha Company to your location. I repeat, lay your weapons down. I am sending Alpha Company to you. Do you understand, over?"

"Yes, sir."

"Wait for them to reach you, over."

"Roger, will comply, over," said L.T.

L.T. repeated the words of our brigade commander over the phone to the rest of the company. "Put your weapons down. That's an order," he said. "Men, we have to wait here for Alpha Company. Put down your weapons and relax."

Sergeant Turner was near me, and so was Tiger. L.T. told all the squad leaders to assemble in one place so he could tell us what to do next.

"Men, we were in an ambush with the enemy. Captain Kenny said that's what happened. Do you understand, men?" Everyone agreed. Then Lieutenant walked away from us.

I couldn't believe my ears. Did he say we got into an ambush with the enemy? Was he in another world? Did he witness something different than the rest of us?

I walked over to Sergeant Turner. "Did you hear that, Sergeant? That isn't what happened." Sarge told me not to worry. "It's OK," he said, "just do what he says."

"Yeah, but he's going to get us killed," I replied.

I went over to Tiger, who was standing around dazed in disbelief. "Did you hear what L.T. said?" I asked him. "Yes, he's nuts, man," Tiger replied. "He's F---in nuts. He started this whole shit thing."

"L.T. yelled, 'Open fire!' and we all followed his orders," I said. "I heard them tell brigade that we were in a firefight with Charlie. They are not telling the truth. It's all a lie. Or am I imagining all this?"

"No man, you're right," Tiger replied with unmistakable anger in his voice.

It was all a cover-up.

The whole company waited an hour and a half before brigade sent Alpha Company to help us. I listened to the orders over the phone. Our colonel told Alpha Company's commander to surround us and that we were not to use our weapons until dawn. We were ordered to take all our bullets from our rifles and to lay them down.

Dyckes found Tiger and me. "Wow, I can't believe it, Stone Pony," Dyckes said. "What happened was bizarre, man. I just kept firing my rifle at our own company. My machine gunner fired at them, too. We all did."

We stayed awake all night. I lay down and closed my eyes, but my mind was racing. I recalled every detail and replayed the horror over and over again, obsessed with trying to understand what had transpired. This was no ambush, I thought to myself. L.T. screwed up and ordered us to fire upon our own men.

Tiger and Dyckes had seen the green tracer rounds, too. So had everyone else we asked. That's definitely Charlie. Only Charlie fires green tracer rounds. He might have thought we were firing at him on the other side of the gully. Charlie saw the whole thing. Maybe he was planning to ambush our company. Maybe, in some perverse way, this whole friendly-fire tragedy had spoiled Charlie's plans. No one knew for sure. We would never know for sure.

What I did know was that the fear of death had hit me hard, shattering me like a rock through a pane of glass. I started to become even more afraid for my life. I was afraid just as much that my buddies Dyckes and Tiger might get killed. Fear ran through my entire body and soul.

It got me thinking differently, like an epiphany, like a light that illuminated my heart and soul. In the dead of night, I walked over to where Tiger was resting. I nudged him on the shoulder and asked him, "Are you awake? I need to talk to you." I went over to Dyckes and nudged him as well. He got up, and the three of us sat together.

Fresh on my mind were the thoughts of Robert, David, and Captain Kenny. My heart was heavy and filled with fear as I spoke to both of them. I needed to tell Dyckes and Tiger how much they meant to me. I might not have another chance.

With a heavy heart I spoke, "You guys mean everything to me. I trust you with my life. I love you more than brothers," I told them. "If anything ever happened to either one of you, I wouldn't want to live."

"I feel the same way as you, Stone Pony," Tiger replied. "Me, too," said Dyckes.

"We are a band of brothers, united by cause and love for each other," said Tiger. Dyckes agreed. "I would die for either of you."

We stood there under the moonlight in silence for a few minutes then Tiger spoke; "We are all in agreement," said Tiger, "We will keep each other alive no matter what the cost."

"I agree, no matter what the cost, so that one may live or may God help us," said Dyckes.

" I looked up at the stars and spoke, "Let God be our witness."

Tiger had a further idea. "When we get back to the States, we will have to reunite," he said. "

The three of us were in agreement. At that moment, we became bound together in a promise that we weren't even sure we could keep. "With God's help," we would keep each other alive and get each other home in one piece.

Like brothers, we surrendered our lives to each other that day. We stretched out our hands in unity. We made an oath, witnessed by God and one another. No matter what happened, no matter what odds were against us, we would watch out for each other. In time of need, we would come to each other's rescue.

This was our sacred covenant — our covenant made in the jungles of Vietnam.

As we feared and expected, Robert did not survive to dawn. Later that day, as we stood somberly to honor and remember Robert and David, our two deceased brothers, we all knew we had just tasted the grim realities of war — in what for most of us was only the beginning of our third week in Vietnam.

To this day, I don't know what happened to Captain Kenny. We never saw him again. We heard a rumor a few months later that he was alive but had both of his legs amputated as a result of his injuries. He had spent time in Japan before being sent back home to the United States. We never heard or saw him again.

CHAPTER 9: HIGHWAY TO HELL – AC/DC

Fear can be a powerful force. My fear of walking point with my lieutenant was only the tip of the iceberg of my anxiety.

Our 199th Light Infantry Brigade was one of the infantry fighting units in Vietnam that could be dispatched anywhere, at any time, under any conditions. The new infantry fighting units of today have learned a lot of tactics and strategy from our combat experience in Vietnam.

Our daily routine was to be picked up each morning by Huey helicopters, APCs (armored personnel carriers), LPCs (landing patrol crafts), or anything else the Army would find to transport us to our destination. We would hike ten to fifteen miles a day. Our mission would last until sundown unless we made enemy contact. That was our daily agenda.

At night, we ran ambush patrols. We rotated shifts, and each squad was on ambush patrol twice a week. Our enemy was everywhere. We walked through villages not knowing if the residents were Viet Cong or friendly. Day or night, we never knew who was against us or for us. We were on constant alert.

We hopped aboard helicopters in a minute's notice in attempts to catch Charlie off guard. We found the best places to hide from the enemy to surprise Charlie. We set out M-18 Claymore anti-personnel mines and booby traps, and then waited all night. Whether in pouring rain, mud, behind rice-paddy dikes, or in the villages, the night hours were always the worst. Charlie always changed positions and set up his own booby traps during the night.

Charlie was on the offense a lot while the U.S. military was on the defense. He was smart, and he knew his terrain. We had to follow orders from our superiors. We had to be able to react instantly or risk getting killed. In Nam, my reactions to noise and sound became razor sharp.

Our missions were called "search and destroy" missions. When we hiked through the jungles, the branches ripped holes through our jungle fatigues and our flesh.

We didn't have to go very far to find the enemy waiting to kill us. A close friend of mine lost both his legs one morning when his patrol started walking just a hundred feet beyond the company perimeter. The squad has just left for ambush patrol when a loud explosion ripped through the compound. I was on the other side of the compound when I heard the blast.

We always had to be on guard because we were in perpetual danger. Charlie watched our every step. I didn't want to get wounded and lose my legs. That was my constant fear whenever I left our company perimeter. No one got too comfortable even if the Army told us we were in a safe and secure area. There was no truly safe or secure area in Vietnam.

I rarely got enough sleep in Vietnam because of that stress and danger. We slept in the mud on riverbanks, in bunkers made from our own hands surrounded by sandbags, or even in trees and on branches when there was no dry land. The dirt was about as safe and secure as it got in Vietnam. So, too, were the dirt-filled sandbags and foxholes we often slept in to hide and shelter us from bullets and mortar rounds. I usually felt safe while I was in the ground or behind a bunker. Those sandbags saved my life many times. Thank God for dirt and sandbags.

Because we were always on alert, we cleaned our rifles every day. If a soldier didn't clean his rifle properly, it could jam, and he could get killed. I fell in love with my M-16 rifle. It was my protector and my security. It was beside me every second of the day.

Given even a few minutes of down time between missions, scary thoughts would flood my mind. I feared the next mission. I constantly questioned who would be the next casualty. Which one of my buddies would get their legs blows off by a booby trap? Who would be killed? Would it be me?

Sometimes those thoughts became unbearable. It was during those breaks that I had time to reflect about my life. The first time I found some down time in Nam, I began to remember events from my school days.

As a youngster, I was very competitive in sports. On the weekends, I played baseball at the elementary school a few blocks from home. I remembered one particular day I was playing baseball with a bunch of my friends. I was ten at the time.

It was the bottom of the sixth and final inning, and my team was behind by one run. We had two outs. Brad's friend was at bat, and Brad was on second base. I knew our chances of scoring and winning were less than great because Brad's friend had never played baseball before, and he swung a bat like a girl.

The count reached 3-2. I went to the batter's box to talk with Brad's friend. "I want you to hand me the bat as soon as the pitcher pitches the ball," I told him. "I am going to grab the bat from you and swing the bat, so you need to duck. Is that understood?" "Yes," he said.

The pitcher pitched the ball. While it was in the air, I grabbed the bat and swung at the ball. Unfortunately, Brad's friend didn't duck — and as I swung, the bat hit him full force on his forehead.

The blow was so powerful that the batter didn't feel any pain. I looked at him and watched as the biggest bump I had ever seen in my life erupted on his forehead. It was about the size of a baseball. When I saw the bump, I started to cry, thinking I had killed him. He looked at me and said, "Why are you crying?"

Everyone ran over to see what had happened. When they saw the bump on his head, they were amazed.

Brad immediately came over and took his friend home. I was scared that he would die. The boy's parents took him to the hospital. He would be OK, but he needed surgery and would have some long-term effects.

The next Monday, a police officer came to our school and questioned me. I thought he was going to put me in jail. For days after that, I was scared of being arrested.

My recollection of that childhood incident was broken by the sound of a gunshot followed by a scream. Immediately, the announcement came over the radio: Someone had been shot in the foot while cleaning his rifle. I felt sick. How could someone shoot themselves in the foot accidentally while cleaning his rifle? Then I realized something: It was no accident.

It happened again the next day. Our company was told that we were going to fly into a hot landing zone. I was the first to hear the captain's words over the radio: "Be ready, men, for some enemy contact. We'll be landing in a hot L.Z. [landing zone]." Later I learned that Alpha Company had one G.I. killed and three others wounded that day. This war was for real now, and everyone felt the stress. The brigade commander had called our company in to support the other units.

A few minutes after the announcement, another G.I. put a bullet in his foot. Immediately after it happened, our company commander ran out to where the soldier was and issued him a court martial. "Take that back to where you're headed, and get the hell outta here," the commander said as he pinned a piece of paper to the soldier's jacket. The helicopters came in and took the soldier away, and that's the last we saw of him.

The stress and fear of the unknown caused these soldiers to shoot themselves. It was one sure ticket back home, but with it came disgrace. It was a coward's way out of Dodge.

I thought about shooting myself many times after that day, but I couldn't bring myself to do it. I didn't want to feel the guilt or pain it brought. Some days, I cared about my life; other days, I prayed to be killed so that I wouldn't have to endure the fear any longer.

We soldiers formed friendships, but trust was very difficult. Most soldiers didn't want to become close friends because there was a risk that their buddy might get wounded or killed.

I counted the days I had left on my tour by marking a calendar I had drawn on my steel pot. Most soldiers kept track that way. The more time I had left in Nam, however, the more risks I took. But as my number of days remaining got fewer, I became more afraid and took fewer risks. I could feel the second's ticking off in my mind as I got closer either to returning home or to death. The thought of death was always in the back of our minds, and that made our days in Nam seem like an eternity. Fear of death was our daily companion, our unwelcome visitor.

While some soldiers shot themselves in the foot, others re-enlisted in Nam in exchange for reassignment to other parts of the world or even back home. Most everyone looked for a means to escape this death trap, but often there was none to be found.

In Nam, our leadership was vital. There was a chain of command from the squad leaders to the platoon sergeants to the platoon leaders. We depended on their leadership and survival skills. We followed their orders and entrusted our lives to them. They were the best.

With the exception of L.T., I deeply respected the Army officers. They were skilled and determined men with an appreciation for life. They deeply cared for their men. They knew they were accountable for us. Many had barely one year of training as second lieutenants before they had to lead their men into battle. They followed the military code of honor.

The officers kept themselves separated from the enlisted men on the social level. They only bonded with other officers in the bush. That was important in order to maintain the respect of the men, and it made a difference when we had to follow their orders.

When we gathered in a funeral gun salute to honor a fallen soldier, it was a solemn time. It was a time to reflect on death, not life, because sooner or later it will be our turn. God only knows when.

When faced with a life-or-death situation, religion plays a role in fear. I went to Mass whenever I had a chance. Our brigade chaplain would make the rounds, asking us questions and trying to be friendly. There were only two chaplains per brigade. The only other time they would come out to us was to perform a service or when someone was killed.

The Army allowed us to express our religious beliefs. The Protestant and Catholic chaplains ministered to men who wanted spiritual help. Most Sundays, the priest would come out to the field to celebrate Mass unless we were too far into the jungles or too close to the enemy.

The longer I was in the Army, the more I realized how some of us were trying to express our God-given freedoms. We all tried to express our individuality as best we could, and no one questioned us. Our drill sergeants, however, didn't like men who were individuals. There was no room for an individual in the Army. We all had to work as a team.

Most of the men would write sayings on their steel pots whenever they sat down for a break. Some drew peace symbols; some drew crosses; some wrote words of hate or fear. Men in my unit wrote things like "Kill Charlie," "Though I Walk Through the Valley of the Shadow of Death," "Make Love, Not War," "United We Stand," and "God Bless America."

During those days, my faith in God and my prayers to him were my closest companions. I told myself that if I died, I wanted to be ready. When I awoke, I prayed. When I walked the villages, rice paddies or jungles, I prayed. I prayed continually.

I tried to make bargains with God in Nam. My conscience exposed me to sin as far back as I can remember. I knew I was a sinner even when I was five years old. I heard it first from the priest during Sunday Mass. But deep down inside, I felt that man was born with this disease. I couldn't hide from my conscience.

When I was young, I always viewed God as a disciplinarian. If I did something wrong, I would get punished; if I did something right, then I'd get better treatment down the road. In my teens, I went to confession at the Catholic Church on Saturdays and confessed my sins to the priest. Confession never seemed to prevent me from sinning, though. It wasn't until 1983 that I learned at church that God accepted me no matter what I did. Churches are filled with sinners, and I happen to be one of them. No one is perfect except God, who provided a way for us to escape from eternal death through his son Jesus Christ.

So I made bargains with God in Nam while I patrolled: If he let me live, I would go to church every Sunday. I vowed to stop swearing and drinking, and I pledged never to cheat or take advantage of others. I resolved to give my money to the Church. I was always talking to God as I walked along the booby-trapped roads and rice paddies of Vietnam, negotiating with him so that I wouldn't get killed.

I would be in my thirties before I read the Bible and realized that God isn't interested in my bargains. He knows I won't fulfill them, but he loves me anyway, like a father loves his child. He loves me unconditionally, without reservations. All I had to do was to accept his love and invite him to live in my heart. He provided us a way to escape from death and punishment by sending his son Jesus to die on a cross as the penalty for our sins. It's our own choice to accept God's son or reject his salvation.

God saved me from getting killed or wounded countless times when the situation really should have been turned out differently. I really felt God often answered my prayers.

CHAPTER 10: YESTERDAY WHEN I WAS YOUNG – ROY CLARK

The day after Robert and David were killed, we received our new company commander, Captain Ronald Wishart, to replace Captain Kenny. We were still in shock when he flew in at sunrise and assembled the whole company to extend us his sympathies about Captain Kenny. He vowed to help us to stay alive and return home to the States. We all believed him, so we gave him our trust and respect. He was only about twenty-five years old, but he would become one of the best leaders I had in Vietnam.

Two weeks later, our company was sent to guard the railroad tracks about five miles west of Saigon. There were rumors of an enemy assault, a second TET Offensive, so we prepared ourselves for a fight.

Captain Wishart ordered our platoon to position ourselves along the railroad tracks. It was a terrible position to defend because the whole platoon would be exposed to the enemy in all directions. There was nowhere to hide. It would be an easy kill for Charlie if he found us. We felt like a sitting ducks in a pond.

Army engineers had flown out a bulldozer to help us dig trenches deep into the ground. I couldn't believe they actually sent a bulldozer to our position with someone to operate it. We dug in, sent out our ambush patrols, and waited.

About six o'clock in the evening, our ambush patrol radioed in and said that they had made contact with the enemy. Gaskins was on ambush that day, and he said he saw about a hundred N.V.A. marching down the dirt road.

"What did you say?" asked our platoon leader.

"I said I see about a hundred N.V.A. coming in our direction," Gaskins repeated. "They are marching in full uniform and are carrying AK-47s. They are headed our way."

Our platoon that day was about thirty-seven men strong, and we were dug in a circle about fifteen feet apart from each other. That was way too close, but that was how our platoon leader had us dig in.

Oh, my God, I thought, we are all going to be killed. I just knew this would be my last day on earth. There was nothing I could do. All I could do was pray and wait for Charlie to throw an R.P.G. (rocket-propelled grenade) and kill all of us. One mortar round or grenade, and it would be all over. "God, help me," I prayed over and over, my head down between my legs, as I begged God not to let Charlie come and kill us all.

A few minutes went by as I waited for Charlie to open fire, and then another few minutes. We kept waiting and waiting, but nothing happened. Maybe my prayers are working, I told myself.

We waited until almost sundown, but Charlie never came. In the meantime, my platoon leader had called Captain Wishart and told him what had happened and that we had spotted the enemy. He told me to order an artillery battery about three hundred meters out in front of our position.

"Echo One, this is Charlie Fox Trout Two, over. I need a Willy peter [white phosphorous explosive] at location Indio four-nine-five, over," I called.

"Roger," answered our artillery commander.

I listened and watched for the first explosion to hit. The willy-peter round was a warning shot that exploded in the air over the location where we wanted the incoming artillery rounds.

The next sound I heard was that of a projectile that came from far off and over our heads and landed exactly where I had requested in the order, about three hundred meters in front of our position. "This is Charlie Fox Trout Two, over," I said. "Fire when ready, over."

A few minutes later, a huge barrage of artillery pounded the area precisely where Charlie was last seen heading toward our perimeter. The barrage kept coming one after the other for the next twenty minutes and then stopped abruptly.

Over the radio came the word from our company commander: "Charlie Bravo Two, this is Alpha Bravo One, over. Pack up and go after them, make contact with the enemy, over."

I was holding the phone and turned to tell Lieutenant. "Captain gave us orders to go make contact with the enemy, sir."

"I heard him, Campos," was all L.T. said.

"What do you want me to tell him, sir?" I asked L.T.

Not one word came out of his mouth. "Sir," I said again. "Captain wants us to go out and make contact, sir."

"I hear you, Campos, and we're not going anywhere," he said. "Do you copy?"

Captain's voice came over the radio again. "Charlie Bravo Two, this is Alpha Bravo One, over. Did you copy, over? Pack up and go out and make contact with the enemy, over. This is the captain speaking, over."

We all heard what our captain told our platoon leader that day. There were four of us in that bunker — Yingst, Sergeant Turner, L.T., and me. We all looked at each other when Captain said again, "Lieutenant, this is Captain Wishart. You will get up and go make contact. That is an order. Do you hear me, Lieutenant?"

L.T. froze. I looked at him and waited for his response. L.T.

grabbed the phone. "No, I'm sorry, I can't do that, over," he told the captain.

Captain Wishart spoke again. "I didn't hear what you said, Lieutenant. I said to get up and out and make contact with the enemy, over. That's a direct order, over."

Lieutenant handed me the phone. "Tell the captain we're losing contact," he told me. I grabbed the phone and said, "Ah, sir, we can't hear you, we're losing contact, over. This is Charlie Fox Trout, over."

"Tell him we are losing contact, Campos," L.T. said sternly. "Tell him we can't hear him, and then hang up."

"Ah, we're having difficulty making contact, sir," I radioed the captain in a murmured voice. "I can't hear you, sir."

"Lieutenant, are you refusing a direct order?" asked Captain Wishart.

"I hear you, and we're not going anywhere," answered L.T.

"Charlie Bravo Two, this is Alpha Bravo One, over. Did you copy, over? Pack up and go out and make contact with the enemy," our commander said again.

"Are you refusing a direct order, Lieutenant?"

We all waited for the inevitable to happen. The situation reminded me again about playing baseball as a youngster.

My brother and I were always playing baseball with his friends in our back yard at home. The park was too far for us to walk, and we didn't have much time before dark.

My brother was pitching the ball to me. The count was three balls and two strikes. I was losing by a run and it was the last inning. I had a man on second and I could score and tie the game. I was excited that this could be the first time I had ever beaten my brother.

The throw was perfect, right where I liked it — belt high. I swung with my full force. Crash, Kabam! The ball sailed straight toward my bedroom window and shattered the window!

There was broken glass everywhere, both inside and outside

my bedroom window. Boy was I scared. I knew that I would get a whipping for that from my father when we got home.

My mother immediately ran outside when she heard the glass break. What are you doing?" she asked. The next words out of her mouth were frightening: "Your Dad is going to kill you when he gets home."

"But Mom, it was an accident!" I protested.

"I don't care. Your Dad is going to be mad and he gets home he will punish you."

For the next four hours, I cleaned up the pieces of glass. But the damage was done, and so I waited until my father came home. I kept thinking about what was going to happen. Fear and anxiety often grips me when I am waiting for the unknown.

That same kind of fear and anxiety filled me again that day in the bunker by the railroad. I knew it was wrong to disobey orders. My orders came directly from L.T., and it would be his butt on the line this time. L.T. ordered me to turn off the radio and to take the battery out. I did what he ordered, and then sat down on the ground and waited. I looked over at Tiger and then I looked at Sergeant Turner. No one said a word.

L.T. turned his head and whispered to the three of us, "We aren't going anywhere, men, you hear? We're staying right here until morning. If Charlie is going to get us, it will be right here."

That would be L.T.'s last order to our platoon. At sunrise the very next morning, a helicopter came to our position. It was odd, because choppers usually don't arrive that early. This day would be different.

The chopper circled overhead and then landed on the other side of the railroad tracks. Out of the chopper walked Captain Wishart and another man who looked like a lieutenant. He walked over to our position and ordered L.T. to get into the chopper.

"Platoon, this is your new lieutenant," the captain told us. "His name is Lieutenant Brinks." Captain then got into the helicopter with L.T. and flew away.

The firefight we were expecting with Charlie never happened. I felt that God had protected me again by removing our platoon leader. I was so worried that he was going to get me killed. After he left, I never had to walk point again.

The Army officers were our best-trained soldiers. We had to trust our platoon leader that he wouldn't get us killed, that he knew where he was sending us and that he would get us back safely. The platoon leader was our key to life or death.

The Army seemed to changed lieutenants about every four months. They would serve a short while and then get sent to our base camp for lighter duty. The rest of us were stuck in the field knowing that the lieutenants had only a few months in combat. It didn't seem right that the Army treated us differently. We grunts were expendable, and our officers weren't. It didn't change my attitude toward officers, though. I had five lieutenants in Nam, and I respected every one of them.

I did not respect my first Lieutenant because of all the personal risks he took, however, I did respect his authority.

The fun came when we got another replacement. The platoon leader needed to be initiated into our platoon, and we were just the men to do it.

When Lieutenant Brinks arrived, I naturally was assigned as his radio operator. I was trained and ready for his leadership, but I didn't trust him right away due to my experience with my previous lieutenant. I was thankful that Lieutenant Brinks didn't walk point, and he seemed to know a lot about the Army. I respected him, but I didn't know how he would react in combat.

Lieutenant Brinks seemed to be a mama's boy. He looked clean, fresh, and barely old enough to lead a bunch of sixth graders. Lieutenant Brinks dressed like he was going to be in some kind of memorial parade. He kept his fatigues pressed, just like back in boot camp. His clothes were clean, and his boots still had a shine to them. Our boots were worn and dirty, and our jungle fatigues had holes and were caked with mud.

There was a rumor that he was from a very wealthy family. He graduated at the top of his class. He was proud and confident — maybe a little too confident for Yingst and me. We felt we needed to change his stature, and we didn't like his cocky attitude. We needed to teach this guy some jungle manners before it was too late, since it was obvious it was his first time in the bush. We wanted to make sure he was ready to lead our platoon.

When we saw Lieutenant Brinks arrive with clean, starched, and pressed fatigues on a hanger with a plastic bag over them, we hit the roof. That was the last straw.

In the first week after he arrived, Tiger and I took care of his fresh-looking fatigues.

"We've got these dirty, muddy fatigues, and he looks so clean," I told Tiger. "He reminds me of a football player who has a clean uniform while the rest of the team is all dirty."

"Exactly, Stone Pony," said Tiger. "We're lucky to get our old, worn-out fatigues cleaned once a week, and here he looks so pretty."

It was cleaning day, the day we would sent our dirty fatigues to headquarters and receive a clean set. Most of the time, we did not get the same fatigues back even if we had our names labeled in them. When the clean fatigues would arrive, Tiger and I would distribute the laundry to the men.

We decided to find Brinks' fatigues and discard them. We went through the bundles and bundles of dirty laundry to find them. After ensuring that no one was watching, we tore the tags off his fatigues and mixed them in with another bundle.

When we arrived back with the clean laundry, we issued all the fatigues to the men. Lieutenant, looked for his, but couldn't find them. He was angry, but we told him they would bring his out the next day. We lied. It would be a week before we got our next shipment.

Each day that his fatigues didn't arrive, he got madder and madder. Yingst and I made sure he didn't get any fresh fatigues to wear, and by now his fatigues were starting to smell from the caked-on mud and sweat.

Tiger and I laughed all week long as everyone else had fresh fatigues and L.T. had to wear the same dirty ones every day. We got particularly dirty that week because we were by the Delta River and had to walk in mud and water up to our knees. By the time we got back to our base camp, our fatigues were literally covered with mud.

"When do we usually get our fresh fatigues, Campos?" asked L.T.

"Well, we usually get them once a week, sir," I replied, "but that depends where we are. Sometimes we have to wait two weeks."

"Two weeks!" snapped Brinks. "Are you sure, Campos?"

Tiger was standing right beside me. "Yes, sir, just ask Yingst," I said.

"Well, it's been two weeks since I had a fresh pair, sir," confirmed Tiger. He and I looked at each other, and I had to turn away to avoid busting out in laughter.

That week was miserable for L.T. Every day after a mission, he would ask if his fatigues were in from supply.

"No, sir, no fatigues today," I would answer.

By the third day of the next week, L.T. was steaming. We had just come back from walking eight miles in knee-high mud and water on a very hot day. We were all hot, muddy and tired, and ready for a clean pair of fatigues. Brinks had had it! He needed some clean fatigues too!

As we came in and put our gear down next to the bunker, Brinks walked over and scrounged through the clean fatigues looking for his name, then yelled out.

"Where in the hell are my clean fatigues!" Damn it, anyway!

Everyone in camp turned and looked at him.

L.T. got on the phone and called base camp. "Sarge, where are my clean fatigues?"

"We sent them out, sir," answered the supply sergeant.

"Well, there not here. Are you absolutely sure, over?"

"They have your name on them with your lieutenant bars on the collar," Sarge replied. "I personally made sure you had some, over"

L.T. looked over at me and then at Tiger.

"Yes, Sergeant, well, they're not here, over" L.T". Said angrily.

"OK, sir, I'll send out another pair for you tomorrow, over."

"Thank you, Sergeant, over and out" replied L.T. Then he slammed down the phone and walked away.

The next day, the laundry had already arrived by the time we returned from our mission. When we entered camp, Lieutenant Brinks made a beeline to find his fatigues. I think by then he suspected we were stealing his fatigues and giving them away to other grunts. When Tiger and I saw L.T. grab his clean, fresh fatigues, we both burst out in laughter.

"What are you two doing?" Lieutenant Brinks asked "It was you two all along, wasn't it?" You dirty bastards. You'll pay for this!"

He was madder than hell. "You two have been taking my uniforms and giving them away! Where are the rest of them?" he screamed. "Where are they, Campos? Yingst? "You two are going out on ambush patrol every night this week. Do you hear me?"

Radio operators should never be sent out on ambush patrol, because they have to monitor the radio. L.T. ended up sending us out on night patrol for the next few days. He had to monitor the radio each night and finally gave in.

After that day, Lieutenant Brinks earned the respect of us and our whole platoon. He was now a full-fledged member of our Comanche Commando team! I ended up liking him a lot.

Several days later, I told him we planned that laundry trick, because we had to initiate him our way. He was our friend from then on. He could be trusted from then on to help us, and we would also help him stay alive. We wanted to make sure he knew this was no game out here in the bush. Our lives depended on him. This wasn't Fort Benning, Georgia, where he had trained. He wasn't back at home living with Ozzie and Harriet Nelson. We were in a war zone. We didn't care if he looked pretty or had his shoes shined.

After a few weeks, he forgot about the incident and started to return to his old self. He started to get puffed up about being in command and would separate himself from the other men like he was John Wayne or something. It made Tiger and me mad because he just wasn't getting it.

L.T. always had to have the driest, safest, and most secure place to sleep. He seemed to be putting himself above the rest of us, and that wasn't good. We shared in the comforts of the dirt and mud. Why should he be any different?

The Army-issued air mattress was our best companion at bedtime. It was four to five inches think when fully inflated, and it felt good. It cushioned us from the mud or water and protected us from some of the insects. It also felt good to rest after a ten-mile hike in search of Charlie. It was the next best thing to a real mattress. These air mattresses held all our weight and all of our gear. They could support the weight of a 250-pound man, his M-16, and all his ammo.

It was time for another lesson for Lieutenant Brinks. So after a patrol, just before sunset, Tiger and I told L.T. we would dig his foxhole and take care of inflating his air mattress so that he could attend his command meeting. L.T. was relieved and grateful: After a long, hard day of walking, it wasn't that easy to come back and blow up an air mattress. It took a lot of strength, and I often had to stop several times to catch my breath. It would take me about a half-hour to fill it up.

He turned away and headed across the compound toward the

site of his command meeting. He would be gone over an hour. That would give us plenty of time to blow up his mattress and make things tidy for him to sleep.

Right after L.T. left, Tiger and I got together. I said to Tiger, "I think he thinks we are his servants. He seems pretty confident we are going to take care of him when we have just hiked all day long."

"Yeah, Stone Pony, he needs to be knocked off the high horse again. He is hard headed and needs to learn another lesson," Tiger said. "He thinks he's back in his Georgia mansion and that his servants are waiting on him."

"Let's show him some good ol' boy, down-home-style hospitality," I replied. "I think I've got an idea that will make him feel back at home on the range. Let's find some rocks or something to put under his air mattress. When he gets back before twilight, he'll never know the difference until he wakes up in the morning to find his air mattress flat and his back in pain!"

Tiger agreed. This happened during the rainy monsoon season, and it had been raining heavily all day long. We were all looking for higher ground that wasn't wet or muddy.

Tiger and I searched every inch of our base camp and brought all the empty beer and soda cans we could find. We collected about twenty-two cans and some large rocks. We tucked them neatly under the air mattress and squashed the cans flat so as not to look suspicious.

"I know what we can do," said Tiger. He got out his Bowie knife and pierced a small whole in the air-intake nipple of the mattress. "That will fix him," said Tiger, laughing. We agreed not to tell anyone about our little diversion.

A few hours later, L.T. came back and asked me where his sleeping quarters were. "Over there, Lieutenant," I pointed. "Tiger and I made a nice place for you to sleep." I turned away and tried not to laugh. Then I looked over at Tiger and winked.

I'm sure L.T. thought he was well taken care of that night — and he surely was!

The next morning, L.T. awoke complaining about his aching back. He also complained about his air mattress being flat. "Do you know anything about that?" he asked Tiger and me.

"No, sir," said Yingst.

For the next two days, Tiger and I did exactly the same thing. On each day, L.T. would wake up with his air mattress flat and complain about his back aching during the long hikes.

L.T. even called back to base camp to have a new air mattress shipped out to him. When the Huey chopper brought us our hot meal and supplies the next day, Tiger and I rushed over and cut a small hole in L.T.'s new air mattress.

We got caught on the third night. Lieutenant Brinks excused himself to attend the command meeting just after we got back to base. I watched him leave and notified Tiger to search the area for beer cans or empty boxes.

Tiger and I had just placed a few beer cans under his air mattress when L.T. jumped out from behind a bunker where he had been hiding while we were scanning the area for beer cans.

"I knew it was you guys!" Brinks yelled. The whole platoon looked in our direction. "You dirty sons of bitches!"

Tiger and I broke out in laughter, but, Lieutenant Brinks wasn't laughing. He started to get mad again, and then he hesitated.

"OK, you two guys, I've had it. You have proven your point. I surrender," he told us. "I understand now. I guess I've been a little too spit-and-polish out here. After all, you guys are the experts. I've only been in the bush for two weeks."

All in all, Lieutenant Brinks was the best officer we ever had. Our whole platoon liked him and trusted him with our lives. I think our little pranks at his expense helped to foster that relationship for everyone. He turned out to be one of the best platoon leaders we had in Nam. We started to like him and trust him. That makes a tight bond of trust and respect that last a lifetime.

CHAPTER 11: TURN, TURN, TURN – THE BYRDS

Our company had just received a fresh supply of new recruits. We called them "green" because they had no fighting experience yet.

It was getting late one afternoon while we were on a mission, and as always we walked and walked in search of Charlie. We came upon a river and had to cross it. We didn't know how deep the river was, so we followed the usual procedure of having one man swim over to the other side, where he would secure a rope for the rest of us.

Our squad started crossing with the help of an air mattress. We would place our hands on the rope and keep our weapons and gear on our air mattress so they wouldn't get wet. I awaited my turn, fairly confident that I would not drown. We had heard reports of soldiers drowning while trying to cross rivers.

I watched as one of the green soldiers was taking his time crossing the river. I could tell he was scared to death. "I can't swim!" he yelled out. Can't swim? He's got to be kidding, I told myself. Everyone knows how to swim.

Well, not everyone. This guy was so scared that he started wobbling the air mattress. He was becoming frantic thinking he was going to drown. I took off my web gear and laid down my rifle.

At just about that moment, he panicked. I dove into the water and placed him onto the air mattress. As he struggled, he dropped his M-60 machine gun in the water. I was so close to him that I held out my foot and caught the machine gun by its strap.

The machine gun was hanging on my foot and the weight was now dragging me under. I somehow helped him make it to safety, but then I was in trouble.

"Hey, I need some help," I yelled. "I have the machine gun on my foot and it's pulling me under." Another guy behind me jumped in to help me.

I risked my life to help another soldier, and in turn I was helped by yet another soldier. The G.I. grabbed the machine gun from my foot, and I was able to swim across the river. When I climbed out of the water, the G.I. who had almost drowned was nowhere to be found.

That's what Nam was all about. You help others, and then they help you, too. There was no animosity toward our fellow combat brothers. We lived each day to help each other stay alive.

★ ★ ★ ★

Late June is the beginning of the monsoon season in Vietnam, and on one particular day our company was on a search-and destroy-mission when we noticed that the sky was becoming darker and darker with rainclouds.

Captain Wishart ordered us to set our perimeter in the Bamboo Fields. Usually that's where we could find Charlie, but not during the monsoon season. Charlie stayed out of the rain, so we usually had a break in the fighting.

Just before sunset, it began to rain heavily. Within an hour, the water was rising to our ankles. This was the heaviest rain any of us had ever encountered.

Captain told all the radio operators to find dry ground so as to keep the radios from getting wet. If they got wet, we could lose all communication. The captain's radio man found a tree branch a few feet off the ground. Most of us figured that was a poor choice. There were bugs, snakes, and scorpions hiding in those trees.

A few minutes later, we heard a loud scream. "I got bit! Something bit me!" the soldier screamed repeatedly. Everyone watched as he stripped off his web gear and flung it into the mud. The next minute, he fell off his branch and onto the ground — and he wasn't breathing.

Captain Wishart ran over to his radio operator to see what had happened to him. He rolled him over and found a brown scorpion walking by his helmet. The captain used his boot to smash it into the mud.

"Medic! "he yelled. "Medic, he's been bitten by a scorpion." Everyone in the platoon heard the captain's screams as fear filled the campground. I looked everywhere to see if there were other scorpions around.

The medic ran over quickly. "Captain, he's not breathing," he said.

"Well don't let him die, give him mouth to mouth," replied the captain. "I'm calling in the medevac."

As we waited for the helicopter to arrive, the doc frantically kept trying to keep the stricken soldier alive. I watched as his lips turn blue. I thought he was dead.

Doc gave him mouth-to-mouth resuscitation and finally got him to breathe again. A moment later, he asked the medic what had happened.

"You were bitten by a scorpion," Doc said. "We have a medevac coming in to pick you up. Just be quiet and lie still."

"Am I going to die?" he asked Doc.

"No you're not going to die on my watch." said Doc. "Mine either," affirmed Captain Wishart.

Then the swelling began, and he continued to have difficulty breathing. Just before the chopper arrived, his heart stopped. Doc revived him again by pounding on his chest and giving him mouth-to-mouth. The chopper finally arrived, and we loaded him onto the chopper. Thank God for the Army medevac pilots.

It was still raining cats and dogs, but now the water was rising toward our knees. I thought we were going to drown before the night ended. I was praying for the rain to stop, but it didn't let up until dawn.

Captain again ordered the radio operators to get high as possible off the ground, but there was no cover. Tiger and I found some C-ration containers and piled them as high as we could. We both jumped up on the containers and sat back-to-back. Then we watched the water rise toward our feet again.

The other guys weren't as lucky as us. They had to stand up against a tree or find a hill, rock, or anything they could to sit on. Most everyone had to sleep in the water that night.

Conditions seemed to keep getting worse by the minute. I knew we wouldn't get any sleep that night. All that was on my mind was that scorpion floating in the water. Where did they go, and how many were there? Usually we found scorpions in groups of five or six. That was one of the worst nights of sleep I had in Nam. All night long, I kept imagined scorpions floating on the water trying to crawl on me. Imagine walking for fifteen miles a day, slopping through mud up to your knees, and then not being able to sleep at all.

Tiger told me to sleep with one eye open. "How can you keep one eye open and sleep?" I asked him.

"I see people do it all the time!" he shot back.

I don't know about Tiger, but I never shut even one eye all that night.

At night, usually around sunset, the B-52 bombers would light up the horizon. It made me feel secure, at least for a few hours. I watched in silence and awe. I always wondered how someone could survive a B-52 bomber raid. Those bombs made huge craters fifty feet wide and fifty feet deep. I was amazed as we would sometimes walk past them the next day on our mission. If Charlie was there, he was blown into tiny pieces.

Thank God we weren't the ones being bombed. How frightfully scared Charlie must be when he knew a B-52 airplane is overhead bombing him into dust! No wonder Charlie dug deep in the earth and hid in holes! Sometimes, while on patrol, we would find severed body parts — feet, arms, legs, fingers — but most of the time we found nothing but a deep bomb crater.

There was another terror in the air — our fighter planes. Our planes were armed with napalm bombs and fifty-caliber machine guns. We would call in the Air Force and Navy to drop napalm bombs and to fire their guns. Sometimes they would miss their target and hit our own troops instead.

Napalm was nasty. It left the land desolate. Trees, plants, and everything in its path would burn. If Charlie was there when the napalm landed, he would burn. But Charlie was smart: He was usually under the earth, in a hole, or in a tunnel.

In the early 1960s, our planes used Agent Orange to destroy the foliage of the jungle and reveal where Charlie was hiding. Our troops had difficulty finding Charlie by traveling through the jungles or bushes. We were warned about Agent Orange contamination, but we walked through it anyway.

When the Huey helicopters would pick us up and take us to our mission, they would often be accompanied by two Cobra gunships. The Cobras were bad-ass. They gave us a measure of security and firepower. They flew back and forth over our heads while we were on our missions. Whenever they circled overhead a few times, it usually meant they had found the enemy.

One time, while we were out on ambush patrol, I watched as a Cobra circled above our heads. He kept circling and circling. He was watching us. I felt the Cobra pilot somehow thought we were the enemy, boy, was that frightening. I kept looking up and wondering what he was thinking. Surely he knew we were patrolling the area. But he kept circling over our heads.

All of a sudden, he dipped the nose of his Cobra toward our

position. At that time, we were walking on a rice-paddy dike to get to our ambush site. I was walking faster and looking back at the Cobra. Then I had a chilling premonition.

"Hey, L.T., I think that Cobra up there thinks we're the enemy," I yelled to Lieutenant Brinks. "We'd better get out here. I think he's going to fire at us!"

The lieutenant looked at me and said, "No, he's not, he knows we're friendly."

"Ah, I hope you're right, sir, but he's starting to point his nose down at us. I think he's going to fire on us," I replied. Then, to my unit, I yelled, "Let's get the hell out of here, men!" We immediately began to run in full stride.

Just then, the Cobra fired a missile at us. I could see the trail of dark smoke coming directly toward me. I thought I was going to be blown into tiny pieces. I ran faster and faster, looking for somewhere to hide, but there was no place to go. We were on top of the rice paddies, and if we were to jump into the water, it would be worse. All I could think to do was run as fast as I could. The rocket hit the rice paddy about twenty feet behind me and blew water and mud fifteen feet in the air.

I was running ahead of Lieutenant Brinks when he called for me to stop. "Campos!" he yelled, "Stop and let me catch up to you so I can call in headquarters!" I handed L.T. the phone behind me. I had slowed down to a fast walk, but I wasn't going to stop. L.T. tried to keep up with me while talking on the phone at the same time.

"Alpha One, this is Charlie One, over… We are being fired upon by a Cobra, over… Captain, tell that Cobra to stop firing at us… Captain, we have a problem here, over… We have a Cobra on our tail firing missiles at us, over…. he thinks we're the enemy, over…"

Lieutenant Brinks handed me the phone and said, "Let's get the hell outta here." We both took off running again down the rice-paddy dike and headed toward our company perimeter. The rest of our squad followed quickly behind us. I think the captain must have been able to reach the Cobra pilot because the Cobra finally stopped firing at us — but not before he had launched another missile. That one exploded in the rice paddies about thirty feet to the side of us, but thirty feet was still too close for comfort. Those missiles would have killed all of us. I was praying and running my ass off at the same time. I thought I was going to be killed that day. God had protected me, and no one got hurt or killed. It was a miracle that those missiles barely missed us.

me, tiger & Dyckes Delta 1968

Hill 41

★　★　★　★

Sometimes even our own men were the enemy. War has a way of making a person crazy, and sometimes weird things happen.

My squad was on patrol one day, and I was walking atop the rice paddies. Everyone was suffering from the heat. Big Jim was walking ahead of me. He was a big, mean-looking guy from Detroit. No one messed with him. He was rough, tough, and bad-ass.

We all were thirsty. We would walk several hundred feet at a time, then stop and rest for fifteen minutes. On one such break, I noticed one of the guys in front of me needed to take a leak.

When you're out in the bush and nature calls, you just go, no matter where you are. This guy stopped a couple of feet in front of me. In front of him, big Jim had just tripped and fallen off the dike and into the rice-paddy water. He immediately climbed back up and sat on the dike to compose himself. I stooped down and watched the G.I. in front of me whip out his penis and take a piss. Then he looks at Big Jim, who was still sitting down, and started to piss on his back.

"What the hell are you doing?" yelled Big Jim. He jumped up, his face turned red, and his whole demeanor changed. The G.I. who was pissing on him started laughing like crazy. I watched as Big Jim took several steps backward, then locked and loaded a magazine of twenty roads in his M-16.

It shocked the heck out of me because I was in the same line of sight as the other guy. I stepped slowly off the rice-paddy dike and tried to get out of range. A few seconds later, he unlocked the safety and pointed his M-16 rifle right at his friend's penis.

"Blam, blam, blam, bit-bit-bit-bit!" came the sound as he unloaded twenty rounds trying to blow the guy's manhood into oblivion. I was in shock. Thank God he missed!

After he missed, Big Jim wheeled his M-16 at the rest of us and put in another twenty-round magazine. What saved us was our platoon sergeant, who walked slowly and deliberately toward the soldier until he was about five feet away and said in a soft voice, "Take your hand off the trigger, G.I. Slowly bring your weapon down to your side."

Big Jim looked around. I could see the faraway look in his eyes as if he was in the "Twilight Zone." The sergeant called out again in a more firm voice, "G.I., slowly bring your weapon down. Take your finger off the trigger and hand me your weapon."

It seemed like hours went by, but I'm sure it was only a few minutes when he finally handed his weapon to the sergeant. We were all holding our breath until he was under control. I thought I was dead, killed by my own combat brother.

After Big Jim got hold of himself and realized what he had done, he looked at his friend and told him, "Brother, I don't care who you are. You're a dead man if you ever do that again."

CHAPTER 12: OH HAPPY DAY – EDWIN HAWKINS SINGERS

Lieutenant Brinks wasn't the only person we initiated in Nam. We initiated every officer who ever transferred into our platoon. We liked having fun when time permitted. We found ways to ease the emotional pain of our fears, and we made some lasting friendships.

As well-trained fighting men, we were eager to engage the enemy and test our training when we first arrived. The sooner we engaged the enemy, the faster the war would end. I personally felt we could have won in Vietnam if given the chance to do it our way.

We truly felt we were making a difference in this country for the South Vietnamese people. We felt proud to be there to defend the world from communism and to bring peace to Vietnam.

Sometimes the Army would bring us back to base after spending four to five months in the jungles and give us what they called a "stand down." Brigade would buy steaks for the whole division, and each company would get two days of rest. Most soldiers spent the time to get drunk and have fun. It was a way for our leaders to thank us for doing a good job.

We had been in the bush for three straight months when we had our first stand down. The commander ordered a show for the 199th and told us we would have a special surprise on stage that night.

We started drinking early in the afternoon, and by the time the show was to start a lot of us were pretty well blitzed. We sat before a huge stage waiting for Bob Hope or someone like that to show up. Instead, the brigade had hired three strippers from the Philippines. The show was a huge success, with drunken guys screaming as the girls slowly took off their clothes.

Suddenly, one G.I. got up on the platform and raced toward one of the girls. The M.P.s (Military Police) stopped him just short of tackling the girl. When another four or five soldiers jumped up on the stage, the situation turned into a near riot. About ten M.P's came from all directions to quell the trouble before the commander came on stage and told us to "get the hell out of here."

Our stand down was over. That would be the only stand down we had in Nam. The brigade commander kept his word. He was disgraced by our actions. We were ordered back into the jungles the very next day.

★　★　★　★

One weekend, I was surrounded by a bunch of guys, and all our eyes were glued to a small television set that one guy had bought with some money he had saved. We were watching the news about war protesters back home in Washington, D.C. The television showed film of thousands of radicals protesting the war, carrying signs that read, "Get Out of Vietnam," "Make Love, not War," "Stop the Bombing" and other such statements. They were fighting their own war at home.

Those war posters made me angry. These protesters knew nothing about Vietnam. They claimed we were killing innocent people. The television newscasters made us look like losers.

Sure, we didn't want to fight and die, but we were here to do a job, to stop communism. We were fighting to win, with or without the support from the public. If these radicals thought we were losing the war and wanted someone to blame, they should blame themselves for not supporting us. We did our job, and we are proud of it!

We exercised our freedom by wearing peace symbols, drawing them on our helmets. We wore them under our jungle fatigues, around our necks, or on our M-16 rifles. Still, we paid the price for wearing peace symbols. The military ordered us not to do anything that even hinted of war protests. Some men had their privileges taken way. Others were treated with disrespect and given extra duties. However, they permitted us to write things on our camouflage bands and our steel pots.

The Army officers and sergeants hated soldiers who wore peace symbols. They thought the peace symbol meant that we opposed the principles of our government. We didn't. We wore them because they were the signs of our generation. We loved our country, and we were giving our lives for that cause. We fought out the love of our country and the love of our combat brothers. We fought out the love of our families, our wives, and our children.

Some of the guys bought radios so we could listen to the latest music and the newest hit songs. The Vietnam radio station was one of the best stations to listen to in Nam. One famous disk jockey in Nam greeted us each morning with "Good morning, Vietnam!" I listened as often as I could as he played the sounds of our generation — songs like The Doors' "Light my Fire," Jefferson Airplane's "White Rabbit," The Birds' "Turn, Turn, Turn," the Fifth Dimension's "Aquarius," Edwin Starr's "War," and Barry McGuire's "Eve of Destruction." We kept up with the music of Country Joe and The Fish, The Mamas and the Papas, The Seeds, The Rolling Stones, the Beatles, Strawberry Alarm Clock, The Zombies, The Brotherhood of Man, The Cowsills, and many more.

★ ★ ★ ★

"Everybody must get stoned," the refrain in Bob Dylan's "Rainy Day Women #12 and 35," describes fairly accurately one of our ways to escape reality for a little while. We needed a break from fighting the war and the elements. We had to find ways to ease the stress we faced and enjoy some moments with our combat buddies.

We had good support from the Army's supply depot. The best part of my day was the hot chow. No matter where we were, the Army would find a way to send us hot chow unless we were in a firefight. It was our special treat.

They'd also send us a ration of beer on weekends. I took it as an expression of gratitude. We were limited to a ration of three beers each on the weekends only, but no one really counted. The booze wasn't much of a problem for me. I didn't want a hangover while walking on patrol or on a mission.

Then there was pot. While I was still in training back at Fort Lewis, a couple of combat veterans told us that the marijuana in Nam was easy to get and that it was the best pot he had ever smoked. The Vietnamese would find a way to bring it out to us, even in when we when entrenched in our sandbag bunkers.

You could buy it anywhere in Nam. It sometimes they came packed in cartons disguised as regular cigarette cartons. They were packed in Marlboro, Philip Morris, and Lucky Strike packages. A carton would cost for three dollars and fifty cents. The joints were rolled just like regular cigarettes with filters on them and looked exactly like American cigarettes. All you had to do was take the filter off and smoke it.

Whenever we returned to our base camp from the bush, it wasn't hard to find someone who had some weed. We were good at hiding our pot from the officers, but I think maybe they were just looking the other way anyway.

When one of the guys bought some pot, we would all share

it. We usually smoked it from a tobacco pipe. Some guys smoked it in a gas mask or even a rifle. It made me cringe when I saw them smoking pot out of an M-16. I wouldn't do that. I knew my rifle was to be used only to kill Charlie. My M-16 was my only security I had in Nam. I wouldn't allow myself to use it to get high.

Some men in our squad found a way to escape other than through booze or Vietnamese pot. One of the guys bought some Thailand weed and gave me a hit. I was so stoned that I was simply out of it for the next two hours. My lieutenant went looking for me and found me sitting in a bunker trying to sober up. I finally walked back to the C.P. and told myself I would never do that again. I was scared, because I needed to be alert in case Charlie popped a couple of mortars our way or I was called to go out on patrol. The next time I did something like that, I would make darn sure I was in a safe area.

When we had a break away from the enemy we treated ourselves to pot and alcohol to escape the fear and the relentless pounding of death in our heads. I'm not trying to say it's OK to smoke pot. It's definitely wrong. But in a way, it was better than beer. Getting drunk would leave us helpless and tired and give us hangovers, but the effects of pot wore off in a couple of hours.

I wanted to get home in one piece, so I tried to limit getting high or drunk. I also needed to stay alert for my buddies. They needed to count on me watching their backs, and I needed them to watch mine. When you live in a tight community of combat friends, you look out for the other guy.

One weekend, Captain Wishart gave us a two-day pass. We had just returned from a search-and-destroy mission in the hot and humid jungles. It had hit 118 degrees that day. We had consumed all the water in our canteens, and some of our guys had passed out from heat exhaustion. Two men had to be airlifted to the hospital. Captain Wishart could see that we needed a break, so he let us have some fun since we were close to Saigon.

Whenever we had liberty, we wanted to do something to take our minds off the war, so Tiger, Dyckes, and I went looking for something to do. We stood by the highway hoping to thumb a ride for the fifteen-minute trip into Saigon. There was always the danger of getting killed by a roadside mine, but who cared anyway? We would go home sooner, except in a pine box, we joked.

I watched as some of our buddies started running out into the highway and stopping motorcycles, buses, bikers, and anyone else who could give us a ride into Saigon.

Yingst ran out into the highway, raised his M-16, and screamed, "Stop, you Gooks! You're taking us to Saigon!" The three of us climbed into the back of the small van, and it took off down the road.

After about five miles, we entered the city of Saigon. Dyckes ordered the driver to stop when we arrived in the city and gave him two bucks. We had our M-16 rifles our ammo with us, and we were wearing a clean set of jungle fatigues. We shed most of our infantry gear before we left. We were looking clean and proper. Most of all, we were ready to have a good time and have some fun.

Saigon was amazing. There were people everywhere. The streets were packed with cars, military trucks, motorcycles, rickshaws, bicycles, and scooters. There were numerous vendors selling everything from guns to Coca-Cola, even many American products. There were bars, massage parlors, and brothels. I had heard that you could buy anything you wanted on the black market there, including drugs. Most of us just wanted a few drinks, some cigarettes, and maybe a good dinner. If you didn't want to drink, you could buy a Coke for a dollar, but the ice to make it cold would cost you two dollars. I thought it would be great to find a bar and get a massage. I also wanted to buy a camera. Tiger wanted tiger fatigues, and Dyckes wanted to send a gift home to his parents.

It was dangerous to go into Saigon. Although there didn't appear to be much of a war going on there, we were warned that there were snipers everywhere. We all heard about rumors of soldiers who entered the city and were killed or beaten. We could not trust anyone. We were always on guard against attack. In Vietnam, we had to be careful about who we spoke with. Nevertheless, we took advantage of our short breaks by trying to forget we were in a war zone.

We just didn't care how dangerous Saigon was. It was better than walking along the rice paddies and stepping on a booby trap and blowing your balls off. Besides, we had already developed a kind of animal instinct that gave us a sixth sense to alert us whenever danger was present.

Most soldiers on leave would look to find a bar with young women and drinking. They would walk into a nightclub for a little taste of being back home. They would dance with the Vietnamese girls, who were sexy and wore long dresses. Whenever a soldier entered the establishment, the girls would approach him and ask him to buy them drinks. The G.I. would spend all his money getting drunk. The girls would dance with a soldier until he didn't have a dime left in his pocket.

The three of us headed to a different section of Saigon in search of a good restaurant. We walked until we got hungry, finally arriving at a street that didn't have much traffic or activity and was uncharacteristically quiet. It was weird. It was a better district then most of the streets you expected to see in Saigon.

We turned the corner and entered a crowded café. There was a sign outside on the building that looked like it was written in French. As the three of us entered the restaurant, the people stopped talking. The whole place became silent. I realized they were not speaking Vietnamese. They were speaking French. I turned to Tiger and said, "We're in a Vietnamese French establishment. It feels weird in here."

"Yeah, Stoney Pony, it's really, weird," Tiger said in reply. "You'd think you were in France and not Vietnam. Who cares, though? I'm hungry. Let's get a drink and order something."

I looked around and noticed the bar had three seats. We sat down next to a man who looked like he was an American. Everyone seemed to be staring at us. Were we somehow intruding on their right to a free society? I could see it in their faces that they didn't like Americans. We weren't welcome there. All we wanted was some good food to eat, something better than the Army's C-rations.

The patrons' stares penetrated the back of my fatigues. I sensed danger, but the three of us were determined to get some good food before we left. What could they say, anyway? We had our M-16 rifles!

There we were, dressed in our fatigues, amid a roomful of men dressed in suits and ties. They also looked taller than most Vietnamese, taller and healthier. They seemed to have a sense of dignity about them. They looked like professionals, and not like the other villagers.

"How's it going?" I said to a man seated next to me at the bar. "What's happening in here? Why is everyone staring at us?"

"You shouldn't be here," the man whispered. "These people don't like G.I.s. They are respected people of the community and don't want trouble."

The bartender didn't even want to serve us drinks until the man said, "It's OK. I know them. We're all friends. You need not worry."

The man at the bar then turned back to me and said, "I'm putting myself in jeopardy, but I like you. You'll need to put your rifles in the corner over there."

"He wants us to put our guns in the corner," I told Dyckes.

"No one's taking my rifle from me, Stone Pony," said Dyckes.

"I think it's OK," I told Dyckes. "Trust me, if we don't put our weapons down, will not make it out of here alive."

The three of us agreed. Anyway, I still carried a grenade in my pocket! We stacked our weapons in the corner, about fifteen feet from us. I wanted to make sure I could get to mine fast in case I needed it. I kept one eye on the crowd and the other on my M-16 as I drank.

Our new friend spoke French to the bartender and waiter. We were in a very affluent setting, and the people seemed to be very wealthy. The man said he was a C.I.A. agent and told us not to tell anyone. "Sure," I laughed to myself. I asked him what he was doing there.

"I'm here doing some counter-intelligence," he said before stopping abruptly. He was a little drunk. I noticed his suit was bulging on the side and wondered if he was concealing a pistol.

I got the impression that he might have been a double agent. I decided that we'd better gather our rifles and ease our way out of there. We all sensed danger and didn't want to get into a shooting match on our day off. We finished our drinks, excused ourselves, grabbed our M-16s and slowly walked out the restaurant door.

We headed back toward the busier streets. Rounding the next corner, we stepped into a bar filled with Marines. The sounds of "Susie Q" echoed from the loudspeakers and flashing lights surrounded us as we walked in and sat down at the bar. We were met immediately by three girls. It felt better to be with our own kind and around people who appreciated us.

The bartender asked us our favorite drink. "I'll take a bottle of Coors," Dyckes laughed. "NO, Tiger beer!" Yingst told the bartender. "That's the best. Three Tiger beers."

"YOU number one, G.I.," the young female bartender said as she handed us three Vietnamese Tiger beers.

We held up our glasses. "TO THE WORLD!" we toasted.

We sat in the bar drinking our Tiger beer and watching the girls dance to American songs. The Vietnamese girls wore long dresses with a slit down the side of their legs. Some of them were sexy and attractive. We were interrupted when a girl walked up to me and asked me if I wanted to buy her a drink.

"I don't think so," I said.

"You want to 'boom-boom,' G.I.?" she asked. "Boom-boom" was slang for sex. She was a hooker, propositioning to have sex with me for a price.

I turned her down. I remembered my vow to God not to go to bed with anyone here. I didn't want to go to hell if I died, nor did I want to get the clap! I remembered the Army warning us of the "black V.D." (Venereal disease). You can't go home if you have the black V.D.

We drank our beers and had fun watching the girls dance on the table in front of us. It was a good time and they made us feel appreciated. Any relief from the stress of war, even for an hour, made my day a little more endurable.

Dyckes, Tiger and I closed the evening by lifting up our Tiger beer and saluting each other.

"Until our reunion in the world!" we said in unison.

Little did I know that it was about the last time the three of us would be together in Vietnam.

★ ★ ★ ★

PART IV: SEARCH AND DESTROY MISSIONS

★ ★ ★ ★

CHAPTER 13: RIDERS ON THE STORM – THE DOORS – JIM MORRISON

Toward the end of June, brigade headquarters decided to split up our units. They integrated men from different combat companies throughout the division so that each unit included soldiers who were skilled and experienced in combat. They had learned a big lesson from the friendly-fire mix-up of more than two months earlier in which Robert was killed and Captain Kenny was badly wounded. It was a smart move.

On July 1, I got orders to be transferred to Charlie Company of the 4th Battalion of the 12th Infantry. Our company commander read a long list of men who were being moved. I never thought that I would be on that list.

We were based close to Saigon that day and our company had set up in a Buddhist temple. We had just arrived after our jungle ordeal in the monsoon rains. Everyone was edgy. I never heard anything over the radio to even hint that our company might be splitting up. We had all trained together, and I thought we were all going to stay together in Vietnam.

Lieutenant Brinks had all of us assembled. "Men, some of you are being transferred out of this company into another company," he told us. "I do not have any explanation except that you have

135

two choices. If you are chosen but do not want to transfer, you can stay in this platoon — if you extend your stay in Vietnam another thirty days."

He walked over and called out the list of men who were transferring. I heard it loud and clear: "Stephen P. Campos, pack your bags." I couldn't believe it. How could they transfer me out? I was the lieutenant's radio operator!

Then it hit me. I was leaving my brothers, Dyckes and Tiger. Lieutenant Brinks didn't seem very comfortable in telling me that I would be leaving, but he did what he was ordered. I was really depressed after that. How could I leave my buds? How could we keep our covenant now? But I had no choice. I had orders from higher up. I was very angry with the Army and the commander for separating us, and I sure wasn't about to extend my tour for even one minute, let alone another thirty days.

The three of us had trained together at Fort Lewis. We fought together, ate together, and laughed together. We vowed to cover each other's back. What would happen to me now?

I accepted the outcome, packed my bags, and started to say my goodbyes. I was angry and emotional. It was hard to talk to anyone.

I always admired Tiger's strength and his friendship. He made me feel supported and more confident. He encouraged me when I was afraid and depressed. He listened to me when I needed to talk about my fears, particularly about walking point with my first lieutenant. We laughed together and enjoyed each other's company.

We were close-knit because we were both radio operators, the only two in the platoon. We held the key to communication for the whole platoon and company. I talked to him a lot while in the bush. We had a secret code all our own.

Yingst and shared together a special kind of courage and fear that united us even closer than brothers. The bond held us together when times got tough. He understood my viewpoint and wasn't afraid to tell others what he thought was right. It was comforting to me whenever he agreed with me.

I didn't get a chance to say goodbye to him. He didn't want to say goodbye. He was angry with me. When I approached him, he turned and walked away from me. He couldn't believe I was leaving.

I found Dyckes and told him. We vowed to write each other and stay close. I had Jim's phone number and address in Rocklin, California, where his parents lived. I would find Jim after the war and get together with him. But I didn't have Tiger's address or phone number in Pennsylvania. We lost touch after that day, and it saddened me beyond belief. My spirit was crushed.

We were Comanche Commandos, though. We were combat brothers no matter what happened, and we would remain loyal to each other until death. Nam was bad enough going through this living hell, but take away some security and that brings depression. I bid farewell to my friends, turned my back, and left.

The closeness I held for my two combat buddies was a force of its own. I remembered our covenant in the jungle to get back together after Vietnam. Deep in my heart, however, I never thought it would happen. Life and death is not in our hands, but in God's hands.

Me and Dyckes June 30th. 1968

★ ★ ★ ★

My new unit was a distinguished fighting unit and had a mean reputation. "Company C" had killed hundreds upon hundreds of North Vietnamese during the TET Offensive in February 1968. They were a tough group of guys with a nasty view of life and a distant stare in their eyes. They had an animal mentality. I didn't think I would fit in with them. I didn't know if they could be trusted. They had killed Charlie. I had never seen a Charlie killed, nor had I killed Charlie my entire tour of duty. Actually, it was in my prayers: I never wanted to kill anyone in Nam.

During the TET Offensive, these men of Company C placed

a black ace on the forehead of each Vietnamese they had killed. All the men carried a deck of cards with only black aces in it. This was a curse on Charlie's forehead and a message to the North Vietnamese: Don't mess with Charlie Company — we're bad-ass! Even the president of the United States awarded Charlie Company with a unit citation. It was a godsend later when I realized how lucky I was to be transferred to a unit that had such distinction and pride.

Even the civilian ARVAN (Army Regular Vietnamese) soldiers knew about the curse. I heard from the ARVAN soldiers that each man in Charlie Company had a bounty on his head. The North Vietnamese wanted badly to kill Charlie Company men because of what the soldiers did to their countrymen. They would pay a price for a dead Company C soldier. Now I had a bounty on my head, too.

I asked a few men in my company what all the fuss was about. They told me that Charlie Company had killed a thousand North Vietnamese soldiers in front of its perimeter during the TET Offensive. The North Vietnamese had sent out their fighting men in waves of four. The first wave carried rifles; the second wave carried ammo; the third and fourth waves didn't carry anything. The plan was that when a soldier was killed in front of them, a soldier in the wave behind him would pick up his weapon and keep attacking the Americans. The TET Offensive was an imaginary battle for me: I wasn't in Nam yet, so I could only envision it as it was described to me.

The day I got transferred, I was lucky that my new unit had been assigned back at base camp for an extended rest. My buddies Dyckes and Tiger were still out in the bush. They were still running patrols from the Buddhist temple out into the rice paddies were I had come from.

I heard from Dyckes from time to time through letters. He told me the 5th of the 12th was getting a lot of action. They were constantly getting the bad end of the stick when it came to assigned missions while the rest of my tour was a hit and miss.

I think brigade headquarters was angry that Captain Kenny had his legs blown off and took their anger by giving my old company riskier assignments.

My new company got the better assignments. We were placed around the outskirts of Saigon to protect the city from the Viet Cong. We rarely saw action unless brigade needed our help. Unless we were sent out to find Charlie in the pineapple fields or the rubber plantations, we were fairly safe as long as we avoided the booby traps. The elements were always our main enemy, whether it was the insects, the monsoon rains, or the clap. Somewhere out there, something was always lurking to get us.

We searched for Charlie every day, but he always ran away from us. All I know is that Charlie didn't mess with us. The word was out: If Charlie was to engage us, he would lose.

Three days after my transfer, I celebrated my first Fourth of July in Vietnam. I still felt displaced, alone, and depressed, still sad about leaving Dyckes and Tiger. I had to make new friends all over again. It wasn't easy learning to trust someone I didn't know anything about, so I avoided getting close to anyone else the rest of my tour. I would fight my war alone for the next eight months.

It took me months to get over the idea that I would fight this war without my combat brothers beside me, but I had to stay positive. I remembered my true friends were Dyckes and Yingst, and I would still honor our covenant if we ever got back to the States.

I dreamed of my home, my family and my wife. I obsessed about having a perfect relationship with Renee. Our relationship was bad when I entered the Army. I wanted to straighten out my past and start over again.

On July 4, everyone was celebrating that night. I looked up

into the high watchtower above my head and wondered what it looked like from that position. I really didn't care if I had gotten killed that night. I had a don't-give-a-shit attitude. I was angry that the Army had separated me from my friends.

I climbed a hundred feet up the tower. When I arrived, I was greeted by two other men. "Let me help you up, man," one guy said. "This is the best spot in Nam, man," he continued as he handed me a joint of marijuana. "And this is the best pot in Nam," he laughed, coughing up some smoke as he did.

After a few hits of pot, all I could do was stare out into space. I could see 360 degrees all around our base. "It was out there," the one soldier pointed, "that we killed a thousand gooks. Man, was it cool. It was like shooting ducks in a duck pond. I killed about a hundred."

I imagined all those enemy soldiers being torn down by our machine guns and artillery explosions. Smoky helicopter gunships sprayed thousands of bullets, killing everything that moved. I heard that my new company had killed so many Vietnamese that it took the Army engineers a week to cover the bodies. They took bulldozers, dug a huge hole, and covered them in the gully right in front of us. There was a huge graveyard of dead soldier's right before my eyes.

I suddenly thought of my life back home, where people were celebrating the Fourth of July. How I wished I was home. I really missed everyone. I imagined the celebration at Del Web Field back in Modesto, where the Modesto Reds played. They were a minor-league farm team for the New York Yankees, my favorite team. My dreams seemed to come true when I was at the ballpark.

Del Web Field was the place to go in those days in Modesto. If you wanted to see the Fourth of July fireworks, you drove to a spot and parked your car, or you got out and sat in the grass outside the stadium. We would take lawn chairs, a blanket, and some snacks and wait until the fireworks started. Those were some great times.

'"What did you say, man?" the G.I. standing next to me asked. "Oh, I was just tripping, man," I told him. "I was thinking about home."

I looked out into the open darkness in front of me and thought of the sacrifice men gave for the sake of freedom. Wow, I thought, I am experiencing freedom right before my very eyes. This is why we celebrate. It is an awesome task to give your life for another. Just looking at the American flag gives me a feeling of pride. It is a privilege to live in America. We have so many blessings.

When I attended elementary school, we started our day with the Pledge of Allegiance. It made me feel good about my country. It helped me show respect to authority and to my fellow schoolmates. It made me feel patriotic.

When I look at the American flag today, I still feel pride. I feel humbled by the sacrifice men give to their country. In Nam, I was proud to be a part of this war, to fight for my country. I have a responsibility to my God and to my fellow soldiers.

I looked up and saw the stars. I wondered how God could make so many bright stars. I wondered if we were the only people he had made living in this universe. I wondered if God was looking down upon me at that moment.

Then my mind shifted to my loneliness. Even all those stars couldn't help me now. I felt depressed and wondered what the rest of my fate would be without my friends I left behind.

Over the loudspeakers came a song that everyone joined in all over the base camp:

While the storm clouds gather far across the sea, Let's swear allegiance to a land that's free, Let us all be grateful for a land so fair, As we raise our voices in a solemn prayer.

God bless America, Land that I love, Stand beside her, and guide her thru the night with a light from above,

From the mountains, to the prairies, to the oceans, white with foam

God bless America, My home sweet home, God bless America, My home sweet home.

A blast of machine-gun fire ripped open the night air. I watched as I saw red tracer rounds arc into the sky from one end of the horizon to the next. It seemed to last for about thirty minutes. There were flares that shot upward in the sky and burst open, lighting the ground beneath. There were explosions of 155 Hosier rounds, and "Bam,Bam,Bam...rat,tat,tat,rat,tat,tat" sounds were everywhere.

That was the weirdest experience. I never expected something like this to happen. I was in Vietnam, and we were celebrating the birth of our nation and our freedom in America. We are free because of good men and soldiers like these. Many men and women have given the ultimate sacrifice. Even if we survived and didn't sacrifice our lives, we certainly sacrificed our youth, some of the best years of our lives.

Most Americans take freedom for granted. They don't understand the value of sacrifice. They want their rights handed to them on a stick without having to work for them. Most Americans will never feel the way we soldiers and veterans do.

I felt proud to be an American, proud and honored to be in the U.S. Army. It was right of us to help the Vietnamese people. They had lived with war all their lives. They deserved a better life.

This was for them, the Vietnamese people. We were fighting to gain freedom and to choose one's destiny. Isn't freedom always worth fighting for?

★ ★ ★ ★

CHAPTER 14: THESE BOOTS ARE MADE FOR WALKING – NANCY SINATRA

My tour of duty was not only about finding the enemy. It was also about fighting the elements. When we weren't battling the enemy, we had other conditions to deal with. The weather was a deterrent in Nam, but it never stopped us from fighting or searching for Charlie. We never quit, even during the rainy monsoon seasons. I learned to watch the sky, the clouds, and the wind to get an idea of what kind of weather was ahead of us.

The heat and humidity were oppressive, and they took their toll on our health. If you had a wound, it would take months to heal. During our missions in the jungles, the heat would sometimes reach 118 degrees. Men would pass out from heat exhaustion. We had to take saline tablets and drink lots of water to avoid dehydration. Under normal circumstances, a grunt would carry one canteen of water; in Nam, we needed to carry two.

To cool off, we would dip our towels in water and put them around our necks. The heat would pound through our clothes, so most of us never wore underwear. It was way too hot in Vietnam for underwear.

In Nam, we either had to adjust to the environment or go

crazy. Whatever the situation we faced, we had to accept those circumstances and harden our emotions.

Mother Nature would warn us before we got drenched. We would see a curtain, a wave of rain, coming toward us before we got hit. A dark sky, blackened by huge rainclouds, would precede the downpour, giving us a little time to run for cover before the storm actually struck. We had only a few minutes to prepare for what sometimes was like a waterfall from the sky, but that would be just enough time to gather our gear and head for higher ground. I would quickly put on my poncho over my gear and rifle to keep everything dry as I looked for cover.

It would rain in buckets, large raindrops, sometimes coming at us sideways, sometimes straight down. It seemed to rain differently every day. On some days, the force of the rain would pound on our helmets and backs. It made a thumping noise, and we couldn't hear a thing, not even the voice of a soldier standing right next to us. It didn't take long before the ground was saturated with water. Our boots and feet would be soaked within a couple of minutes. When we walked, our feet would slide into the mud up to our ankles.

That wasn't the worst of it. Vietnam is largely a jungle, and with it came many perils that had nothing at all to do with the war. The rain disturbed the insects that were hiding under the ground and in the trees. We slept in our fatigues because of the insects. We had to be careful: The Army told us to keep our sleeves buttoned so that the insects, leeches, and snakes wouldn't crawl into our clothes while we were sleeping. I always looked carefully in the streams of water because I could see scorpions, centipedes, and snakes floating downstream, looking for a dry place to land.

Vietnam was filled with poisonous snakes, bamboo vipers, centipedes that were eight inches long and could give us a mighty sting, malaria-carrying mosquitos, and scorpions whose bites could be fatal. All the insects seemed huge, at least twice the size of those we had seen in the States. Then there were the army ants that could eat right through clothing and embed themselves deeply into our skin. Boy, did they hurt!

The mosquitos would bombard us as we tried to sleep. They would buzz overhead, searching for a place to sky-dive into our skin. The noise often kept us from sleeping. I always sprayed myself with insect repellent before going to bed. I would spay a circle around my body on the ground when I slept at night. I thought the insect repellent would protect me from snakes and other night critters, but I was wrong.

I watched as the insects found cover on boxes, on lids, and in our trenches. I couldn't help but imagine something climbing on my back or on my clothes. I was like a dog fighting off fleas to make sure he didn't get bitten. But some soldiers did sustain insect bites and had to be evacuated to a local hospital.

Soldiers also got jungle rot — a severe fungal infection of the feet — from walking in the water of the rice paddies, rivers, or mud. Some men got it so bad that they couldn't walk and had to be treated. Everyone had jungle rot. No one could get away from it. Our feet were always wet. Each grunt carried two pairs of socks in his backpack, but that didn't help. It was just a matter of time before we had to have medication. No one could keep his feet dry long enough to get the rot to clear up.

While on patrol, our point men sometimes would fall into bunkers with holes or into pongee pits. Pongees were sharpened bamboo sticks. Charlie would dig holes several feet deep and cover them with brush and leaves. The bamboo sticks at the bottom of the pit were razor sharp, pointed upward, and dipped in poison, so that anyone who fell into the pit would be gored and killed.

We were told it was against the Geneva Convention to use that kind of warfare. Maybe Charlie didn't get the memo.

✦ ✦ ✦ ✦

As bad as they were, the jungles of Vietnam reminded me of some fun times from my youth.

All my aunts, uncles, cousins, and I would get together several times a year at my grandfather's home, and almost always during Easter. It was truly a family reunion, with lots of fun and food for all of us. Our family became very close over the years, and my grandparents loved having all the family together.

Usually, my cousins and I would play together all around my grandfather's neighborhood. One time, when I was around twelve years old, one of my cousins was down the street and needed to go to the bathroom. Instead of returning to my grandparents' home, he ran behind some houses. There he discovered a huge forest. He realized that he had found some previously unknown territory, so after he relieved himself he ran back to tell the rest of us about the forest.

That forest became our "jungle," as we called it. That is where I learned how to become a mighty warrior and destroy the enemy. I pretended to be an Army soldier. We made toy guns and rifles in my grandfather's workshop in his garage. We were always on an expedition to find the enemy with our make-believe rifles and bullets. My cousins and I lived the life of make-believe soldiers. My cousin Ronnie was the leader of the pack because he was the oldest. The others were Wayne, Gary, Pat, Mike, Chris, Ronnie, and sometimes Joan, his sister (she was the nurse), Tim, Jerry, Rick, my brother Roger, and me.

My cousins and I would enter "the jungle" and follow a path into the unknown until we reached the other side. It usually took us several hours to reach the other end of the forest. When we were ten and twelve years old, it seemed to last forever.

We had a pecking order in our squad of infantry soldiers, and I was one of the youngest. The oldest were Ronnie, Wayne and Gary. Ronnie was the commander, and Wayne and Gary were officers. Since I was one of the youngest, I would always get shot first and die. I had to climb over brush and trees to clear the way for our officers. The jungle looked frightening to any boy. It had an element of the unknown.

We were always looking out for some type of wild animal who could kill or attack us in the high brush. But rarely did we encounter anything, and when we did it was always a dog or cat running away from the noise we were making.

The jungle had tall trees that extended as high as you could see. The foliage and brush hid all the homes, so we were really in a world of our own. It was filled with all different kinds of trees and plants, just like a real jungle. It was our secret place where no one else knew where we were. We all made a vow never to reveal it to anyone.

On our trips to the jungle, we only carried the essentials — graham crackers, chewing gum, and candy if we had any. Usually we ran out of the candy first. The oldest would always get more than the youngest.

It was scary walking through that dense bush. Yet it was always the highlight of our reunion until Grandpa died in 1963. Our family stopped getting together for ten years after his death, and the jungle trips were put on hold.

We grew older, but we never returned to our adventure jungle. Finally, around 1983, my cousin Ronnie let the cat out of the bag and told our aunts and uncles about the forest at the Thanksgiving family reunion. I was twenty-eight years old at the time. Everyone laughed, because no one had said a word for all those years.

In Nam, chewing gum, candy, and make-believe guns just wouldn't do. The essential equipment was necessary if we wanted to survive. Each man in his jungle fatigues wore his steel pot on his head, his jungle hat, and a towel for the heat and sweat. We carried three to four cans of C-rations, two pairs of dry socks, one set of dry fatigues, web gear weighting about thirty pounds, two canteens of water, a bayonet, five hundred rounds of ammo, a rifle, four grenades, two flares, a gas mask, a first-aid kit, a shovel, several sandbags, a poncho, some writing material, pistol belt, flashlight, and other personal belongs.

We placed our cigarettes on our head and insect repellent on the side of our steel pots to keep them from getting wet. Most men carried pictures of their wives, girlfriends, or favorite pinup girl. Of course, I carried the radio, so I had an additional thirty pounds. With all this gear, we would go looking for Charlie.

Everywhere we walked and walked, it seemed to be a different type of terrain. We walked through rice paddies, swamps, and streams. We searched for Charlie in pineapple groves and rubber-tree plantations. We rode on Navy boats in the delta waterways and other rivers. Sometimes they called us "river rats."

We chopped our way through the jungles and climbed over hills and cliffs. We slept in water and mud filled with leeches and rats. We trudged through mud up to our waist. We walked cautiously on the rice-paddy dikes and through villages, stepping lightly, not knowing if we would hit a booby trap.

At night, it was usually so dark that we couldn't see two feet in front of us. Imagine closing your eyes and going into a dark closet with no light. You open your eyes, and its pitch dark. That's what it was like at night in Nam.

Nighttime was a terror. I prayed for dawn to come, and always arose early to watch the sunrise. The sunrise brought safety because I could see again.

The stars and moon didn't seem to shine on Vietnam. Could it be that God didn't like this country?

$$\star \quad \star \quad \star \quad \star$$

CHAPTER 15: 96 TEARS – QUESTION MARK AND THE MYSTERIANS

Mail call was a very special time of the day. Once a day, usually in the afternoon, we would receive our mail from home. If we were still out on a mission, then we would get it the next day. Mail call was like Christmas: It meant somebody cared, someone loved us.

The mail gave us another reason to live. In Vietnam, a soldier could give up and take unnecessary risks. Having someone to live for gave us hope. A soldier's mail was his personal acknowledgment that the outside world still existed …and cared.

When the mail came, we would sit and read our letters privately and guardedly. Some soldiers would become distant because hearing from loved ones back home would cause them to well up with emotion. No one wanted to be seen in tears, so we would read our mail the way a mother lion protects her cubs.

Some letters were sweet and romantic, such as from a girlfriend or a wife. Other letters could make a soldier tremble and shake. Some men would receive boxes with cans or cookies in it, which made the rest of us a bit jealous. The Army censored every communication, incoming and outgoing. Sometimes a soldier would get an envelope with nothing in it but a note saying that the Army had censored the entire letter. We were constantly warned about revealing details about our position in our letters home. If Charlie were to intercept the mail and get wind of our location or find out anything else about us, he could use it to his advantage and rocket or mortar our location. We were also told not to write anything that was X-rated.

With that in mind, I didn't have much to say to my wife and family back home. I would write letters to my family whenever I got a fifteen-minute break, but I never talked about the battles or the elements. It was hard to write home and say what was really happening. I didn't want say what Vietnam was really like. I didn't want my family to worry. So I kept things inside and talked instead about my coming home to get my mind off this place. I wrote about working for my father's business or about how much I had changed. I was nineteen years old, and I wanted everyone to think I was a man. My letters home must have been pretty boring, but I didn't want to give Charlie anything that he could use as propaganda.

Remembering our families and wanting to come home to them is what sustained us in Vietnam. Sometimes that's all we lived for or thought about. For me, it became a driving force. It made me stay alert and watch my steps in the bush. Loving my family and my wife gave me the will to live.

Letters from home helped relieve the horror and fear that was with me every day. During those times, I would focus all my hope on returning to work for my father's business and to resuming my life with my wife, Renee. She would send me pictures of her, and my G.I. buddies were all envious of me. She was so pretty and she was onl9 19 years old. I had to guard those pictures because someone might steal them. I put her pictures under my steel pot.

Sometimes a soldier would receive a "Dear John" letter, one of those shocking notes from a wife or girlfriend stating that she had found someone else and was ending the relationship. We could always tell when a soldier got one of those. His face would show his utter despondency. "Dear John" letters caused great destruction, not only for the spurned soldier but to all of us. We were brothers in combat, and we cared for each other. When a man received a letter like that, it was emotional cruelty — and we all felt it. It was seen as a loss of love and respect for our cause. It made us feel worthless.

When a soldier received a letter like that, he stopped caring about his life. Because of that, he couldn't be trusted by the other soldiers. He might become reckless and take unnecessary chances with his live and even the lives of others, and no one wanted to be around someone who was reckless. He would be like a walking time bomb. You didn't know how he was going to react. It was frightening for everyone.

I remember two men who received "Dear John" letter and then went ballistic. Both volunteered to walk point on patrol. I know of other men who re-enlisted in the Army for another four years after they got their "Dear John" letter. A "Dear John" letter was like a kiss of death.

My friend German was in my platoon. He was our point man. I can still see his face when he read the news after he received a letter from his girlfriend back home. At the time, we were guarding Hill 41 outside of Bien Hoa, just twenty miles south of Saigon.

I watched German's face as it transformed from a smile into a frown. His eyes filled with tears. I asked him what was wrong. All he said was that it was a "Dear John" letter, and then he turned away. I tried to console him, but he lost it. He didn't say a word. He just got up, found a bottle of Jack Daniels, and downed the entire fifth. It was a sad day for all of us. We all shared his grief.

German remained depressed for the rest of his tour. He stayed drunk as much as possible, too, and was generally withdrawn. I could see the melancholy in his face and in his posture when he walked. He never held his head up high. He no longer cared what happened to him.

I was concerned that he might kill himself with his M-16 rifle.

On one occasion, we actually had to restrain him from grabbing his weapon. He was even more distant after that and never got close to anyone again. He even stopped talking to his buddies, and we likewise kept our distance when we were around him. I started to recall another incident in our platoon;

Our company had just come from patrolling the Pineapple fields near the Cambodian border and we were cleaning our rifles. Over the radio I heard the crackling sounds from Brigade. We had received fire from Charlie. One of the helicopters had taken a few rounds. We would be heading back where we just came from.

There was a complete silence in my squad. You could feel the stress see the fear flow like a fog rolling in from the sea.

Intelligence reported there was a division of North Vietnamese troops in the area we had just patrolled. We had to quickly put back on our gear and prepare for an assault. Our camp was silent. You could hear men thinking out loud. Someone is going to get killed

And then a heard gun shots that echoed from around the camp. Someone's been hit? Where and who?

A few minutes later Captain's words came over the radio.

"What the hell was that, over? Give me a response, now, over.

Ah, this is Delta-Tango. We have one man that has appeared to shot himself accidentally in the foot, over.

"Son of a bitch", were captain's reaction.

"If that G.I. put a round in his foot on purpose I'm going to give him an article 15 right on the spot. I'm heading your way, over".

Fear and anguish can paralyze a man, also, depression.

When I saw German's face I knew he would never be the

same. The hope of having someone love you can keep you alive for another day.

What scared me more than getting killed by Charlie was receiving a letter like that one.

After that experience, I vowed that if my wife ever cheated on me while I was serving in Vietnam, I would leave her, even if I found out ten years later.

However, I never received any bad news from home. My family was pretty faithful in writing me once a week. When I didn't receive any mail, though, it felt like no one cared. I felt even more alone. It's not good to be alone, especially in Nam.

One day, I received a large package from my brother. I was really excited about opening it. At the time, I had been in Nam for only about two months. I was happy to know that someone back home cared about me. They must know I'm starving out here, I told myself.

I opened the package slowly, hoping and imagining that it contained a batch of homemade chocolate-chip cookies. That would have been delicious right about then! But when I tore open the box, I saw something green and plastic. What the heck was this? I can't eat this, I thought. I unfolded the wrapping and found it was a green plastic rain suit. My brother, who lived in Washington, D.C., had sent me a full-length rain suit! No cookies, just plastic! I had a good laugh at that.

There I was in Vietnam, fighting for my country, and craving some good home-baked food or snacks. And what do I get? Plastic! I looked around to make sure none of the other guys saw what I got. I was a little embarrassed.

My brother must have been watching the news one night and saw how hard it rained in Vietnam during the monsoon season. I guess my brother thought I needed some rain gear to help me stay dry. Good thought, Roger, but I can't wear this over my Army gear, brother.... It would make way too much noise in the bush! If Charlie heard that squeaking sound, he would shoot in my direction!

There was more in the box, so I kept digging and looking for something to eat. All right, I found a bottle of hot sauce! Now that would be useful. I could use the hot sauce on those awful cans of C-rations! Hot sauce was a prized commodity in Nam, and it went fast. I used it on everything.

After receiving my brother's gift, I wrote him a letter:

Well, things are pretty good right now. It has just stopped raining. It's been raining for three months straight. It rains day and night. The ground is always wet, and your feet never dry out.

Oh, by the way, that rain suit was really cool, but I couldn't use it over my gear. It made too much noise. It did become useful, though. I hope you don't mind, but I traded it for eight chocolate chip cookies! They were delicious, and the guy I traded with really liked your rain suit. I hope you don't mind.

Roger always sounded like he was having a good time in the bars. It really made me angry to read how much fun he was having while I sat in this hellhole waiting for the next mortar round to rip my balls off.

Now here is the letter I really *wanted* to write him:

Dear Roger, it sounds like you're having a lot of fun and screwing a lot of women. Save some for me! I really appreciate the information about how everyone back home opposes the war, but I don't want to hear about it. I don't give a rip how the war protesters in D.C. are desecrating the flag. I don't really want to hear about all the fun you're having, either.

If you want to send me something, send me some food. I'm starving to death, and all I can eat are the Army C-rations. However, the free love and sex sound pretty good to me right now.

Oh, I just heard some news today about one G.I. that had a day off and got the clap from a Saigon whore. He was in excruciating pain. He is on penicillin and feels much better now, though.

The Army is always warning us about not getting venereal disease, especially, the "black V.D." There was circulating a rumor that a soldier would be sent to the Philippines for treatment and would not ever be allowed to return home to the United States...

★ ★ ★ ★

It was dangerous to enter the Vietnamese villages. We never knew if the villagers were friendly to the American side or allied with the communistic Charlie. Whenever we walked in the villages, we were ordered not to fire our weapons unless we were fired upon first. It was strange, because the enemy could fire on us out of nowhere. I felt like an easy target, even when patrolling around "friendlies."

The Vietnamese people who lived in the villages seemed to know that Charlie was close by. They wouldn't tell us anything, even if he was living with them. They were afraid they would get killed. But whenever Charlie left the village, they would tell us.

Vietnamese homes were more like huts made from palm trees. The sides and roof were held together by four posts made from tree branches. The floors were dirt, and there was no electricity and no bathroom. Most huts had only one large room where everyone slept. In the middle of this room was a pit where they kept rice and food utensils.

For their bathroom needs, they used what they called "bathhouses," even though there was no bath inside. They didn't have toilets, either. There would be a wooden plank with a hole in it, and a person would set his or her bare butt over this hole. Usually these bathhouses would be positioned out over a river or stream, and so the human waste went directly into the water — water that very likely was also used for washing and drinking downstream somewhere. The bathhouses were made out of wood, and there would be two stalls — one for men, and one for women — with entrances on opposite sides.

Only a cloth sheet separated the men's side from the women's side — not even remotely as private as our bathrooms in America. They would bring their own toiletries; if they didn't have any, they would search for discarded newspaper nearby. It wasn't a place to be modest, and you didn't have many choices. The only other places to go were the bushes, and that was not recommended because that's where Charlie placed his booby traps.

Every day as I walked through the villages, I could see the *mama-san* (oldest woman) outside sweeping out the hut. Her duties included not only cooking, but also sweeping bugs and branches out of their dirt-floor huts. They had to do that in order to keep snakes, centipedes, scorpions, and other insects from entering their homes.

Papa-san had lighter duties. The oldest did nothing but smoke dope. He would sit all day long just looking at everything and everyone, with never a smile on his face. His eyes were bloodshot and he had a long beard, usually grey, long, and stringy.

Unless the family happened to have a shop or a piece of the black market, everyone else in the family worked in the rice paddies or raised vegetables. Many of the young women were used as prostitutes, with a brother serving as the pimp. The rest of the family did whatever they could do to earn money to survive.

The huts were lit by a candle to see at night. At sunset, however, it was lights out. The villages feared that lights would attract mortar fire from Charlie. As soon the sun went down, the villagers would go into their huts and not emerge again until morning. If anyone went out, they were considered the enemy. The Vietnamese people lived in constant fear.

On the first of every month, the Army passed out our paychecks. We got extra duty pay for being in a war zone and extra duty pay for different levels of seniority. I was paid $175 a month when I first entered Nam. After two months, the Army raised my pay to $225 a month. When I was promoted to sergeant, I received $275 a month. It was enough to live on, and I kept $50 to spend on the essentials.

The Vietnamese always seemed to know when we got paid, and they were always trying to make money off us. We could count on them finding us on the first of every month. They would ride their sand-pan boats filled with iced-cold Tiger beer to our base camps. They would walk the rice-paddy dikes to find us in the bush and sell us watches, ice, Coca-Cola, cigarettes, fake cigarettes filled with marijuana, lighters, and all kinds of stuff — a lot of the same goods we could buy in Saigon on the black market. They wanted to make money, and they did, because the American dollar went a long way in Vietnam. The U.S. military had its own currency, which we preferred to use instead of regular U.S. currency because the value was about thirty to one.

The Vietnamese pimps would even send their prostitutes out to find us. Young girls would walk to our base camp and stand just outside our perimeter waiting for someone to nod his head. They would take him behind a bush for $10. Some prostitutes would go from tent to tent having sex with any man they could. Prostitution was big in Nam.

Most soldiers didn't care much about getting venereal disease. The biggest concern was staying alive. The Vietnamese girls were just making a living. A lot of soldiers spent all their money on sex or booze.

I had made it up in my mind when I first arrived in Vietnam that I wouldn't have sex with any Vietnamese girl. I didn't want to get the feared "black V.D." I had vowed to wait until my R&R (rest and recuperation), when I could arrange to be with my wife again for a few days. I had never practiced sexual abstinence since I was sixteen years old, but I knew I could do it with God's help. I wanted to be right before God in case I got killed. I wanted to go to heaven. I didn't want to go to hell.

I loved the Vietnamese people and their simple way of life. I especially fell in love with the Vietnamese children. They would run up to us in the streets and beg us for food, and we played games with them. Seeing them laugh and play was a breath of fresh air. They seemed to love and appreciate us, and I really enjoyed giving them chocolate. The kids would call out our names: "Hey, G.I., YOU number one!" If we gave them a treat, they would call us "number one"; if we didn't, we were "number ten," the worst!

I believed these children and people were the real reason we were fighting in this land. Growing up in the Catholic faith I believed all people have the right to live in freedom. We soldier's hoped to build a free Vietnam for the next generation and the generation after that. Ironically, like all wars, innocent people would be killed. But, for the Vietnamese they had to live with the threat of not seeing another day. Sooner or later, "death" would come knocking on their door or ours.

As I patrolled through the villages where the Vietnamese people lived, I watched the expression on their faces. The older Vietnamese adults were sometimes cold and insensitive, even sinister and hateful. They turned away from us and wouldn't look us in the eye. They had lived through wars all their lives and trusted no one.

They had high respect for their elders. They were treated by everyone as wise.

"Wise", huh, I thought. If he were so wise he would get the hell outta Nam. I'd be on a boat to Singapore! Why stay in this hell hole!

Watching them daily as we patrolled in the villages I deeply wanted them to know of the freedoms that we enjoyed back home — growing up without fear, feeling safe and secure in their homes, being able to walk to the store unafraid was dream, never to be experienced in this land of the dead.

There was always the other side of war, the war I hated. Some of the children we saw had arms missing or faces with the scars of burns from a grenade explosion. Some were orphaned, their parents having been killed in this war. In the adults, too, I could see the sad expression of death written all over their faces. Many had lost loved ones, spouses, parents, siblings, and children. Many were supportive of us because we brought them hope. They wanted us to win so that this war would end.

The bigger vision of a FREE Vietnam and free of communism gave us another reason to fight on and live for one more day. And yes, their lives were worth fighting for. We were fighting on a distant land and freedom is the same no matter where you fight. So we fought for the future of Vietnam.

★ ★ ★ ★

CHAPTER 16: WE GOT TO GET OUTTA THIS PLACE – ERIC BURTON AND THE ANIMALS

Our training back at Fort Lewis helped us to react to situations in combat, but our training never produced fear. The Army tried to provide training situations so we would experience fear and learn to make good decisions in frightening situations. But, real fear only exists in real combat, and then a soldier may react differently. A person can fake a situation in training, but you can't really fake it when someone is trying to kill you. I don't ever remember being scared in our training as much as I was in real combat.

So, the Army assigned an Army chaplain to each brigade unit. The chaplain would travel out to meet us whenever he could, and his presence was comforting. The chaplain celebrated Mass for the Catholics on Sundays and gave us Communion. The war kept him busy, though, for there were a lot of men killed and wounded each week. He would give the dying the last rites and preside at services for those killed. On average, I would see the chaplain maybe once a month.

I prayed a lot in Nam. I believe that it was my faith in God and his almighty hand that helped me to stay alive. It gave me hope that I would stay alive and have a good marriage with my wife Renee. I promised God that I would make everything better if I returned home from Nam. I told God I wouldn't swear anymore or cheap. I would give the church my tithes. It was all a lie, to myself. I could never keep a promise.

Several of my fighting buddies went crazy from the stress of fear in combat. They had a faraway look in their eyes. They would look into the distance like someone was looking at a wall. Combat and fear brought despair. Men, like that you left to themselves. They could snap and kill at a moment's notice.

I remembered one time our unit was patrolling in the pineapple fields of Cambodia. We were told by brigade not to tell anyone we were in Cambodia. It was a big secret. We were not supposed to be there, according to the military, but we were there anyway, and we went several times. Cambodia was supposed to be a neutral country, off limits to military conflict. We went in because that's where Charlie was reorganizing and resupplying.

But, Charlie knew that the U.S. soldiers weren't supposed to enter Cambodia. Cambodia was off limits to U.S. troops. The Cambodian government was declared a neutral country but, housed North Vietnamese troops. Figure that one out. Our government is so stupid sometimes yet; our leaders never mentioned and did nothing about this during the Paris Peace talks.

So, Charlie had camps there and enjoyed freedom from our troops and from our B-52 bombers. He was dug in deep and had many underground trenches to hide in. Charlie got fresh supplies, food and rest there. Charlie would counterattack us and then go back to Cambodia to hide. It was a cat-and-mouse game. Some of our generals secretly sent us in there anyway: We would fly in quickly, under the radar to kill some Gooks and then fly back out.

The next day brigade choppers picked us up early that morning. The word was out: We were headed into the pineapple fields again. Something was up. We knew we would be fighting Charlie today. The Army pilots warned us before we landed. We would be touching ground in a hot landing zone.

As we approached our spot to land, I prepared to hit the dirt. Just before the choppers touched down, the door gunners started blasting with their machine guns, sprayed bullets in all directions. If Charlie was there, this would be our way of saying hello — with M-60 machine-gun bullets!

We got out of the helicopter and walked swiftly in columns into the rice paddies. We walked on one rice-paddy dike after another as we made our way toward the enemy — until our chaplain warned us that we were in a trap.

"The enemy is all around us," announced our Catholic chaplain, Father Angelo Liteky, who was with us on this mission. Chaplain Liteky had won the Medal of Honor for saving the lives of some 20 soldiers under enemy fire in the Asha Valley the previous December. "I've seen this happen before," he told our captain. "The enemy is hunting us. They're trying to draw us in. It's a trap."

Then I saw two N.V.A. enemy soldiers walking on the rice-paddy dikes right in front of us. I was walking twenty feet from our captain when he asked, "What the heck are they doing?" My platoon knelt down and watched as the two North Vietnamese soldiers walked back and forth on the dike. It was like they were taking an afternoon stroll in the country. Something just didn't feel right. I had never seen Charlie walking out in the open. Usually Charlie was underground, but not this time. What was he up to?

"They're trying to lure us into an ambush," whispered Chaplain Liteky to Captain Woodward. "This is *déja vu*," he said. "It has happened to me before. They want us to follow them so that they can ambush us." Our chaplain sensed the danger. A firefight was about to ensue. Everyone felt the tension in the air. You could cut the stress and fear with a knife.

I remember praying as I lay there on the dirt. My body was in the rice-paddy water while my head peeked over the dike to watch what happened next. "God help us," I prayed.

Captain then asked Chaplain Liteky, "What do you think we should do, Chaplain?"

"Lay down a heavy round of fire, and let's see what happens," Chaplain Liteky said.

Captain got on the radio to the squad leaders. "I want you all to lay down a heavy round of fire on my command, over." He wanted all our squads to fire a hundred feet from where Charlie was seen walking on the dike. Then Captain ordered, "Open fire!" and we all began firing.

"Bam, Bam, Bam," went the M-16s, and "rat-a-tat-tat-tat" went the machine guns as the mortar gunners popped their M-79 grenade launchers across the field and into the rice-paddy dikes. It was like we were at the target range. I was waiting for Charlie to return fire at us. We were all anticipating him to fire back at us, but he didn't. Nothing happened.

The gunfire lasted about ten minutes before Captain ordered, "Cease fire." We waited and waited. Charlie didn't react.

'This is not good, Captain," said our chaplain. "I think Charlie is going to box us in. He's going to surround us and then pick us off like flies."

Our whole company was exposed. We were out in the open between two rice-paddy fields. We were sitting ducks. All Charlie had to do was surround us and begin firing. We all could be killed easily. I could hear and sense a trembling in Chaplain Liteky's voice when he told Captain, "We'd better get outta here."

The captain was listened to him. He hesitated at first, but then called in the choppers to pick us up.

"Air Command, this is Alpha Charlie One, over."

"This is Air Command, over. We need a lift-fast, over."

"Roger that, Alpha Charlie One, we're on our way, over."

We kept quiet for twenty minutes until the choppers came over our heads. Smoke flares were popped, and we were lifted out of there. Thank God, I thought as I got into the helicopter with my feet tangling over the skid. I felt relief from my fear as the chopper headed us back to base. I remember looking down from the air to see if we could spot Charlie. All I could see was rice patties and bush. No Charlie.

It was a forty-five minute ride back. We were in Cambodia, the forbidden country. We would get punished from our government if they found out we had been there. I was anxious because every single time we were sent into Cambodia, an American had been killed. I didn't want to be the next victim.

The choppers landed at our base. We jumped off onto the dirt and walked briskly away from the helicopter blades. I waited as the last helicopter arrived and our men jumped off and onto the dirt.

We had only been on the ground for five minutes when an order came over the radio. Lieutenant ordered us back on the choppers.

"What did you say?" asked my platoon sergeant.

Captain ordered us back onto the slicks (slang for "helicopters"). He had a message from brigade. One of our choppers had received enemy fire as it left the area. Our brigade commander had ordered to return to the Cambodia rice paddies and pineapple fields to engage the enemy.

Uneasy and with spirits low, I re-boarded the slicks. I watched the choppers behind me fill the air as we flew in a V-formation. This time, we would be without our chaplain. Brigade didn't want to risk our chaplain's life.

I settled back with my head against the metal seat preparing myself for action. I grabbed the extra ammo that was on the floor in front of me. I put another sling of magazines around my neck filled with twenty rounds in each magazine. I hoped it was enough ammo to last me in case I needed it. All the way back, I sensed death. I prepared myself as best as I could, asking God's help in prayer.

Fifteen minutes before we landed, the pilot announced we were landing in a hot landing zone. As we approached the area where we were to be dropped off, I watched as the other choppers landed and our troops exited around a yellow layer of smoke.

"We're unloading you, and then you're own your own," remarked the pilot as he turned his head just before the drop-off point. I knew this time we had to jump off the slick about five feet off the ground. He didn't want to risk getting his helicopter shot up. It would be easier for him to fly off before Charlie fired and launched rocket-propelled grenades at him.

I scooted my butt toward the door and put my feet over the side and prepared myself to jump out. When the pilot reached the landing zone, he lowered his Huey five feet off the ground. I jumped off the slick and hit the dirt. The impact threw me on my back, and I rolled a few times against some bushes. I got up to run for cover, anticipating incoming gunfire. I dove into the bushes safely.

After I realized Charlie wasn't firing at me, I caught up to my squad. We headed through the rows of pineapple groves. I was walking toward the rear of my squad when I heard machine-gun fire at a distance. They weren't coming in my direction, at least not yet.

The pineapple groves reminded me of the grape vineyards back in Sonoma County, California. That's where the best wine was bottles in California. There were vineyards after vineyards in the Napa Valley, and plenty of wine-tasting places to visit. But this wasn't California.

We could not find Charlie. The trees were silent, and I knew he could see us. The bushes were so thick, we couldn't see on either side of us. We were walking in single file. All Charlie had to do was aim his AK-47 down our row and he could have killed all of us.

We made our way slowly until a few shots rang out in front of me. They were from an AK-47. Charlie's machine gun erupted as we hit the ground. Our point man had encountered Charlie, I thought. The firing continued for about fifteen minutes. I waited for the next order from my sergeant, who had been leading us through the thick groves. He was green, a rookie, and didn't know what to do next. He had only been in the country for two weeks, and this was his first firefight. He was scared. He froze without saying a word.

"What's happening?" I whispered to the G.I. in front of me.

"The company commander is pinned down," he responded. "One man has been killed, and our point man has been hit." The whispered news was traveling fast. Within minutes, everyone knew.

"Our point man is dead, too. It's Peter," he told me with the second wave of news. My heart sank. I couldn't believe it. Peter was on point? I knew him well. We were in basic training and AIT together at Fort Lewis. But he was our M-79 grenadier, and grenade launchers aren't supposed to walk point.

"Sergeant had him as point man today," the soldier told me. "He's crazy, man. No M-79 grenade launcher ever walks point. Only riflemen do. That stupid son-of-a-bitch sergeant! You don't put a grenade launcher on point. Sergeant doesn't know what the hell he's doing. Campos, tell Sergeant he needs to get an M-16 up front."

"Why don't you tell him yourself?" I whispered back.

"Because I'm a short-timer," he answered. "I only have thirty days left in Nam."

Peter and I had been transferred together from our original platoon back in early July. I knew him well and liked him. We weren't too close after we were transferred, though, as he made friends with another bunch of grunts. We were in the same platoon, but never in the same squad. Men in the same squad were closer than the other men because they fought side by side.

The soldiers in front of me were passing Peter's lifeless body back toward the rear of the line, still hemmed in a single file in the pineapple grove. When the body reached me, I saw the bullet hole in his head. It had gone right through his helmet.

"Steel pots don't stop AK-47 bullets," the soldier in front of me answered. Peter's eyes were closed, his face expressionless, his body lifeless. It made me cringe.

There was also a bullet hole at his heart. My buddy ran his

finger over the bullet hole on his head and then his heart. "He died instantly. He never knew what hit him," he said. "God rest his soul. He won't have to worry ever again. He's with God now."

Man, when you see someone dead it rocks your soul. It feels like someone just knocked you aside the head with a big rock. It hurts and there is a numbing pain in your whole body. You want that person to be alive. You touch him so he will wake up. You touch again and nothing happens. He doesn't open his eyes. He never will ever again.

The soldier had tears in his eyes. "We were best of friends. We lived in the same city," he sobbed. "Oh, my God, why him"? He continued to stare at Peter's body for several minutes. "He must have been dead before he hit the ground."

I waited in silence as Peter's friend composed himself. "Rest in peace, bro," he said quietly as he slid Peter's body back to me.

The lone bullet hole on the front of his steel pot had hit him directly at the intersection of the three lines in the middle of the peace symbol he had drawn on his helmet. The bullet went right through the center of that peace symbol and out the other side of his head. That was eerie.

The story came out that Peter had seen Charlie hiding in a deep hole underground in the bushes. When Peter saw Charlie, he fired his M-79 grenade launcher, but it jammed. An instant later, as he tried to fix the jam, Charley fired a quick burst with his AK-47, killing Peter, and then immediately retreated back down his hole.

We couldn't see where Charlie was hiding. No one had seen him pop up except Peter. Now, Peter's friend was getting angrier by the moment. He barely restrained himself as he muttered under his breath, "Get an M-16 rifleman up front, Sergeant, you dumb shit."

"You need to get an M-16 on point," I radioed to the sergeant. The rest of the squad was about thirty meters in front of me now, and I couldn't see anything because of the high grass. No one else said a word. Most of the other men in my squad had only been in the country for several weeks. I was a veteran and had been in combat for five months.

Sergeant thought about it for a while and then said, "OK, you, Campos, and then you get up here right now. Move it up hear".

"Ah, I didn't mean me, Sergeant," I told myself. "I'm way back in the rear of the squad." I'm not as point man. You go up there. You're the leader" Shit, I could get killed.

Sergeant called out again. "Campos get up here with your M-16. You're on point."

"Okay" I hesitated and then crawled forward. I kept thinking I would be the one killed next. Shit, Peter just got killed, just like that and now I was going to be on point. Charlie would sure see me next.

"To hell with it, here I come".

It took a while before I reached the spot where Peter had been killed. I got on my knees and stayed very close to the ground. Slowly, I scanned the area looking to find Charlie. I wasn't going to let him pop up and kill me the way he did Peter. If he did try I would be ready for him.

I took out all my M-16 magazines of ammo and placed them on the grass in front of me. I took two grenades out of my web gear and placed them in front of me. I would get my chance to fire first. I would surely get Charlie or die trying.

I slowly took the safety off my M-16. I didn't want to make any noise to give off my location. Then I started firing into the bushes about a foot off the ground. I went through about three magazines of twenty rounds each. I sprayed the entire area in front of me and to the sides in the bushes where I thought Charlie might be hiding.

Then, I got angry. I was angry that Charlie had killed my friend Peter. That f--in Gook is going to die! I sprayed another round of bullets and stopped.

I listened and listened for Charlie to make a sound. But, I

heard and saw nothing. It seemed like an eternity. I waited for Charlie to pop up his head and shoot me.

I could sense Charlie was right there a few feet in front of me in the bushes. Maybe he's dead, I thought. I reached down, grabbed a grenade, pulled the pin, threw it toward the bushes on the right side of the mound, and watched the grenade roll into the dirt.

"Short!" the G.I. behind me yelled. The scream startled me, and I buried my head and body into my steel pot while lying flat on the ground. The grenade exploded with a loud impact and threw dirt and scrap metal all over me.

I popped my head up and looked, still no sign of Charlie.

A few minutes later, I heard the sergeant command, "Okay, Campos, that's enough, move up."

Move up? He didn't say that, did he?

Oh, shit, I thought. He's got to be F-ING kidding! I'll be moving right past Charlie and he'll shoot me in the back. So, I stood up and started to take a step forward.

"CAMPOS, came the words behind me! Captain has ordered us to retreat back. We're heading back.

"Oh, my God," I knelt down. Just in time. I looked out ahead of me.

Next, time Charlie. It's you and me.

It had been a horrifying experience. If our captain hadn't ordered us back, I probably would have been the next to die. I was thankful that I was alive.

When I reached back to the spot of the entrance I was asked to carry Peter's body with the help of three other men.

I took out my poncho liner and laid it under him. The other men took out theirs. We made a stretcher with them using our M-16 rifles to help keep his body off the ground. We lifted his dead body and started carrying it back to the Command Post.

It wasn't easy, as rigor mortis set in his body got heavier and heavier. We had a mile top travel and it was raining hard. The dirt switched to mud. It was slippery and we struggled to keep his body from flip flopping out of the rig. We walked over the rugged terrain and through a stream. We dropped his lifeless body several times but, picked up and continued to get closer and closer to our C.P.

It seemed to take forever to walk those several miles, but we finally reached our destination.

When we laid his body down next to the captain's RTO. He was also killed by the N.V.A. And then it hit me like a ton of bricks. I knew this man. I couldn't believe he was dead. I wanted to sob, but I couldn't.

I kept thinking about the way he was killed. I pictured in my mind him seeing Charlie as he approached. He was the only one who saw Charlie. He picked up his M-79 grenade launcher and quickly aimed and fired. It didn't fire. He looked down to see why it didn't fire and then Bam, Bam, Bam. One round hit him in the head. The other round hit his heart. He went down on the ground and it was over. That's how fast it was to die. In a split second it all happened so quickly.

My hope was that he never felt a thing. But, he was at peace with God now. I held my breath before my body burst into convulsions of tears.

I struggled to gain my composure. I had to separate myself from his death or I would lose it. I thought about his parents or a girlfriend back at his hometown. They would all hear the news that a hometown boy lost his life in Vietnam.

I imagined the Army sending someone to his parent's house. The officer would pull up in a military car. He would get out and shut the door behind him and approach the front door. He had a letter in his hand that read, "The United States Army regrets to inform you that you son was killed in action in South Vietnam. .Peter's platoon leader had the responsibility to personally telephone his parents. He was a brave soldier, that he died with honors and distinguished himself on the battlefield.

And to us, the soldiers who lived with him his last final hours? Well, he was doing his duty for his country, the Vietnam government and his fellow combat brothers. He had sworn an oath to the United States of America. He will be missed by us all.

Peter was only twenty years old when he died in Vietnam, three weeks short of his twenty-first birthday.

We had set Peter's body down next to Captain Woodward's RTO.

I watched my company commander pace back and forth through the mud and water. He had his head down and wasn't saying a word, but I could tell he was disturbed.

Captain said, "I was standing right next to him when he got shot," "I went over to him to help and he was dead. There was nothing I could do for him. That's what started this whole damn thing."

I sat down in the mud next to the two bodies and put my head between my legs. I silently recalled every over and over.

Captain Woodward had lost his R.T.O., but he needed to call in artillery support so that

Charlie wouldn't attack us. A few minutes later, I heard him make the call out loud.

"Does anyone have experience on the radio?"

I didn't say a word. I was waiting for someone else to speak up.

"Does anyone know how to use the radio?" he asked again. "I have just lost my radio

operator."

I finally responded. "Yes, sir," I answered. "I carried the radio for my lieutenant with the 5th of the 12th."

"What's your name, son?" he asked me.

"Campos, sir, specialist fourth-class, sir," I answered sharply.

"Campos, you are my radio operator," Captain calmly said. "From now on, you will be

with me." He grabbed the radio and handed it to me.

"I've called in artillery support and it should be arriving in shortly. I want you to monitor the radio while I attend to some business," he ordered.

I took the radio and put it on my back and waited for artillery support to arrive.

About twenty minutes later I heard the thundering of 155 Hoister rounds heading our way from a long distance out.

Every night on patrol we called in artillery support around our position as a way to keep Charlie away from our perimeter.

A few minutes later I heard the whistling sounds of incoming artillery. It sounded close so, I covered my heard.

Kam, Kabam, Kbam.

The incoming rounds were coming in on our position. Everyone scrambled to get out of the way.

Kabam, Kbam, Kbam. The rounds had entered our perimeter. I watched as the rounds hit the mud all around me. Another round landed twenty feet away, and then another about ten feet away.

"Hit the ground, caption screamed

"Campos" give me the horn. He reached over and grabbed the phone.

"Stop your firing!" he yelled. "You're killing us, and they're coming into out perimeter! Stop your firing!"

Next, we say and explosion. A round landed thirty feet away where three men were on guard. The artillery landed on top of them.

I heard men screaming.

Captain said to me, "Let's go, Campos." We both ran in the direction of the explosions.

The screaming got louder as we approached.

We both reached the area quickly. I saw three men sprawled in the mud. All three were wounded. One had taken the incoming round directly in his stomach.

I watched Captain Woodward take out his flashlight and illuminate the area where the men lay.

Some of the other men had reached the position and was

trying frantically to hold his insides from gushing all over the mud. Another man was yelling. "No, No"!

"Oh, my God," screamed Captain. "They've hit our own men."

"Medic! Medic! Get over here now. We need help, medic! screamed the captain,

"Call in the DAMN medevac, Campos," Captain said. He looked over at me and remembered that he had only given me the radio five minutes ago. I didn't know the codes for our company. I hadn't received that information yet.

"Never mind" Captain grabbed the phone and called in the dust off.

I was really scared. A few more rounds keep came in and hit outside the perimeter.

And then it stopped. Thank God! Finally, the artillery stopped.

We now had three men seriously wounded and two others dead. What was going to happen to us next?

The night was just beginning. We had just arrived at our C.P. when this happened. Now, we had to wait for the dust off.

That was the worst day of my Army tour, a real nightmare from hell. I prayed silently for sunrise and for God to protect me.

"Campos!" yelled Captain. "Get over here and hold this strobe light and guide in the medevac."

I walked over and he handed me the strobe light and I held it in the air while it flickered in the night air.

"Keep this in the air until they arrive," Captain said. "It's so dark. The chopper will not be able to see our position."

"Yes, sir," I said.

I stood there in the dark with my arm and hand held high holding that strobe light that would guide in the helicopter to pick up the wounded and dead. All the while thinking I could be next again to be killed. For Charlie could also see the reflecting strobe light from his position.

But, that was my job and it did what I was told to do.

Captain said, "Don't leave my sight, Campos. This night has been bad enough. I don't want to lose any more men.

"Yes, sir," I answered.

I got a promotion in the field that night. I became Captain Woodward's radio man. From that day forward I would be his radio man.

Early the next day the company moved out and searched the area where Peter And the other RTO had been killed. We searched and searched but found nothing. Charlie had been there, all right, but he had retreated back into Cambodia.

Two months later I was again promoted to radio operator for the Brigade Commander, who's previous RTO had gone home to the states.

For the next month all I did was sweep out the Colonel's tent and put water in his shower each morning. I also helped sell beer and stack beer pallets. Boy was that was fun!

That duty didn't last long because, next, I would be reassigned to a hospital — not as a radio operator, but as a patient.

★ ★ ★ ★

PART V: LAST DAYS IN NAM

CHAPTER 17: BAD MOON RISING – CREEDANCE CLEARWATER REVIVAL

We were all told we would get R&R (rest and recuperation) at some point in our 365-day tour. Usually it was after about six months of service. We could choose Thailand, Singapore, Australia, or Hawaii. The Army would send us there for one week and then return us back to the bush.

I would choose Hawaii. I would fly Renee there so we could be together for the week. It was all I could think about for three months. It gave me hope to stay alive another day. And one day at a time was all I had.

Serving in Nam felt like an eternity. Each day was filled with terror and the unknown. So, it was great to have a few days off from war.

After R&R was over, it was hard to get into the mindset of war. All I could think about was coming home. I wanted out of Vietnam. I wanted to come home where it was safe. I wanted out of this hell hole and this land that God even seemed to hate.

The days got longer and more difficult emotionally. I didn't want to fight anymore. But I had a job to do, and I knew it. No one was going to play patty-cake with me. The Army wasn't going to make it easy for me, either: They sent me right back into the bush the day I returned from Hawaii.

The Army was good to us, though. R&R was a godsend. It gave me something else to live for, the hope of returning back home. Hope is essential for survival.

In the fall of 1968, Charlie Company, the 4th of the 12th, was shipped by trucks to a malaria-infested area. The doctors had told us it we were at risk to get sick with malaria. The area had an enormous population of mosquitos and water, and that was a breeding ground for infection.

I knew something about malaria from the war movies. A person could die from the malarial fever. The doctors and the captain told us to make sure we took anti-malaria tablets.

Medics distributed malaria tablets every day so that no one would forget. But there were days when we had to go out on ambush patrols and were out of camp for several days. At those times, we wouldn't get the malaria tablets again until we returned. When we returned, the medics would give us extra to catch up from the days we missed, but that doesn't always work.

At that time we were working with the Australian Marines. We would go out on patrol with them for several days at a time. Sometimes we would stay at their camp. They were a great bunch of guys, and I admired and respected these young men greatly. We also worked with Korean forces for a time. I was impressed that they risked their lives to fight the North Vietnamese even though it wasn't their war. Some of these soldiers died in Vietnam for us.

These soldiers didn't have war protesters back in Australia or Korea. When they returned home, they were treated like war heroes. They were honored and respected. Not so in our country. Our combat troops were hated by many of our fellow Americans. The Australians told us that Americans were their role models. They said it was a privilege to serve with us. They respected America for standing up and helping poorer countries.

To hear them say that it help to be an honor. It made me feel proud.

The Australians were young and courageous, a different

breed of soldier. They were very polite, and they wore their uniform proudly. I liked their attitude of welcoming combat as a privilege, a privilege? Maybe their government treated them better. I learned later that I was right: They did get better perks and rewards for their service duty. Not so, here in America.

Sometimes, back at base camp we could watch a small T.V. someone had purchased from Japan. We all sat around watching the news and the war protesters. We saw men burn their draft cards. Freedom! Is this freedom! Sons of bitches should have been sent to Nam and not us. We love our country and are willing to fight for our freedom. Let them go to Canada, pussy assholes!

It was the beginning of November 1968. We were on a reconnaissance patrol with the Aussies for two days straight with no malaria tablets. When I returned to the compound, I felt like I had the flu. I went to sleep in my foxhole with a slight fever, a mild headache and body aches.

The next day, I couldn't move. I reported sick. It was the first time in my Army service that I had reported for sick call. I am the kind of person who works in spite of being sick. I never thought I would be one of the causalities of malaria. I always heard about it from people but, never knew anyone who got the disease.

The Hong Kong flu epidemic was in full strength back then; too, so I thought maybe, just maybe, I had caught the flu virus. I couldn't eat anything for a week straight.

That evening, the medic sent me and a few others back to Lon Binh. I boarded the truck for the three-hour ride to base camp. As soon as I arrived, I walked over to see the doctor. My temperature was down to only 102 degrees. He told me I probably had the Hong Kong flu, gave me some aspirin and told me to rest. He said I would be fine the next day.

As I walked to the barracks, I just knew I had malaria. But, how could I convince the doctor when my temperature was down? I lay down on the cot in the barracks.

For two weeks, I was unable to get out of bed. I would sweat all day and have chills all night long. I lost thirty pounds in two weeks from the fever.

One day I was feeling pretty good so I got up to eat. I headed down to the chow hall. When I entered, I got my chow and sat down. I noticed the doctor eating across the room and decided to visit him.

"Doc, I think I have Malaria," I said.

"What are you doing eating, then?" he said.

"This is the first time I have been able to eat in two weeks, sir," I told him.

"You got the Hong Kong flu, son," he said and he kept eating.

"Sure, Doc," I replied, as I walked back to my seat.

The fever of malaria would come and go every other hour. My temperature would rise every hour, from about 101 to 104 degrees daily.

Later that same night, I was feeling a lot better. I felt good enough to go outside the barracks and watch a movie. I guess it was the food that made me feel better. I was getting tired of sleeping all day and all night.

Back at base camp the soldiers were able to watch a movie once a week. Not a great selection. Usually, there were just two to pick from, either John Wayne's "To Hell and Back" or Frankie Avalon's "Beach Blanket Bingo." Everyone loved John Wayne because; he was always the hero and won the babes. We all said, "To Hell and Back, Sarge"!

I took a seat in the rear. We were about one-third of the way through when we were interrupted by the sounds of sirens all over the compound. The sirens usually meant that Charlie was in our compound or that rockets were headed our way. "Incoming, incoming, take cover!" someone yelled.

We all headed for the nearest bunker, twenty feet away. It was no big deal. I had heard these sirens before, but Charlie had missed us by a mile. Still, we walked briskly toward the bunker. We never knew where those rockets would hit.

We were all told in basic training, when you don't hear the

artillery; it's coming right on top of you. Well, that's comforting Sarge!

"Kabam, kabam!" I watched as a rocket hit the ground twenty feet away. My walk suddenly turned into a run. The blasts were getting closer and closer.

The next rocket landed on top the barrack about fifteen feet away from me, tearing a large hole in the metal roof and sending shrapnel flying everywhere. I hope no one is in there, I thought. I ran my ass off and turned the corner. Once again, I feared for my life.

Just before I entered the bunker, I saw a flash of light. The chair I had been sitting on at the movie exploded. I was really scared now. I entered the foxhole bunker and hid in the corner. My ears were ringing from the percussion, especially my left ear. I had forgotten I was so sick that night. I was lucky, damn lucky. I hadn't been hit or wounded. I was just scared to death.

A few minutes later, the rockets stopped. We all waited for the sirens to start again signaling it was all clear. The sirens sounded about thirty minutes later and I returned to my barracks.

I couldn't sleep that night. All I could think about was how close I came to becoming a casualty of this war. Charlie had us zeroed in that night. If he used one more rocket, I 'm sure it would have had my name on it.

The next morning, I was still shaken from the night before. I kept thinking about Charlie and those rockets. Charlie knew where we were. He had a spy in our camp. (Probably, one of the prisoners that surrendered and we made a scout)

That was it. I had made up my mind. It was safer out in the bush. So, I packed my bags, sick and all. Screw it. I would take my chances elsewhere.

I boarded a small truck and headed back out to my company.

I reached back to base and stepped off the truck. I was met by the doctor who was making a few calls.

"What are you doing, Campos?" he asked me. "How many

pounds have you lost, son? You look horrible. Son, get back on that truck. You're going to the infirmary." He took out a piece of paper that said admit.

"Yes, sir," I said. I turned my back, stepped onto the truck, and sat down. I put my head down toward my legs. I was ready to pass out, delirious with fever and jaundiced.

Our superiors and officers looked down on soldiers that got sick or wounded in our company. It felt humiliating, as if I was trying to get out of my duty. I didn't want anyone to think I was a weak or a coward. I never went to sick call, even if I had a wound, until now.

I was raised by my parents never to go to the doctor. "You couldn't trust the doctors", my father told me. He never went either. "They were all quacks", he said. So, I rarely went to the doctor.

The only time I had gotten hurt was when I was ten years old. My brother and I had been at Camp Jack Hazard for two weeks during the summer of 1958. It was a Boy Scout camp in the forests of Stanislaus County where we were taught about survival skills.

We returned back to Modesto after two weeks. The bus dropped us off at Garrison Elementary School. The buses were early, so we waited for our parents to pick us up.

Two hours went by and still no mom or dad. We were two of only five kids still waiting for their rides. We were playing on the school basketball court on the other side of the fence when someone yelled out, "Roger and Stephen Campos, your father is here to pick you up!"

I rushed toward the tall wire fence and decided to climb up and over. It was a shortcut, the fastest way to get to the car. I climbed up to the top of the fence and put one leg over. As I swung my other leg over to jump down, my trouser cuff caught the top of the fence. I fell straight down; head first, toward the cement, bam, my head and arm hit the solid cement.

When I awoke, I tried to get up. "Are you all right?" a boy standing next to me inquired. "Ah, not really," I said as I got up and walked woozily toward my father's car. I was holding my arm. I couldn't move it, and it was completely numb.

I reached the car and said, "Dad, I think I broke my arm," I got into the car.

"No, you didn't," he said.

"But Dad, I'm sure it's broken," I can't move or feel it.

"We'll wait and see tomorrow," he replied.

I was in pain and agony all night long. When I awoke the next day, I expected him to take me to the doctor. Again I said, "Dad, I'm sure my arm is broken. I can't move it."

"OK," he said. Wait until this afternoon and see how you feel."

Later that afternoon, he finally took me to the doctor. The X-ray showed that my arm was indeed broken. The doctor placed my arm in a cast, and I had to wear it the rest of the summer. That was one of only two days I remember having seen the doctor as a kid. The other time was when I thought I had broken my leg playing football at a Davis high football game.

Still, not wanting anyone to think I was a wimp for taking sick time I boarded the truck back to base camp.

When I got off the truck, I could barely walk. I was delirious. I went to the Army infirmary, where the nurses took my temperature and told me to lie down.

Two hours later, I began to slipping into a deeper sleep then I had ever experienced before. In my delirium, I started to see people. "Hi, Mom, what are you doing here?" I dreamed of my mother visiting me. There she was looking at me.

"Hi Mom, what's for dinner tonight?" I always loved my mother's cooking. As soon as she appeared next to my hospital bed, she disappeared.

Then my life began flashing before my eyes. I remember I was with my brother in our two-bedroom home. I was five years old. Roger and we were in our bedroom taking a nap. I was four years old.

"Stephen, let's crawl out the bedroom window and play outside," Roger said. "Okay," I said.

Then my father's image flashed before my eyes. He was standing next to his tortilla-making machine. "Stephen, why are you here? You should be in Vietnam," he told me.

Next, I remembered Renee and me getting married in Reno. I was standing next to my mother and her mother outside the Reno City Hall. We were waiting to get our marriage license.

"Hey, pussycat, what are you doing here?"

The nurse ran over to me and checked my forehead. She put a thermometer in my mouth and started undressing me.

"I'm taking your clothes off," she said hurriedly. "You'll be Okay; I won't look at your privates."

She yelled to the other nurses, "Get me some ice quick, he's going delirious! Pack him in ice and pour in the alcohol."

Several nurses rushed came over and put me into a large tub. Then they poured several large bags of ice on me. They poured about fifteen bottles of rubbing alcohol into the tub with the ice. I was totally submerged, except for my head. The head nurse kept talking to me, "You'll be all right," she said several times.

And then I started to shake. I felt like an iceberg. My teeth started to chatter. I was freezing cold. My body was shaking frantically and I couldn't stop it.

The nurses screamed for the Army aides to load me into the jeep. They were sending me to Bien Hoa Hospital. It was outside the perimeter, Charlie territory. It was about a forty-minute ride over dangerous roads.

When the truck finally arrived they unloaded me and wheeled me into a large tent that served as an emergency room. I looked around and I saw several beds with wounded soldiers. They were ALL around me. All the men had been shot or wounded. There was blood on the sheets and on the ground everywhere.

I was in full shaking convulsions. I couldn't stop from shaking.

A nurse attended to me while the doctors and nurses worked frantically on the wounded men. I looked over and watched while they tried all they could do to keep the patients from dying.

And then I started to feel guilty for having malaria. I was

sick and they had been wounded by Charlie. I felt like a coward for being in the same room as these men who were wounded in combat. And here I was, a combat soldier that was just sick, I felt guilty for even being in the same room with those heroes.

A few minutes later, some men rushed in a wounded G.I. who had scrap metal wounds all over his legs and groin. The nurses and doctors scurried over to help him when he first arrived. They used scissors to rip open his fatigues and his jungle boots. They worked frantically until he was completely naked.

The doctor asked the nurses what had happened.

"It was a booby trap hit, they said. I think a Bouncing- Betty," someone said.

A Bouncing Betty was a Chinese made bomb, usually placed under water, as designed to blow up between the legs, injuring his penis, legs and feet.

I could see the blood streaming down his legs and feet. His privates were exposed and there was blood all over him. The explosion nearly tore his balls off. He was screaming and moaning. The nurses were on a frantic pace to save him. They gave him several shots that sent him to sleep.

My first thought was that he was going to lose his manhood. He would never be able to have children. Damn, I wouldn't wish that on anyone.

I prayed, "God this man needs your comfort". Please help him.

I stayed a few hours in that room. They would bring in one after the other with bullet holes or scrap medal in them.

I spent a week in the hospital in Bien Hoa Hospital and then I was transported to Cam Ranh Bay. Cam Ranh Bay was the big hospital where men from the Central and Southern part of Vietnam were sent to heal or be sent back home to the states.

Cam Ranh Bay was a beautiful inland port off the South China Sea. It was by the most beautiful ocean I had ever seen. Even growing up in California I had never seen such beautiful water or beaches. The water was turquoise and warm.

Man, this is heaven. It felt like I was on vacation — except for the warning sirens. They reminded me each night that I was still in a war zone.

A month later I started to feel better. I was taking quinine tablets and aspirin to keep my temperature down. I was also given time off to go to the beach during some of my breaks. The ocean beach was only four hundred feet from the hospital ward. I would walk out like a vacationer and spend an hour on the beach and I would dream of Renee. I would look out across that ocean and try to see her looking at back at me from the other side. The only thing was that she didn't know about me being sick because my letters would arise two weeks later.

Even though I was in a place of healing there was still death near by my bedside.

The first night I was in the hospital ward, the nurses wheeled in a man and set him up in the next bed. He was a sergeant, a "Lifer" — a career Army man. Twenty years is about the normal length of active duty for a Lifer. How anyone could anyone stay in the Army for twenty years, especially under these conditions?

I could hear the nurses and doctors whisper as they wheeled in the sergeant. "He has been in the Army for nineteen years" one nurse said. "He only has one year left before his retirement", another answered.

The doctor told the nurses that the sergeant is an alcoholic. They had found him cold-stone drunk on the floor. He passed out from being drunk and hit his head on a cement brick.

"I don't think he's going to make it, Doc," the nurse said.

"Well, we can't give him anything until the booze wears off. It may kill him. We just have to wait nurse.

"The best thing we can do right now is keep a close watch on him. He might go into a coma if we give him an antibiotic. Tell me when he sobers up. We have no choice but to let the alcohol wear off. Keep a close watch on him, and check on him every hour."

As the doctor walked away, I remember thinking to myself: Here we are in a war zone and this guy gets drunk, passes out, and hits his head on the cement. If he dies, he'll never know what the hell had happened to him, nor will his family back home. The Army wouldn't tell the family he got drunk, hit his head and died. What a way to die as a soldier. Or anyone who had died from Malaria, I thought.

After, the nurses and doctor walked away I had a bad feeling about this man. He was on the verge of dying from alcohol and no one could do anything for him but wait.

I tried to watch out for him myself, but I was falling in and out of sleep that night. My temperature was rising and falling as usual. It was about two o'clock in the morning when I looked over at him to see how he was doing. I didn't recall seeing the nurses for the last two hours. They usually make their rounds every hour. They may have forgotten about the sergeant and me.

When I looked over at the sergeant, I noticed he wasn't moving. He's dead, I said to myself. Finally, one nurse came by to check on him. She looked and then screamed, "I need help, and he's not breathing!" I felt panic for a moment, but then I thought the nurses would be able to revive him. He was fine just two hours ago.

"Oh, my God," said another nurse, "He's gone.

They covered his body with a blanket and wheeled him out fast.

I felt guilty for the next couple of days. I should have said something to the nurses or asked them why they didn't come around to look after him. But, I guess it was just his time. That's what it was like a Nam. It was on a time clock and sooner or later you're number was on the clock.

What a way to die in Vietnam — not from the enemy, not from a bullet to the heart or a booby trap or old age, but from just being drunk.

NOTE: ALCOHOL CAN KILL YOU

CHAPTER 18: WHAT'S GOING ON? – MARVIN GAY

It was just before Thanksgiving when I wrote to Roger again. It was my first Thanksgiving celebration in Vietnam and my last, thank God. We were still set up in a mosquito-infested area in the mud, but I was feeling better again after my bout with malaria.

I wrote:

The monsoon rains were cruel last night, but today the sun is shining. I am thinking about you and the relatives meeting for the Thanksgiving holiday reunion. I am writing on top of a couple of C-ration boxes with my feet in the mud. I am holding my tin plate full of the Army-issued turkey dinner, and it's not bad at all.

We were told on the G.I. news today that Charlie would honor a cease fire on Thanksgiving. Charlie cares about our Thanksgiving holiday? He's probably planning to throw a rocket-propelled grenade or mortar into our midst.

I didn't want to think about that possibility, so I quickly changed my tune and thought about our traditional Campos family reunions at Thanksgiving.

Every Thanksgiving, all of the Campos relatives got together, just like we did every Easter. It was a very special holiday that honored my grandparents' escape from Mexico to America, and it was always a big crowd of fifty or so relatives. We were thankful that my grandfather had the courage to leave Mexico and enter the United States.

My grandfather was a quiet man. He was tall and spoke little English. He worked hard for my father and was in charge of opening Campos Foods' tortilla factory early in the morning.

I respected my grandfather and always wondered what he thought about. I wondered if he missed Mexico and why he never returned to visit his homeland. I wanted to know more about his parents and family, but he never spoke about them. He was a very humble person and didn't talk much. He lived with my grandmother and her sisters for many years. My aunts seemed old to me. I think they were in their eighties when I left for Vietnam, and they had medical problems.

When we would visit their home, I would ask my Aunt Concha how she was feeling. "*Como estás?*" I'd say. She would always take her hand and pat her chest over her heart. "*No, no muy bien,*" she said in Spanish — "not very well."

"My heart, my heart" — she claimed she had a bad heart. I think she was afraid she was going to have a heart attack. She died at the age of ninety-one, many years after I returned home from Vietnam. My aunts and grandmother all died within a few years of each other.

Jarred back to awareness of the present moment, my mind shifted to Charlie. I wondered if he really was taking Thanksgiving Day off like we were. I wondered if he was being thankful or perhaps just thinking about his home. I didn't think he was getting a turkey dinner — it's an American holiday anyway — but maybe he was eating rice. He always ate rice.

Charlie and I were both far from home without our families, though. We were both fighting to stay alive so we could return home to our loved ones. How ironic: Charlie and me, we had the same intentions!

Thanksgiving Day seemed a little more somber than usual. We all were sitting around enjoying our meal when the silence was broken.

"Incoming!" someone yelled, and everyone ran for cover. Bam! Bam! Bam! The mortar rounds started exploding three hundred feet from our base camp. Kaboom! Kaboom! Another barrage of mortars hit that same area. It was quite a way from our perimeter, but everyone ran for cover when we heard the first mortar hit the ground. Fortunately for me, I had eaten my turkey dinner. Some of the men dropped their plates while they were running to find safety.

Within a few minutes, the sounds stopped as suddenly as they had started. I think Charlie was trying to harass us and let us know this was no holiday vacation.

Two weeks before Christmas, we were invited to watch Bob Hope do a show for our troops. I couldn't believe that I would get a chance to see Bob Hope. What a thrill! I had watched him perform on television for years, and now he would be in Vietnam with his team of entertainers.

I didn't realize there would be television crews and that we would be filmed during the show. I was hoping none of my friends or family would see me on television. They might think I was enjoying myself over here and not really fighting a war. No one knew that I almost died of malaria. I stopped writing letters for three weeks while I lay sick in the hospital. I didn't want anyone worrying about me. I was too sick to write letters, and besides, what could I say? "Hi Mom, I'm having a great time lying in the hospital. The fever comes and goes from hour to hour, you don't worry about me, I'm OK!"

On the day of the show, we boarded trucks wearing our blue infirmary uniforms. All the wounded and sick who could walk were sent to a site with a huge tent. No one knew what to expect. I didn't realize I would be one of five thousand soldiers who would watch Bob Hope in person.

We were the first to arrive. We were dropped off around nine o'clock in the morning and waited. We were told the show would be starting that afternoon, but we were the only people there for the longest time. We sat on the dry ground, since there weren't any chairs. The Army had dumped us off with neither food nor water. We didn't bring anything. We had no idea about the show, when it started, or when it would end. All we knew was the Army had dropped us off, and we were to wait to see Bob Hope.

It felt like the hottest day of the year, maybe 120 degrees, but maybe that was just a relapse of my malaria fever talking. Around three o'clock in the afternoon, we figured we needed to get some food and water. So we sent two guys out to look for food and water for the ten of us. This place was about three to four miles from anything. What poor planning! I think they dropped us off to get rid of us.

It was a little before five o'clock that they returned. They both were drunk! They had bought two cases of beer and three bottles of whiskey. No food, no water — just hot beer and Jack Daniels.

Have you ever drunk a hot beer in the heat? Well, that's what I did. Two cans of hot beer is all I had. The rest of the guys drank the whiskey and the rest of the beer. There was nothing we could do. What a combination, hot beer and heat!

Finally about five o'clock, other troops began to arrive. The stage was set, and all of us were waiting impatiently for Bob Hope to show up. We had great "seats," about a hundred feet from the stage, front and center.

We finally learned that Bob Hope's show wasn't to begin until seven o'clock that evening. By the time he arrived, most of us were blitzed!

It was six-thirty when his chopper flew over our heads, and by then the crowd had swelled to about five thousand people.

Someone announced over a loudspeaker that his chopper

would be landing soon. We watched as it touched down on the ground a few hundred feet away from the staging area.

I watched as Bob Hope climbed out of the helicopter, wearing a G.I. uniform and carrying his famous golf club in his hand. Following him were several beautiful girls. One took hold of his arm, and then another one grabbed the other as they happily walked toward the stage.

As soon as Bob Hope's name was announced, there was a huge roar from the audience. What a sound! It reminded me of the cheers at the Stanford vs. California football game.

Finally, the show was about to start. Everyone was excited. There were chants and shouts of "We want Bob Hope, we want Bob Hope."

It took the longest half-hour you could imagine, but finally he entered the stage.

"Hello, men, I'm Bob Hope, and I have a great show for you tonight," the crowd booed. "With me are the beautiful Ann-Margaret and the current Miss U.S.A." The crowd cheered and clapped. "We also have some men from our band," Bob continued. The crowd booed louder.

"I have to go back to my tent because I forgot my jacket in case it rains," Bob said. The crowd booed loudly again.

I thought Hope was joking until he turned around and left the stage to a continuing chorus of boos from many of the five thousand soldiers.

A few angry drunk patients started throwing beer cans onto the stage. Next, they threw an empty Jack Daniels bottle.

I was embarrassed... I was sitting right next to these idiots!

We had been waiting all day for Bob Hope and then he turned around and left the stage. It was the last straw. We were all angry.

But, Bob finally come out and put on a really great show. It was worth not eating all day in the heat and waiting eight hours to see this hoary comedian.

The crowd finally settled down after Ann-Margaret came out

to woo the crowd. The few soldiers who were throwing the cans passed out from the heat and the rest of us relaxed and enjoyed the show. It was an awesome experience as one entertainer after another came out and treated us with their talents.

I got to see the sexy and beautiful Ann-Margaret. She was my favorite of the evening. I had always admired her beauty and dancing talent since I was a teenager.

However, I was embarrassed because of a few fellas who almost blew it for the rest of us.

Bob Hope has since passed away, but I want to thank him posthumously for giving us his time and making us laugh. He lifted our spirits, and helped us forget about war — if only for a few hours.

As the year 1969 began, I was out of the infirmary and back with my unit. We were protecting the Ben Dinh Bridge, which provided a direct route toward Saigon about five miles away. It was an important position for our military: If Charlie got through there, he could take Saigon easily. We had to stop Charlie right here at this position. For us, this was Custer's Last Stand.

The position held two companies. Alpha Company was on one side of the perimeter, and my Charlie Company held the other side. As usual, we ran search-and-destroy and ambush patrols out of this perimeter. We had many firefights with Charlie at the Ben Dinh Bridge. It was on Highway One, possibly the most unsafe highway in South Vietnam. Charlie hid mines in the roads and ambushed troops every day and night on that highway. The Ben Dinh Bridge was a slaughterhouse for the enemy during the 1968 TET Offensive.

I remember coming over to this position when our company first arrived. Sometimes when we needed to cross a deep river, we would use a "sand pan," a smallish, rickety boat usually owned by some old *papa-san*. It was the only way to cross the deep river and in this case there was one right next to our fighting position.

The Army didn't have sand pans, of course, so we borrowed one, you might say, from an old *papa-san*, who agreed to drive us across. We would return it when we were finished.

When it was my turn to cross the river, there were two other men with me. It was getting late, and we were one of the last groups to use the old sand pan wood boat, which looked to be as old as *papa-san*! It was made out of wood and was about twelve feet long. It reminded me of something Tarzan and Jane might have used. As I stepped into the boat, it rocked from side to side. I set my other food down gently and grabbed onto the sides of the sand pan. There wasn't much room once the three of us and our duffle bags were on board. I sat on the floor and prayed we would get to the other side.

We headed across the river to our new base camp. It wasn't that long before I realized the boat was sinking. It was dipping lower and lower into the water. I looked at *papa-san* and he looked back at me.

"Hey, *papa-san*, *vin tou*! [Hurry up!]," I yelled at him. "We are starting to sink. We aren't going to make it to the other side of the river!" He couldn't understand my English, but I think he understood that we were going down. He seemed a little frantic as he tried to rev up the motor. We aren't going to make it, I thought. This boat is going to sink with me in it and I am going to lose all my gear!

On the other side of the river was the rest of my company. They were all watching and laughing their heads off at us. This was no laughing matter, I told myself. I was going to drown in this river. Then it became a game. All the men started chanting, "You guys better start paddling! Paddle-paddle," they shouted.

"Paddle with what, my M-16"?

I think they were making bets on whether we would make it to shore or not. They were screaming, laughing, and yelling at us at the same time. "You're going to drown, G.I." yelled one soldier.

What a way to treat a fellow grunt, I thought.

"You'll never make it!" another yelled. I didn't say a word. I just keep looking at the front of the boat going lower and lower into the river.

As we approached the shore I motioned *papa-san* to get closer to the shoreline just in case we sank fast.

"Throw your bags onto the shore," one G.I. screamed.

I couldn't stand up because I would rock the boat. I reached over slowly, grabbed my bag, and held it over my head. I slung it as hard as I could toward the dry bank. It landed safely as one G.I. caught it before it hit the water.

Thank God, I thought. All my clothes, my camera, and all my personal belongings were in that bag. I had saved things from almost every mission. It contained all my letters and pictures of my family.

The guy next to me wasn't so lucky. Just before the boat went under he tried to throw off his duffle bag onto the dry bank. It splashed into the water.

I threw my M-16 to a guy standing on the shore. He caught it with one hand.

Then we sank.

I started frantically to swim to shore, but it is hard to swim with combat boots, helmet and your gear on.

Fortunately, I was five feet from the shoreline.

All the guys standing on the bank were laughing their heads off. I was angry about getting wet but. I looked back and remember *papa-san*. He was struggling in the water. I reached out and took his hand and helped him to safety.

After the incident was over, the captain told us to help fish *papa-san's* boat out of the river. It was the least we could do.

CHAPTER 19: DUST IN THE WIND – KANSAS

Vietnam, in a sense, was a war of numbers. The enemy used our media and television broadcasts while we kept daily records of the dead and the wounded.

The Army kept track of every combat encounter and relayed the information and statistics to headquarters. Each report would state how many enemy soldiers were killed — at least those we could count. We killed a lot of enemy that we never found. The N.V.A. was good at quickly picking up their dead and wounded.

Yet some things that happened in Nam were unexplainable. This story tells of one of the many times my own life was miraculously spared.

In late January 1969, my squad was walking to an ambush site. It was another one of those very dark nights. We had to walk through a village ten miles northeast of Saigon.

Every night, we could count on Charlie rocketing us. I could hear the rockets from a distance, and I'd pray that he missed his target. The incoming rounds whistled through the air heading in our direction. We retaliated after hiding in our foxholes while the brave mortar platoon tried to find their location and fire back with our own mortars.

Sometimes Charlie's mortars found their way into the nearby village. The explosion meant someone's family had been killed. The next day, we'd be sent out on a hunt to find the dirty culprits.

By the end of the morning, they were long gone. We would return back to base just in time for chow. By noon, we were ready to be airlifted to our next search-and-destroy mission.

On one such night, my squad was chosen to go out on patrol through the village and look for Charlie setting up us his mortar gun. Most of the time we went out on patrol, it was away from the village, but not this time. Charlie was getting closer to us, and brigade wanted us to find his snipers. It was dangerous to walk through a village at night. You never knew what to expect. That night was one of the darkest nights I had ever seen. I could barely see two feet in front of me. The stars weren't shining, and it was pitch black.

We walked cautiously, using our infrared starlight scope to look out for booby traps. There was something different about this night. There wasn't a sound in the village except for one thing: I heard the sound of a water buffalo. I sensed that he was about ten feet from me.

The snort of the water buffalo made me stop dead in my tracks. I was walking with my hand placed on the G.I. in front due to the darkness. I didn't want to lose my way with the rest of the squad. Then I heard the sounds of a chain clanging back and forth.

I bent down in panic, and my sixth sense told me I was in danger. I looked at the horizon and saw the silhouette of a huge water buffalo on a chain digging his heels in the dirt. Next to him was an elderly *papa-san* trying to hold this chain with all his might. "Watch out! That bull is going to charge!" said a voice my side.

Water buffalo hated U.S. soldiers. I think they could smell us. We had a different smell then the Vietnamese because we washed with soap daily. The Vietnamese washed maybe once a week. I saw them charge at our troops several times before as we were patrolling around the village. I watched my captain kill one that was threatening our whole company and had almost killed him the week before. They weighed up to seven hundred pounds and had long horns with which they could gore us to death. We were afraid of them, and they were afraid of us.

Papa-san's water buffalo was snorting and pounding his horns in the dirt. The old man was holding on to his chain for dear life. Suddenly, the man began screaming, "G.I.! G.I.!" He couldn't hold the chain any longer, and the water buffalo came charging toward me. The whole squad panicked, and guys started running in every direction.

"What the heck is that guy doing here?" the G.I. next to me asked.

"Run for it!" I said. "He's going to ram us!"

I turned and started to run to my left, crossing in front of the G.I. next to me. At the same moment, the G.I. opened fire at the beast with his M-16. I was directly in the way of his rifle. It all happened so fast...

I felt the muzzle blast hit my side as I crossed. I fell to the ground and yelled in pain. I put my hand on the side of my rib cage where the impact was and lay there in pain, moaning and screaming, "I'm hit! I'm hit!"

Everything went dark before my eyes as my hands searched for the blood that no doubt was pouring from my side. I realized I was still alive, so I got up quickly and ran because I heard the pounding hooves of the water buffalo coming toward me. I turned again and ran before the bull's horns rammed me into oblivion. I kept running from the bull until my feet crashed through a piece of wood. I guess the shots frightened the bull and he didn't charge in my direction.

I knew I had been shot by the G.I., though. I ran in front of his rifle. I felt the blast. I felt the pain. Yet I could find no blood. I realized then that I hadn't been hit. How could that happen?

The piece of wood I stepped on covered a small well about twenty feet deep. The wood snapped under my weight, and I fell down into the well. My backpack caught the sides of the well and stopped me from falling further. I came to a halt, and then everything went dark.

Then something happened to me that I'll never be able to explain.

I thought I had died. I don't remember how long I was out but, it felt like a long time. A few minutes later, I saw a huge flash of brilliant light that lit up the entire sky. It started on one horizon and went to the other. Light was all around me. I was transported into heaven. It surrounded me, everything was as white as snow and I felt at peace. A peace in my soul that all was safe and well. I also felt love that filled my being and I saw a single tree in the horizon.

My entire life raced before my eyes. I was about four years old, and I could hear my mother call my name, "Stephen." I could feel her love for me. My mind raced forward to another moment. I was at our home on Maplewood Drive, where I grew up and went to school from five to twelve years old. I was seven, and it was Christmas time. My father and mother were by the Christmas tree. I searched and found some presents with my name on them. I had three big presents. I opened the first one, a gun and holster set. I was really happy. The next present was the caps and ammo. I finally got a gift that I really wanted for Christmas. I was extremely happy.

My mind raced further ahead. My father was purchasing my first car. It was a black 1957 Chevy. I sat in the seat and imagined being behind the wheel. Now, I could get all the girls I wanted because, I had a cool car. Wow, was I proud!

Next, I was twelve, and I was playing baseball. I was at Beard Brook Park. The bases were loaded. I hit the next pitch over the left fielder's head and raced home to win the game. When I touched home plate I was surrounded by my teammates. They all hugged me.

Next, I thought about my brother Roger and my sister Cecilia and then heard Renee call my name, "Steve, I love you.

" The scenes of my life were flashing before my mind.

Then, next, the warmth of light seemed to draw me closer to the hillside. I sensed someone beckoning me to come closer.

Suddenly, I realized I was in heaven. But was I dead? Was God calling me to enter his heaven? I felt beckoned to come into the light. I started to sense someone was walking out to get me. I wasn't afraid anymore.

In an instant, the light went out, until it was dark again.

I opened my eyes and I realized I was stuck in this damn hole. My feet were dangling down a well. I had fallen straight down into a pit that was used for drinking water. It saved my life. I could have been crushed by the water buffalo that was charging right after me.

"HEY, can somebody help me, I'M STUCK" I called out.

A minute later, a G.I. extended his hand and pulled me out of the pit. It was the guy that nearly killed me. He was crying. "I'm sorry, man, I thought I killed you. I'm sorry".

The imagines flashed in my mind. "I had felt the impact of his M-16 on my side. I felt the bullets and blow to my side. I thought I was shot. I felt my side to feel the blood, but there was none. I felt again to make sure. Wow, no blood, but how?

"I'm Okay, man. Don't' do that again. Quit crying. I forgive you!" But, don't even do that again. Keep your rifle on safety. Got it?

I was out of the hole by then and trying to collect myself.

"Keep quiet. Let's find the rest of the squad".

I still don't know what happened that night. I don't know what happened to the bull, either. I hadn't been hit. It was a miracle! God must have sent his angel to protect me that night, to shield me from those bullets.

In Nam there was a spiritual presence of good and evil in war that is hard to describe, but it is very real. You could almost touch it. It spoke to your mind. I was in constant prayer why I walked the muddy rice parties, traveling up high in gunships or trudged through the thick jungles.

Another time, I was spared while on ambush patrol. It was early January 1969. Our squad patrol was on ambush patrol again. The moon was shining while we headed our way next to a canal to set up our ambush.

We set up our Claymore mines and machine guns on the river bank and slipped down below the dirt mound for cover. The canal was about six to eight feet deep and twenty feet wide. The location wasn't very good because, Charlie could see us at a distance. The moonlight exposed our position.

In Nam, we had guard duty in shifts. Each shift lasted about an hour or hour and half, depending how many men were in our squad. This night, we had seven men.

One-hour shifts were assigned and those who were not on duty that hour went to sleep.

My shift didn't start until around eleven o'clock. It was cold that night, so I took out my poncho liner and stretched it over me.

The U.S. Army poncho liners we used were lightweight and would keep us dry and warm. We used them for sleeping, as a cover for shade from the heat, a blanket and a poncho for the rain, or almost anything. We carried them everywhere we went. They rolled up tightly in our backpacks when we were not using them.

Nighttime could be a death trap for a combat G.I. if you got caught sleeping on his guard shift. In basic training, our drill sergeants warned us about soldiers who had fallen asleep during their shifts. Charlie had entered the compound and slit their throats. I didn't want to be killed, so I made sure I did my part.

I never got a full night's sleep in Nam. I made sure I wanted to live.

While, I was sleeping, I sensed something was wrong. My sixth sense of danger took over, and it alerted me. I quickly learned to react when I sensed something different so I turned over on my stomach. At the same time I heard a huge explosion.

I thought the enemy was attacking us. I clutched my poncho as tight as I could around my back and shoulders and got my rifle in the ready position.

It was like slow motion. I heard the blast and imagined the dirt flying in the air but, it was for real. Dirt and mud splattered all over me. I felt a thud of falling shrapnel hit my back.

I thought we were being attacked by Charlie so I waited for incoming fire but, nothing happened.

Next, the soldier next to me starts screaming at the top of his lungs. "I'm hit! I'm hit! I'm dying!" "I'm dying".

"Shut the hell up, man," our squad leader ordered. I'll take a look. He crawled over and took out his in fared flashlight.

"You've got a small piece of shrapnel l on your hand and it's bleeding," the squad leader said. "Stop your screaming. You're not going to die."

I whispered, "Hey, Sarge, something hit me on my back. Would you take a look? I slipped off my top and exposed the area where I thought I had been hit.

My mind raced back at a time when I was a fourteen years old and freshman at Davis High School in Modesto. It was a last football game of the year. I was playing quarterback and defensive back on a rainy and muddy day. It was the fourth quarter, time was running out and we were dead locked in a scoreless game.

We had three minutes to play. I was in on defense. The Turlock quarterback faded back. The wide receivers ran down the field. I withdrew back following a receiver. The quarterback threw the ball. It was headed in my direction. I jumped up and caught the ball. I started to run with the ball. I headed down the playing field and suddenly was hit by two big Turlock linemen. The impact spun me around and buried my helmet in the mud.

My eyes rolled over into the back of my head and it knocked the wind out of me. I lay there and couldn't remember a thing. I didn't know who I was or where I was for a few minutes.

"How many fingers do I have held up?" said the referee? "Uh, three, sir," I answered back "I think".

"He's OK. Let's play ball," yelled the ref.

My teammates picked me up and I got into the next huddle. I was the quarterback. Still stunned and not knowing where I was, I called a play. "Twenty–five sweep, on three," I said.

"What?" my teammates said. "We haven't done that play since our first practice."

"I said, twenty-five sweep, on three." We broke huddle." Break".

When the center snapped the football, the halfback, the fullback, and my whole team ran the end sweep to the right side of the field — everyone except me, that is. I reached over to give the ball to the halfback, but he was too far away from me, so I kept the ball.

It felt like I was in slow motion. Instead of handing the ball off, I turned and ran around the opposite direction. I still had the ball as I rounded the other side and crossed the line of scrimmage.

Bam! I was hit hard and knocked out of bounds.

"I can see a big red spot, and that's it," the sergeant said.

I would have been seriously wounded that night if it weren't for that tightened poncho liner and who knows what else.

Our squad leader calmed down the wounded G.I. and then asked, "Is everyone else OK? Did anyone else get hit?" No one had.

I kept playing out those events in my mind repeatedly trying to figure out the truth. What caused the explosion? Years later, I would be told that is a symptom of PTSD. You constantly think about the situation in your mind. You recall every second, every event. That anxiety may creep in years later when you have a confrontation, a stressful situation. A divorce may cause it or a death in the family or a job loss. I found a way to cope and that was through prayer and learning to go to recovery meeting or reach out to someone who can help you.

★　　★　　★　　★

Apparently, Charlie had placed a booby trap on the other side of the canal about twenty feet away from our ambush site. We were either really lucky or blessed by God's intervention because, we didn't set up walk on that side of the canal.

Evidence in the light of day suggested that a big Vietnamese rat was scampering down the rice-paddy dike when he tripped the booby-trap wire. The mine detonated, throwing shrapnel, dirt and rat parts everywhere. Poor Rat!

Day by day my tour was coming to an end. I only had three months left before I would come home.

The next month, my company commander allowed me and two other short-timers not to go out on ambushes or patrol anymore. He ordered us to guard the base-camp perimeter.

Okay, so here I am with only two the soldiers in Vietnam guarding our side of the perimeter. Alpha Company guarded the other side of the perimeter with 115 men.

We had constant guard duty all night long so, we slept during the day. Thank God the other side of our perimeter had men a few feet away. Charlie could have easily overrun us, but didn't.

I last days in Nam were frightful. The fear was so overwhelming at night, so positioned eight Claymore mines in front of my nighttime position. I reinforced my bunker against the enemy with extra ammo, hand grenades, and flares.

Fear gripped me like a suit of armor. I had to be ready for anything, at any time.

Every night was a day last lasted an eternity.

★ ★ ★ ★

CHAPTER 20: CALIFORNIA DREAMIN – THE MAMA'S AND THE PAPPA'S

Two weeks before I was to leave home for home intelligence told us Charlie was planning to attack our position. A thousand NVA was reported to overthrow our position.

"Oh, shit" I', going to be killed. My number was approaching fast.

That day I re-supported my position with another ten Claymore mines and ammo.

I had twenty-two Claymore mines in front of my position. If I was going to die I would be prepared.

On the very next day, in the afternoon, our base camp got pounded by mortar rounds. I heard the first two hit the outside of our perimeter. Ka-plunk, Ka- plunk, Ka- plunk. They were hitting the dirt and mud. Each round started getting closer and closer to my position.

Instead of watching the rounds I decided to get inside the bunker.

Just as I entered the bunker another round landed ten feet away. The next one would be on me. Shrapnel flew into my bunker and sprayed dirt all over me.

A couple minutes later, the mortar rounds stopped.

I listened and waited until it was all clear before I came outside. I grabbed my M-16 and waited.

I stayed up all day and night waiting and waiting for Charlie, but he never came.

The next day was Sunday. Sunday was a day for the Catholic priest to share with us a mass and Holy Communion. I anxiously waited for him to arrive as I was in a state of panic and anxiety. I needed something my body was shaking with fear.

But, that Sunday would be different alright. Our Chaplin had a day off.

It was just before chow time, around four in the afternoon, when I heard the sounds of a motor boat engine revving up in the river. I walked over toward the river edge and couldn't believe my eyes.

I saw a sand pan in the water boat in the middle of the river and a soldier was bobbing up and down with a wooden plank sticking straight up out of the water. In the sand pan was another soldier reviving up the engine enough to pull the guy out of the water. The sand pan was about ten feet in front of him. The soldier in the water was holding onto a rope that he had tied to the boat like he was going to waterski.

Across the other side of the river was a *papa-san* who was screaming and yelling his lungs off. No one could understand what he was saying, but he was angry. *Papa-san* was making so much noise that everyone in the company came over to see what was happening. Pretty soon there was a crowd of soldiers watching and a crowd of Vietnamese watching, too.

"Hit it!" the G.I. in the water yelled. "Hit it"!

The other soldier, who was reviving up the engine tried as best he could to take off. Those boats didn't have enough power to pull a water skier!

Rum, rum, rum, when the engine. It sounded like it was going to explode.

By now, everyone was screaming and encouraging both men.

I couldn't believe my eyes. Here we were in a war zone, and these guys are trying to water ski down an enemy-infested area. If Charlie saw this, it would be like shooting ducks in a pond.

He was also a short-timer. He was going to be shipped back home the following week and he decided to take the risk of getting shot. He was determined to water ski in Vietnam! This was definitely a crazy war. I thought I'd seen everything, until then.

A few minutes later I heard a shout.

"You guys have one minute to stop that before you both get a court martial," captain yelled out to them. "You've got two minutes to return that sand pan to that *papa-san* and get in here."

The event broke my anxiety and depression for the day. I had a big laugh. We all did!

I had only four days left on my tour when the Army sent someone out to tell me to pack my gear.

It was March 30, 1969. I was still out in the bush while most other soldiers went back to base camp. I thought the Army hated me for keeping me in the boon docks so long. I was never going home. They had forgotten all about me.

Later that day a helicopter landed. Out walked a soldier and headed in my direction.

"Sergeant, Stephen Campos. I am here to pick you up and take you back to base camp. You're going home"

I was stunned. I grabbed my bags quickly before he changed his mind. I walked out into the loading pad and boarded the helicopter. It took off into the horizon.

As we were heading up into the sky, I looked down over the countryside. I wanted to remember this moment.

The helicopter banked toward the horizon. I looked out as far as I could see.

I thought. This country seems very beautiful up here. It has green fields filled with rice growing. It's a poor farming community. I see Vietnamese tending to the rice with water buffalo pulling their old fashioned plow. I'll bet they have been doing it this way for thousands of years.

It looks peaceful and serene. But, that's up here. Down there are bobby-traps hiding to blow off out legs and you're balls. There are pongee-pits waiting for us to fall in to cut through our boots, feet and legs.

No, I thought, I wouldn't miss all the excitement of those booby traps, rocket attacks, pongee pits, ambushes, nightly patrols, always looking for Charlie's incoming bullets or mortars.

I wouldn't miss the mosquitos, army aunts, scorpions, bamboo vipers or king cobra snakes, wild boars, insects that crawled on you at night and would bite you.

Nor would I miss the foul odor in Vietnam. I wouldn't miss walking through the villages trying to distinguish friend from foe or the sting of trees slapping me as we cut through my flesh, leaving cuts on my arms, hands and face. Nor the 130 degree heat and the heavy down pour of monsoon rains.

I wouldn't miss waking up every four hours for guard duty, nor the jungle rot I had on my feet that wouldn't go away all year.

I wouldn't miss the pitch-black darkness or the fear of Charlie finding me. I wouldn't miss the C-rations, sleeping on the rice-paddy dikes, hiking ten-miles in hot and humid weather or walking in the soaking rain. I wouldn't miss the leeches in the rivers or traipsing through mud up to my knees.

I was excited about going home, damn excited! Wow! Is this really happening? Am I going home? Really?

Then I thought: What about them, the Vietnamese people? What will be their fate?

They'd have to stay right here and live in this hell hole of a country filled with death and despair, sorrow and without hope. This was a country without the feeling of home. This was a country being reborn yet, waiting for the day of delivery. And I was a part of this new creation. It felt good to know I was a part of freeing a people from the chains of Communism. It felt good. I had accomplished something worth living for and something I could feel proud of all the days of my life.

The chopper arrived an hour later back at Long Binh base camp where things seemed normal.

Long Binh was a big Army post. It was like a city inside the thirty feet high barbed wire fences. I got out with my gear and headed over towards my company command center. I entered headquarters and reported to the First Sergeant.

"Campos, Stephen P., reporting to leave country, first sergeant," I said.

"You're not going anywhere until all your gear is accounted for sergeant."

"I may have lost a few things, first sergeant. I've been in the bush for the last three hundred and sixty one days."!

"No worries, son, the army will take it outta your pay!

"I'll take that weapon first. Make sure it's clear.

Wow, I looked down at my M-16 for a long time. It has been my best friend and pal. It was beside me for the entire year. I didn't want to give it up. It saved my ass many times. It was my security and my life.

"Son, you're weapon" the sergeant replied.

"I guess I don't need this anymore," I answered as I slowly handed back to him. "No son," he said.

I hesitated. I just couldn't hand it over to him like it didn't mean anything to me.

"Come on son, give me your weapon," he commanded again.

Reluctantly, I took the strap off my shoulder and held my M-16 rifle. "Sure," I said. I reluctantly handed him the love of my life. It was like being NAKED without it.

"Now the steel pot and all your ammo and grenades," he muttered.

My steel pot was my fortress. It had kept me safe from the enemy bullets. It kept my cigarettes and mosquito repellent dry. I had used it as a seat and as a digging tool. It had saved me from being shot up my ass when I flew in those helicopter missions. I used it to shave and clean the mud and dirt off my face and arms.

"Can I keep my camouflage cover"?

"Sure. It's yours" replied the sergeant.

I took off the head band around my steel pot and then took off my camouflage covering. I neatly folded my camouflage and put it in my pocket.

After I had turned in all my gear and weapons I felt empty inside, like I had lost twenty pounds. It was an odd feeling to use to. I didn't need these anymore>

I had writing on my camouflage covering the calendar days of my tour. I marked off each day in Nam. I also, had my personal expressions of my personality. I wrote these words, "Thou I walk through the valley of the shadow of death, I will fear not evil". Psalm 23.

I had a Peace symbol placed right in the front in the middle. On the right side it read, "Kill Charlie," and on the left side were the names of my combat brothers, "DYCKES & TIGER and my nickname, STONE PONY". Underneath our names were written," Comanche Commandos."

I watched the sergeant place my stuff on the supply rack behind him. He turned back to me and said, "That's all, sergeant, you're excused."

I slowly walked out of the supply room.

Why had the Army waited so long to bring me back to base camp? Why did they do that? They must not have liked me. Maybe it was because I wore a peace sign on my steel pot or maybe because I was from California. There was prejudice in the military.

I walked over to the barracks, lay down on the Army cot, and closed my eyes. I thought about what I had been through for the last 361 days. I was angry that the Army had left me out in the boondocks so long. I guess they needed me to guard our perimeter.

Yet there was nothing I could do. My tour was almost over.

I thought about my combat buddies Dyckes and Tiger. What had they experienced after I left their platoon? I didn't know what happened to them. I asked around, but no one would talk much. Everyone seemed to be in their own world of shock and disbelief, as they, too, were going home.

I believed Dyckes was already home in California. He had arrived in Nam two weeks earlier than the rest of us. I wondered what had happened to Tiger, I never heard back from him since I left the platoon in July. Tiger was my best friend and I let him down, because I didn't extended my tour to stay with him and the platoon.

There was nothing I could do now. It was coming to a close. My war was coming to an end, I thought!

My mind shifted to the reunion with my wife Renee and my parents.

Years later, I would come to realize that my combat experiences would stay deep routed within my soul.

Two days later, April 3, that special day had finally arrived. I boarded a military truck with forty others headed to Ben Hoa airstrip.

We arrived and got into a long line and waited and waited.

While we were waiting in line, the soldier next to me sadly told me about a friend of his. Two days before his buddy was leaving Nam his squad got rocketed at Long Binh. A rocket had exploded right beside him. The explosion blew his arms and legs off and left him brain damaged.

He was a vegetable.

"Man, this is Nam, anything can happen, even while we're standing in this line, he said. He continued, "Man, all I want to do is forget about this whole damn trip. When I get home I'm never going to think about this ever again".

I think that was the normal way of thinking in Vietnam. War is hell and more, but you don't think it will have an effect on you later in life.

We waited in line from eight o'clock in the morning until four-thirty in the afternoon that day, before finally boarding another Pan American jetliner.

I walked in line with the rest of the men. I walled up the stairs to the top.

I was first greeted by a pretty stewardess who said, "Welcome, come on in." She had a big smile on her face.

I rounded the corner and found a seat. I took out the seat belt and tightened it around my hips. Then I leaned my head back and took a deep breath.

This was the first time since in the last three hundred and sixty-four days that I was starting to feel safe and secure. No one was shooting at me and I wasn't trying to kill someone either.

I turned to the soldier next to me "Man, I can't believe I am sitting here," He turned and nodded and then looked away from me again. It was weird, but no one on this airplane was speaking.

We sat there waiting and waiting to take off. Thirty minutes went by and then we heard the plane's captain over the loudspeakers:

"Men, the runway is being rocketed. We have to sit here and wait until we have clearance. Keep your seat belts tight".

A sigh filled the cabin and then from, behind me came some words.

"Those damn, Gooks, they're still trying to kill us, little assholes".

"We should have killed them all", another soldier shouted.

Another ten minutes went by and then over the loudspeaker came another message.

"To hell with it, we're going to make a run for it, men. Fasten your seats belts and hold on to your caps, said the captain. What can they do to me"?

" Oh my God! I closed my eyes and prayed for help. God help us! Please don't let a rocker hit this plane or have us run into a bomb crater and crash.

Next, the plane started down the runway. It built up speed and then finally lifted into the air.

"HOORAH!" a big roar filled the air plane.

We headed up, up and away into the clouds. The airplane finally leveled off.

"Damn"! I was leaving Nam. I was leaving hell. I was leaving this war and I never wanted to return. Boy was I glad Charlie didn't have airplanes!

I started to relax and then looked around behind me. I wanted to look at my comrades. I wanted to see their faces. I wanted to remember this moment.

When I looked back most of the men were silent in their own thoughts. No one was laughing or smiling. There was no playing around, like when we first arrived in Vietnam. No one looked out the windows. No one looked around or talked to each other. It was strange. It was like a morgue.

Then the loudspeaker broke the silence. The captain said, "Rest easy, men, we are headed for the U.S.A.!" A huge cheer went out again, and then it was back to the silence.

When I boarded the airplane in Washington State year ago there were 362 men in my company. I took a head count. I counted only fifty-eight. What had happened to the rest of the men? Some, no doubt, had been transferred or had re-enlisted; others had been wounded or killed in action. Tiger and Dyckes crossed my mind.

I sat back and closed my eyes and tried to sleep.

I told myself. I never want to think about this war, ever again. It's a done deal and I have survived. I've made it out of hell!

I was proud of my duty. I was proud to be an American. I was proud of our fighting forces in Nam. I was proud to see our military forces working together to fight and conquer Communism. I was happy to be involved in helping the cause for freedom of the Vietnamese people. Someday, they would be free, just like us.

I was proud of my combat buddies. I actually knew what it was like to fight for my country. I had been promoted to the rank of sergeant in the U.S. Army. I was proud to wear my uniform and my sergeant stripes.

I had made it out of Nam not being wounded. I had my arms and legs all intact. I had my eyes. I felt thankful that God had spared me while living in hell. And I really thought everything was going to be great from now on. I would never have another problem!

PART VI WAR PROTESTERS AND A NEW WAR WITHIN

CHAPTER 21: I JUST WANT TO CELEBRATE – RARE EARTH

It took us nineteen hours to fly back from Vietnam with one stop in Guam and a refueling in Hawaii. Everyone was knocked out trying to catch up the hundreds of hours they lost since first arriving here.

All I could think about was home. I was proud to be a soldier and proud to have served in this war. Our military was doing a stellar job in the field. We had won every single battle we fought in Nam and now it was time to let the public know of how our troops were winning the war at home.

I thought about a GREAT celebration waiting for us. Surely, the US Army band would be there. There would be husbands, wives, children, parents, grandparents and the media there to greet us and ask us a few questions about Vietnam. I really was expecting a welcoming home celebration.

It was all for not.

It was about the last five hours before we arrived in California that we all started to get excited about coming home.

"Man, I'm going to kiss the ground when I arrive", said one man

"I'm going to find the nearest bar and get drunk", said another. "Man, I just can't wait to have some good ole home cookin! My Nana's the best cook in the state of Alabama!"

'Oh, yah, bro? Well, you aren't had nothing till youze got

some of my Mama's corn bread and baked beans"! Yah! She got da best here cooking round daze parts!

The men were really getting stirred up, alright. And me? Well, I was thinking about some good Mexican food cooking and fresh tortillas at my father's manufacturing plant back in Modesto.

Yes, sir, we were all on cloud nine and no one and nobody was going to rob us of our victory and share of the spoils.

Some of the men were singing, while others were starting to dance in the aisle. One man grabbed a stewardess and starting dancing in the aisle with her.

"One hour more and we'll be in California men"! the captain said over the intercom.

A huge "ROAR" filled the airplane.

"Aren't nothing! Gunna stop me now! When, I gets a home, me and my girl are a getting hitched", said the G.I. behind me.

"Well, my wife's waiting for me", I told him.

Half hour later, the words of the captain. "We're on our decent men, buckle in, we're a headin- in"!

When the airplane landed there was a huge applauds and a huge RUMBLE. Men were going crazy as the airplane was taxing down the runway. Men were getting out of their seats. They were throwing pillows at each other and playing grab ass. They were singing and laughing.

Then, the moment finally came. Our plane stopped. A few minutes later the stewardess opened the hatch door and let in the cool California air.

"CALIFORNIA BABY! Man, let's me da hell off this plane. Man, I gots-ta to get off dis plane and get me a good ole steak dinner", said the soldier, as he stepped up to the front of the line.

All the men stood as we started to deplane. As I waited my turn, I looked out the window to see what the guys ahead of me were doing. I watched as some men were kissing the ground.

others were jumping up and down. Each one displaying his own happiness as his foot hit the soil.

"Come on man, let's get going. I want off this plane man! It's been long enough. I want to see my wife and my kid's. Man, let's move it!" Keep it movin!

I was just as anxious just to get off the plane too. I guess I was just enjoying the moment, as I watched every man take his turn.

When I reached the doorway, I looked down the stairwell and watched every man's reaction. Some men jumped up and down on the asphalt. And several men did indeed bend down and kiss the runway! Yuck!

And then our joy turned into a nightmare.

Someone mentioned that they saw a small group of war protesters on the other side of the airfield. Everyone stopped and looked.

About two hundred feet away on the other side of the fence were a group of hippies. They were carrying signs, "Stop the War" another sign read, "We Want Out" and the one that was most hateful read, "FUCK VIETNAM" And then they started yelling to us, as we walked off the down the steps yelling at us, "Baby Killers", Murderers" Losers".

That was it. Man was SO mad and wanted to KILL them all and so did the rest of us.

Baby killer? I was no baby killer. Neither I, nor any of my combat buddies had killed any babies, women or children. Yes, there were people being killed. Yes, war IS HELL and innocent people do die.

I averted my gaze, but I couldn't help from being HURT by those words. I thought my war was over, boy, was I wrong. It had just started.

As I went down the stairway and into the base building, I remembered a Christmas back when I was four years old.

I was very anxious that year to see my name on those presents under the Christmas tree. I still believed Santa Claus was real then, so I wrote a letter to him:

Dear Santa, I would really like a new bike. My bike is old. I like it, but my father bought me this used bike. All my friends have new bicycles. I feel stupid compared to them. Their parents must really love them more ne because, they have new clothes and new toys. I always get used stuff and the hand-me-downs from my brother.

But in case you can't get me a bike, I'll take a gun-and-holster set. My brother and I are always playing cowboys and Indians or Army games. I don't have anything to shoot him with Santa. I made a gun out of wood, but it just isn't the same when you shoot somebody. I have left you some milk and cookies. Love, Stephen.

My mother always told me that if I was good all year, Santa would bring me presents. I worked harder on being a saint those last couple of months before Christmas. I always have thought if I were a good person God would reward me for my good behavior.

I put the cookies and milk under the Christmas tree and went to my bedroom to wait until Christmas day.

I couldn't sleep all night. I must stay awake and hear Santa. I just he's going to come down the fireplace. How he got down the fireplace I didn't care!

It was four o'clock Christmas morning when I went to sleep. I didn't hear anything all night long.

An hour later it was five o'clock.

"Hey, Roger, do you think Santa cam last night?" We were sleeping in the same room.

"What time is it?" he asked.

"It's Christmas time," I said.

"Well, go see, T-bone". He closed his eyes.

I got out of bed and walked down the aisle. I peeked past my parent's room. They were sleeping. My day was snoring so I kept walking.

I went by my sister's room and peeked in the bed, "Hey, Cecilia, wake up, it's Christmas," and then continued down the hall until I reached the living room. I peeked around the corner.

The tree had a bunch of presents under it. Man, was I excited.

I ran back down to tell Roger.

"Roger, Santa came, it's Christmas, get up!"

I ran down the hall yelling Santa cam, Santa came. It's Christmas wake up"!

That was one of my best times because of the way I felt that Christmas morning. The anticipation was not to be denied.

I felt the same way walking down the steps from the airplane. It felt like Christmas. I was excited to be home. I had anticipated a victory celebration with bands playing, news reporters asking questions, and people screaming, "Welcome home!" "You won the war!" "We're proud of you!"

But, there wasn't any band. I looked across at the building expecting the news reporters to run out to get our stories. There were no news reporters. I walked forward looking for all the greeters, but there were none. NO one came to greet us. There were NO cheers. NO band playing. NO parents waiting. NO girlfriends greeting us. NO one came. I was **extremely** disappointed. But, I had learned in Nam to hold back my feelings.

I was in shock. I couldn't believe it. You can't image how disappointed I felt. Then I got angry. I waited for someone to say something, but no one did. NO one appreciated us. NO one knew of the hell we had been through.

Well, maybe my family would understand. I would tell my friends about the war. They would be proud of me. They would understand. They would listen, I thought.

I wanted them to know how proud I was of our military. I wanted them to know that the Vietnamese appreciated us being there and helping us fight for THEIR freedom.

The Military Police arrived quickly, as they heard the war protesters, so they rushed us down the hallway and placed us in a long line. The Army is good at making you wait.

I got to the door and looked inside. There were files on each table starting with A to Z.

We walked in and gave them our name, rank and serial number. They found our file and we were given a ticket for a paycheck, a ticket for a bus ticket or airplane, and a ticket for a steak dinner. **That was our welcome home**.

Men who had been drafted were immediately released from their duty. There was No thank you, NO welcome home, NO NOTHING, except, "move forward soldier, keep the line moving". Keep it moving forward".

I received my tickets and walked down the hall and got into the chow line.

I grabbed a tray. A soldier slapped a steak on my dinner plate. Next, another soldier slapped on a baked potato, then a salad, next some bread and then a slice of apple pie.

I took my tray and sat down next to a guy wearing civilian clothes.

"Where are you going?" I asked him.

"Arkansas," he said. He slammed his food in his mouth as fast as he could.

"I got drafted and I'm out of the Army now. I'm free! I don't know what the hell I'm going to do, except find the first bar and get drunk for the next thirty days!"

"I just came out from the bush," I told him. "I have one year left. They're sending me to Fort Riley, Kansas."

"Kansas, ah? Heard, there's nothing there but dirt! "Got to go, man. Got to catch a plane.

He got up and walked away. I never saw him again.

What a way welcoming committee. The Army gives you a lousy steak dinner and then sends you home. Like, it meant absolutely nothing, to serve your country.

Is this the thanks we soldiers get?

It made me angry that a soldier would be getting off the airplane and immediately be set free. I couldn't imagine how hurt and confused a man who was drafted must feel.

Oh, well, maybe he will get some appreciation when he gets home. Everyone will be waiting for him when he arrives, I thought.

Unfortunately, it wasn't true. Most of our families didn't know when we were would be coming home. The Army was hush- hush, because they didn't want the media to use propaganda against us.

I had a year left to go before getting out of the service. Those men were used as a number. From Hell to freedom. It didn't feel right.

After, I ate my meal I telephoned my mother and told her I would be arriving at the bus depot later that day.

I boarded a Greyhound bus to Modesto and took a seat.

It would be a two-hour drive from Travis Air Force Base to Modesto. The bus was filled. I was in my Army uniform.

I was still proud to be alive and make it home while not being mortally wounded. And I was happy to be coming home to see my wife and parents.

I looked around to see if anyone would speak to me. I was the only one in a uniform. I was actually, wanting someone to say something. After all, I had first-hand knowledge of the Vietnam War. I knew what it was like to kill or be killed.

But, the bus was filled with silence. I noticed that no one wanted to recognize me or my Army uniform. It was a silent rejection. People purposefully looked away not wanting to engage in conversation.

"That's okay", I said. "When I get home I will be welcomed in my hometown". I sat back in the seat and waited for my hometown arrival.

I had a secret. I knew the truth. I had lived in a faraway country for one year. I was in a land that had NO freedom. I knew what Nam was like.

Only a combat veteran would experience the hardship we had to endure. Only the men who fought in Vietnam could talk about what really happened there, but most of us didn't.

When I arrived in Modesto, it was the same type of rejection. I walked around inside the bus depot feeling proud. I made a trip to the restroom. Surely, someone would recognize me.

It was the same rejection issue. NO one would look at me. NO one wanted to ask me about Vietnam. NO one would look at me. I felt the rejection and their internal opposition for my war effort.

I called my mother to come and pick me up and waited outside. It was the same outside. NO one said a word. It was like I had leprosy.

Finally, my mother arrives. She got out of the war and rushed toward me and gave me a big hug. She hugged me so hard and didn't release me for a very long time. She was crying.

"I'm so glad you're home and safe now. I love you son.

This is what I was looking for and desiring. She would be the only one who really appreciated my efforts in Vietnam.

I thought everyone would want to hear about my experiences in Vietnam, but I soon learned that wasn't true.

My friends were actually *angry* with me serving in the Army. They were all in college opposed the war. They shut me out and told me not to talk about Vietnam. Some told me, "We were losing the war and innocent lives were being lost for nothing".

"FOR NOTHING", soldiers were dying for nothing"?

"MY BEST FRIENDS FOUGHT AND DIED IN VIETNAM---- AND THEY DID NOT DIE IN VAIN".

Wrong! Absolutely wrong!

OUR SOLDEIRS WERE COURAGOUS—THEY WERE HEROES. They were fighting for freedom, from a country of communist control. We fought to stay alive and each other. We fought so that generations could live a life of opportunity like we have in America.

Casualties of the Vietnam War

NVA casualty data was provided by North Vietnam in a press release to agency France (AFP) on April 3, 1995, on the 20th. Anniversary of the end of the Vietnam War.

US casualty information was derived from the Combat Area Casualty File of 11/93, and The Adjutant General's Center (TAGCEN) file of 1981, available from the National Archives.

ENTIRE WAR

Killed in Action Wounded Missing in Action Captured
US Forces 58,193 304,704 2,338 766
ARVN 223,748 1,169,763 NA NA
South Korea 4,407 17,060 NA NA
Australia 469 2,940 6 NA
Thailand 351 1,358 NA NA
New Zealand 55 212 NA NA
NVA/VC 1,100,000 600,000 NA 26,000
NVA/VC= North Vietnamese and Viet Cong
ARVN= Army Regular Vietnamese
There were an additional 10,824 non-hostile deaths for a total of 58,202.

Of the 304,704 WIA, 153,329 required hospitalization. This number decreases as remains are recovered and identified. 114 died in captivity. Does not include 101,511 Hoi Chanh

In 1968 there was 14,594 US Forces KIA and 87,388 WIA. There were an additional 1,919 non-hostile deaths for a total of 16,511. In 1969 there was 9,414 US Forces KIA and 55,390 WIA. There were an additional 2,113 non-hostile deaths for a total of 11,527

TROOP LEVELS as of January 1 1968. US Forces total strength 409,111

In January 1969 US Forces total strength 440,029

The figures for relative strengths assume then following.: On January 1, 1969 there were 110 Battalions in Vietnam (98 Infantry, 3 tank, and 9 artillery. An Infantry battalion had 656 infantrymen (4 companies per battalion with 164 men per company). An armor battalion had 204 tankers (3 companies per battalion with 68 tankers per company). An artillery battalion had approximately 300 men. Therefore, the number of actual "trigger pullers" added up to 67,600. Note that this was" authorized strength". Most battalions were not even to their full strength during the war, with many infantry companies operating with 80 men. This was true despite the fact that the parent divisions reported being at, or slightly over, authorized strength.

The Agency France Press news release of April 4, 1995 concerning the Vietnamese Government's release of official figures of dead and wounded during the Vietnam War.

Translation from French to English:

The Hanoi government revealed on April 4 that the true civilian casualties of the Vietnam War were 2,000,000 in the north, and 2,000,000 in the south. Military casualties were 1.1 million killed and 600,000 wounded in 21 years if war. These figures were deliberately falsified during the war by the North Vietnamese Communists to avoid demoralizing the population.

Sources:

A Bright Shinning Lie,Sheedan Neil,New York; Random House

After TET, Ronald H.Spector, New York: Random House,1993

Code Name Bright Light,Veith,georgeJ.New York: The Free Press

Inside The VC and the NVA, Lanning, Michael, New York: Random House, 1992

The Rise and Fall of an American Army, Stanton, Shelby L., Novato, CA: Presido Press, 1985

The Vietnam War, Nalty, Bernard., New York: Smithmark Publishers, 1996

CHAPTER 22: EVE OF DESTRUCTION – P.F. SLOAN

After the rejection and disillusionment I experienced upon my return from Vietnam, I learned not to think about the war. I set my mind on having fun and escaping reality. I felt I deserved the good life. I was back home now and living in the land of the free.

Renee had a party for me the next week and invited all my friends over. There was beer, wine and marijuana. The apartment was filled with the sounds of Rock and Roll music, smoke and plenty of friends who all wanted to party.

I don't know how or when it started by I soon began to talk about my experiences in Vietnam. I thought my best friends would be curious as to what it was really like.

It was the first time in American history that some real live broadcast were televised in homes throughout the nation. But, the media seemed always to display the bad. They would talk about men being wounded and killed or friendly fire killing innocent Vietnamese. This made our military look foolish and seem as though we were losing the war.

I started to talk to Paul, "I just got out from the boon docks in Vietnam last week. I was protecting our perimeter and".

Paul interrupted me,"No one wants to hear about fuckingVietnam, Campos". "We're losing the war and men are dying for nothing".

"Wrong, man we're winning in Vietnam. We're winning on the battlefield". The media is portraying the soldiers like we are losing, but man, I was there", I angrily fired back.

The arguing continued and other joined in. "We don't want to hear about fucking Vietnam, Campos, shut the hell up, said Eddie.

That's was all I could take. There was pushing and shoving and then Renee intervened and grabbed my arm and took me outside.

"Did you hear what they said?" Those stupid ass holes don't know shit. They weren't in Vietnam. I WAS. Stupid bastards", I said.

"You shouldn't have said anything. No one wants to hear about Vietnam, Steve". They all oppose the war", said Renee.

"Well, that's it. They are not my friends anymore. I've known then most all my life, but today they are NOT my friends. They are nothing to me, but cow dung.

"Your drunk, Steve, don't let it bother you. Come on let's go back into the party.

'I'm outta here. I'll be back later", I said.

I turned my back and headed out to door to find my car. I needed some space.

I couldn't cool off from that attack on my fellow combat brothers. They would never understand what I went through in Vietnam. So, I started to isolate myself. No one could understand my true feelings. Not even my wife. I started to hate her too. From that day forward I disowned ALL my friends and started to internalize me anger.

I had one year left and the Army sent me to Fort Riley, Kansas. Renee and I would drive our 1967 Volkswagen way across the

Rockies Mountains. I hadn't reached my 21ˢᵗ. birthday yet and she had just turned twenty years old.

I would spend the final year of my three-year obligation to the Army before receiving an honorable discharge.

With my newfound freedom at home I started to idolize the hippie movement. I especially was drawn to music that was sweeping the nation. There were the Beetles, the Rolling Stones, the Doors, Jefferson Airplane, Country Joe and the Fish and lots more.

America was changing. The youth of America was confronting our parent's authority.

Blacks wanted freedom from oppression and equality. The Hippies wanted to drop LSD. Smoking Marijuana was very popular and getting high was the norm while being in the Army was NOT popular. I started hating my Army life too.

I had seen too many things in Nam that I didn't agree with. It was a political war. We were not allowed to win. Our government wanted an easy way out to silence the people.

So, I started to look to the Hippies for answers. There was peace and love in the air. There was freedom to do what you wanted to do. It was cool to wear long hair, beads, dirty jeans and t-shirts. This was the Age of Aquarius alright and it was time to party!

Renee and I filled our apartment with psychedelic posters. We plastered the entire studio wall with rock and roll posters, pictures of marijuana plants, flowers and hippies.

We partied on the weekends, getting drunk and smoking pot occasionally, until my duty ended.

The day after I returned home to Modesto, I phoned Dyckes. It was June 1970. I wanted to see how he was handling his new life. I wanted to see how he was coping with the trauma of Vietnam.

I needed to speak to someone who knew what I might be going through.

He invited me to a party in the foothills in Grass Valley, California. At that time, Grass Valley was known for its hippie population and war protesters. "Sure", I said, "I'll be there."

Two weeks later, I arrived at his house in Auburn. He was renting a room with some college students. Auburn is a gold-rush town in the foothills outside Sacramento. I walked inside. It was a hippie pad.

We drove me to a farmhouse in the country. I didn't know where we were headed until we got there. He parked his car by an old farmhouse, and we got out and walked down a long dirt road. When we entered the house, we were greeted by twenty or so war protesters. They wore jeans with holes in them. They had long hair, wore beads, and head bands.

The girls wore sleek see-through tops without bras — that's cool — and had long braids holding their long straight hair. Everyone wore peace symbols and had beards or mustaches, colored sunglasses, and they were all high from LSD and pot. They kept passing a pipe filled with hash. Someone passed around a bag of red pills — "reds," they called them.

It was odd. I felt out of place. For the first time I felt I didn't belong. I was still in my Army and Vietnam world. I didn't know who I was. I was not a hippie and not a soldier. I was in no man's land. I started to feel like a **VICTUM**.

I sat next to Dyckes not mingling with anyone else. I couldn't trust anyone as we listened to rock music. There were bands playing and everyone getting high.

An hour later, the party ended when someone yelled, "Tear gas!" Some tripping dude thought the cops came to gas us when in reality it was a pest exterminator. The whole group freaked.

"Cops", someone yelled. Everyone got up and ran in opposite directions.

Dyckes and slowly walked away and we laughed our heads off!

That was my last time I'll ever party with protesters, I told myself. I'll never attend another party with those people who don't back our country.

My Vietnam experience has left a burning impression on me within my soul. I tried my best to forget every detail that I had experienced.

I felt guilt from time to time for not being wounded or killed in Vietnam. It seemed I was running away from the fear, the hurt and the pain that haunted me.

I said my goodbye to Dyckes. I saw him one more time briefly in 1982. We would write to each other from time to time over the years but, it would never feel the same as it was in Nam together. Sometimes, I wish those days were back.

I went back to work for my father at Campos Foods and attended Modesto Junior College and started to isolate myself from others except my wife Renee. After the incident with my friends she never asked me questions about the war. I was silently hating my marriage and wanted out.

I would work for my father for several months and decided to try something on my own at a hippie clothing store called, "Berg's Men's Room". That's where I finally found some acceptance from my co-workers and the public. They liked me, and they liked the way I dressed. I expressed myself by wearing the latest fashions. I received a lot of attention. I let my hair grow long, and my mustache grow. The attention was addicting, and it felt good for a change. I had found a source of happiness in a world that owed me a favor for risking my life in Vietnam.

One day at work, a shopper asked me if I wanted to come over to his home that evening. He said his name was Sean. He was friendly toward me and seemed to have a positive attitude toward life. I surprised myself by accepting his invitation even though I didn't know the man.

That evening, I drove my car over to his house and knocked on the door. He greeted me with a big smile and invited me inside. We sat down around a big wooden reel table.

"Where did you get this table?" I asked him. "I got it from the telephone company," he said. It was one of those wheels upon which they transport cables and that sort of thing. "Wow," I said, "this is really cool." He smiled and handed me a silver cigarette holder and said, "Open it up."

I opened the lighter and looked inside. There were twenty joints of marijuana neatly rolled into cigarettes. "Take one out," he said. I withdrew one joint. He held out his lighter, and I took a hit. Then I took a couple more puffs, "Wow, man, this is the best pot I have smoked since returning home from Nam!" I told him. "I've smoked Thai and the best weed in Vietnam. I just got out of the Army two months ago."

"There's more what this comes from, LOT'S more", said Sean.

I glanced down at the table, and there was an impression of "the Zig Zag Man" burned into it — the bearded guy whose face is on the Zig Zag brand of rolling papers. I looked up; Sean looked exactly like "the Zig Zag Man"!

I was impressed with Sean and his hospitality that day. He seemed to want to share everything — his home, his food, his pot, and even his girlfriends. He was becoming my best friend. He was fun and made me laugh a lot. I was liking my new life style and stayed away from Renee. We separated and I sought other girls to my liking.

Six months later I relocated to San Diego in 1971, because I was threatened by a group of motorcycle bandits to live with my brother Roger in San Diego. I found a job at another clothing store. After two months of being alone, I invited Renee to live with move. The loneliness, anxiety and depression set in that I thought it would relieve the pressure. It did for only a short time until I found another group of hippies to party with.

San Diego was not different. I started to get in trouble, because of my drinking and party life style. Renee and I had our final slip up. One and half year later I moved back to Modesto after I received another threat on my life.

In 1974, I moved back to Modesto to manage my father's new Señor Campos Restaurant. I didn't know anything about the restaurant industry, except that I liked the Mexican food! My father seemed to trust me to run the operation and told me I would learn the business.

I worked long hours, which became a key to my social life. Now, I had the money to go out to clubs and party after work. My lifestyle had changed now to DISCO man!

I dated several women for a while until I finally settled on Stacy, one of the Señor Campos waitresses. She was a beautiful woman and I was very attracted to her charm and sexy figure. I couldn't get enough of her so after five or six months, Stacy and I were living together. At twenty-seven years of age, I was starting to think about remarrying and settling down. I was even thinking I would like to have children.

Back at Sean's house again and the influence of drugs I started to get more addicted. Then a new drug entered our party scene — cocaine. A friend of mine introduced me to it, and I started liking the power it had over women. It was amazing to have a small bag with me at the nightclubs. It was the favorite party drug in the 1970s for the rich. Having cocaine identified you with a higher class of people. I found out quickly it was like a magnet that attracted the wrong crowd. Later, I started selling cocaine to finance my alcohol problem.

A year later, Stacy and I got married and had a son. The marriage didn't last. A year later she filed for divorce. The depression, anxiety and loneliness set in harder this time. The hopes of having a family. So, to try to overcome those feeling I continued to set out on a course of self- destruction, the party, alcohol and drug scene. That lasted fourteen years.

In 1980, it was the Disco Era. Saturday Night Fever" was sweeping the nation. There were Disco-Tecs at all the bars. One of my most favorite was Familia Garcia. I was friends with the owners, his sons, who were bartenders and all the cocktail waitresses. I drank and partied four to five times during the week and made it my handout for women. I didn't realize it then, but my life was about to change.

I drove home one night. I had just left the bar one night around one thirty in the morning. My friends and I had been drinking shots of tequila and snorting a few lines of cocaine. I was pretty drunk, but not enough to drive, I thought.

I remember driving down the road where there weren't any light. Next, on the radio a song filled the car with the sounds of "Run Through the Jungle" Creedance Clearwater Revival. The music put me into a trance. I started to have flashbacks about Vietnam.

I was in village with my squad. It was very dark. I couldn't see my way. I heard the sounds of a water buffalo snorting. The sounds of chains ringing as the Papa-Son was trying to hold him made me scared. I turned to run to my left. The soldier next to me opened fired his M-16. I remember the blast hitting my side and I fell to the ground.

Next, I think I blanked out at the wheel. I suddenly opened my eyes just as I hit the backend of the car I front of me. Tires screeched and my head hit the windshield breaking the glass and knocking me unconscious. The car was totaled. I was nearly killed.

The next thing I remember was policeman asking me to step out of my car. "Have you been drinking?" he asked me.

"Just a couple of drinks, officer," I said.

I was taken to the hospital, where I was given a blood-alcohol test and a breathalyzer test. It was more than twice the legal drinking limit. Right after he read the meter, he cuffed me and put me into the back of his patrol car and took me to jail. This my second time I had been put into jail for drunk driving. A year ago I had been cited for a DUI.

At that time I was back to work with my father driving deliveries to the grocery stores. My license may get revoked so in order to keep my driver's license, I volunteered to go into C.A.R.E. school. It was a school for alcohol education.

No big deal. That won't stop me from drinking, I thought!

CHAPTER 23: SYMPATHY FOR THE DEVIL – THE ROLLING STONES

The recovery program I attended, Comprehensive Addiction Rehabilitation Education (CARE), lasted one full year. In addition, I was ordered to attend twelve Alcoholics Anonymous (AA) meetings and have weekly meetings with David, a counselor. We would meet every Thursday, and he would always ask me how many drinks I had during the week.

David was a godsend to me. He always seemed to know whether I was lying or telling the truth. He made me think about what I told him. I appreciated David and considered him wise, because he had been sober for over twenty-five years. I asked him to be my A.A. sponsor and mentor. I realized that I couldn't get sober on my own.

As was typical of me, I waited until the last couple of months to attend my twelve A.A. meetings. If I were to fail to attend the meetings, I would lose my driver's license, so I was forced to comply.

I'll never forget my first AA meeting. I was in the slum part of Modesto, next to the old Modesto High School. I parked my car and walked around an old building that looked like it had been condemned. As I approached the doorway, several people were outside smoking cigarettes. I nodded my head in passing and made my way into the room.

I was hoping that no one would recognize me. After all, I was Art Campos' son. My father's business was well known, and I had grown up in Modesto. As I looked around the room, however, I couldn't believe my eyes. The room was packed with what seemed to be about two hundred people. Every seat was taken.

When I had entered I was greeted and welcomed by everyone. People came up to me and said hello, and that made me feel I was in the right place. I made my way past the rows of people and stood in the back of the room. Deep inside me, within my spirit, I had a feeling that I belonged here. Those people made me feel welcomed and loved and appreciated.

I recognized some of my parents' friends, and some of my own friends. I didn't look at them and I didn't want anyone to recognize me. I was there because I had to save my job, but why where they here? I wasn't an alcoholic, I told myself, but all these other people surely were. I had seen some of them before under the Ninth Street Bridge. Some of them were bums. Others were successful in their careers. I recognized an attorney, a realtor, a manager of a grocery store, and a lot of other people I wouldn't have expected to see.

Later that night I witnessed and felt something strange. For the first time in years, I felt like I was in the presence of God. I remember a light coming from the ceiling. I felt serenity and peace. I also started to hate myself and the way I had been living my life. I started to envy the people who seemed to be sober. I couldn't even picture myself sober, nor did I want to.

In that A.A. meeting, I felt a love without restrictions. There was no game playing, and no one pretended to be something they were not. There was humility and tranquility with most people around me. There was celebration and victory.

That light of love and sobriety stayed with me after I returned home. During the week that followed, I felt at peace with myself.

I knew I couldn't lie any longer. I wanted to go back to church. I needed something, but I didn't quite know what. I searched for God to help me with my compulsions and anxieties. As I continued to attend meetings, I began to desire a different lifestyle. I desired it, but I wasn't able to go cold turkey on my drinking. I was, however, cutting back on my party life and womanizing.

I made day meetings and night meetings for the next two weeks to complete my twelve A.A. meetings. Each time I attended, it made me feel good about myself. I was making new friends, and wanted to become a better person. I still didn't think I was an alcoholic. I didn't know what I was, or who I was, but I knew I was a liar. I had lied to myself, to my friends, and to my family. I used foul language, and I used the bar scene at night so that I wouldn't be alone. I think that was one of the reasons why I drank. I hated the silence when I came home, so I drank myself to sleep each night.

In 1979, toward the end of my recovery program, someone special came into my life. Jackie and I first met at a country bar, of all places. I didn't consider myself country. I was Hispanic! Yet there I was at the Cowboy Club, the local hangout for country and western music.

As I stood at the bar, I noticed a tall blonde woman sitting there with another woman. I was attracted to her glimmering blonde hair and her tight jeans. She was laughing with her girlfriend and seemed to have a spirited and friendly personality.

Before she left the bar, I got the nerve and walked up to ask for her phone number. She told me she didn't have anything to write with, but as she headed out the door she gave me her last name and said, "I'm in the phone book."

After that night, Jackie and I spent every day together for the next year. I would go over to her house, or she would come over to mine. I loved being with her, and we never had a single fight. She was so caring and affectionate. I loved how good she made me feel about myself.

I was feeling really good about how my life was slowly changing. We were getting serious with each other, but I wasn't ready yet to commit to marriage. I didn't think Jackie was ready to get married, either. She was having problems with her ex-husband and her daughter. By the end of the year, she asked me to move in with her. I had to think about that because I was committed to paying rent to my brother while I was living in his townhouse. We spent a wonderful Christmas together, and I was trying to figure out how I could move in with Jackie and break the commitment to my brother.

Less than a week after New Year's Day, on January 5, 1981, the unexpected happened. Jackie told me told me that our relationship was over.

I couldn't believe it. We were the best of friends. We had been together for a year. I felt it was one of the best relationships I had ever encountered. We never had any arguments or fights. We always had fun together, and we shared a lot in common. She was a good cook, a great mother, and a wonderful lover. We had all the ingredients for a good marriage, I thought.

I was in a complete state of shock. Anxiety hit me gain like a TON of bricks upon my chest. I went into a deep state of anxiety. I couldn't shake it. My felt like it weighted fifty pounds.

Those next few days, I drove myself crazy. I kept blaming myself for the breakup. If only I was a better person or made lots of money, then she wouldn't had broken up with me. I thought about my past relationships and how I hurt other women, dating them and using them. I was rotten to the core. I was a bad person. I hated myself. I ruined every relationship I ever had. I had even used my parents. I used my father's business, and I stole money from him. I was a failure to myself and to everyone else. I also ruined my first and second marriage. I HATED MYSELF. I was NO good to anyone. I had become a BAD person.

On the third day after the breakup, I drank a bottle a wine and tried to go to sleep, but I couldn't. I couldn't stop thinking about Jackie. Like in Vietnam my mind was racing and recalling ever detail about her. I had hoped the wine would ease the anxiety. It didn't. Nothing worked.

Finally, I got up the nerve to call her. I wanted her back. "What is it", she asked.

"I need to see you. I have something to tell you", I said.

A few hours later, she arrived at my front door. I asked her to come in and sit down. I poured the champagne, and then I had her open the silky nightgown. I proceeded to ask her the question.

"Jackie, I know I have been wrong, and I haven't been the best person. I would like another chance," I told her.

She looked at me and then turned away. She looked back at me again and replied, "No, I can't do that. It's over between us." My anxiety and depression seemed to release after all I expected her to give me a second chance.

"NO. I'm sorry, it's over", she said. She put down the gift and the drink, turned and walked to the front door. "I have to go now," she said.

We stood there for one brief moment. Then I watched her walk out of my life.

After she left, I drank the rest of the champagne. I was in a deep panic. I was deeply depressed. I had NEVER felt this depressed before.

My mind was going crazy. I was shaking with depression. "Why didn't she love me? For the next several minutes I was in heavy battle with my emotions and my mind.

The bad things kept flashing in my mind like a movie in slow motion. And then I heard voices call out to me.

"KILL YOURSELF," the voices shouted to me in my head. "You're NO good. You're a SINNER. No one will ever love you. You're a coward. You let your best friends down in Nam".

"You're going to hell. No one loves you because you're evil. You're a looser". Kill your-self- you're going to hell anyway".

I need to stop the pain in my head. And then I started to cry. I sobbed about my life. I cried about what I had done to people and how bad a person I was. I thought how could I be so heartless and selfish? I'll never have a decent relationship again. My life was a mess.

The tears kept coming. I wept uncontrollably. I closed my eyes to ease my mind. The craziness was so intense that I started to pray. And then, deep within my spirit, I started to really pray.

"God, help me. God, help me," I cried over and over. I hadn't prayed, since Vietnam, when I was scared of death. I recalled how many times God had saved me from harm. "God, help me, I need help," I prayed over and over for hours until I finally fell asleep.

PART VI: BORN AGAIN

CHAPTER 24: HOMEWARD BOUND – SIMON AND GARFUNKEL

That night of January 8-9, 1981, had to have been the low point of my life. I had failed to woo Jackie back after she had so abruptly ended our relationship. My gifts had been rejected. I was in a state of panic and anxiety, and I felt like a fool, a loser and now the voices of darkness were talking to me.

I was praying do hard I fell asleep. But in the wee hours, something happened that would change everything for me.

It was around two o'clock in the morning I was suddenly awakened out of my inebriated sleep. I was awakened by a light in my room. Something was in my room. I could see the light envelop around me. I knew it was God.

I lay there not moving a muscle. I was afraid that I might be struck dead if I were to do so.

What followed next was quite strange. Something deep inside of me began to stir. It began in the lower part of my stomach and slowly moved upward until it reached my mouth.

Out came the words, "I love you." It sounded like my voice, but I was not speaking. Then it happened again, the same way as before. Deep within my bowel, "I love you."

The words were expressed with unconditional love. It eased

my fears and broke my depression. And then the light faded and it was dark again.

I still cannot explain what happened that morning. All I know is that the words were real. I WASN'T talking to myself. Why would I tell myself, "I love you"? I hated myself, and I only wanted Jackie back in my life, not God.

I looked behind me, but no one was there. I looked over to the rosary that was hanging on my bedpost. It was my grandmother's rosary, which I had placed there after she died. It was made of wood, like the cross upon which Jesus was crucified.

My grandmother's rosary had a special meaning to me. Now it had even a greater significance. I used to watch my grandmother pray in her home nightly when we visited. I watched her pace the floors of the hallway with her rosary in her hands. I always wondered what she was praying for. Maybe she had been praying for me.

Eventually I fell asleep. When I awoke, I felt different. I was at peace. My fear and trembling had vanished.

Around noon that day I attended my first REAL A.A. meeting. I wanted to attend. I wanted to hear how people were staying sober. I was hungering for God.

When my turn came, I said. "I'm an alcoholic. My name is Stephen. All I can say is this: God is Love. I know this to be true. God is Love."

That was my first Tuesday of my new life of sobriety. After that, I couldn't wait for Sunday so I could go to church. I hadn't been to church since Vietnam. I was hungry to know more about God AND I wanted to receive communion.

For the next NINETY days, I attended AA meetings. I made noon meetings and evening meetings. Slowly, my life began to change. One day at a time, I started to like myself again. I made new friends who were sober and truthful. Finally, I found people I could trust.

Day by day I was living sober. Sometimes I had to pray,

second by second, one minute at a time, but I managed to stay sober and work the twelve steps of Alcoholics Anonymous.

Sobriety has a cost. You learn to deal with your emotions. I felt so badly about the demons of my past that I wanted to make amends. I was living a new life of sobriety now, and I needed to be truthful, even if it meant pain from embarrassment. Being truthful open and honest is essential for sobriety.

Alcoholic's Anonymous meetings became one of my lifesavers and my answers to my prayers. I knew I needed help with my depression and anxiety. It became willing to do anything to change and to get help and feel better.

I knew nothing about the Veterans Administration. They have programs now to help Veterans with depression, suicide, PTSD and anxiety. But, in the 1980's the VA didn't want to help veterans. Nor did they have the funds or the programs they do now. We can thank the veterans who have returned from home after the Iraq War. PTSD was brought to light from that war. NOW, there is help from the V.A., thank God!

★ ★ ★ ★

A few months later, my life started to change again. I was on a delivery route to Familia Garcia when I met the most beautiful woman I had ever seen. She was working as a waitress at one of the very places where I used to drink and party.

It was on a Tuesday afternoon that I saw her while she was making coffee in the back kitchen. She was tall and had beautiful eyes. She was around nineteen years old, though — too young for me? No! I was already thirty-three years old.

Still, I was interested in her. I wasn't thinking about getting married. I had dated during the five years since my divorce. I was feeling uneasy, because I had never asked anyone out on a date while I was sober before! But I worked up the nerve and asked Tony, one of the owners, if she had a boyfriend.

"Oh yes. That's Sharon. She just broke up with her boyfriend," Tony told me.

"Well, do you think she would go out with me, Tony?"

"I think she likes you," he replied. "Why don't you ask her?"

It took me the rest of the week to figure out what to say to her the next time we met. I practiced all week on my route so I'd have it down pat. I was driving on deliveries all day long, so I had plenty of time to practice. But the week went by, and I still hadn't seen Sharon again. I thought I had lost my chance and my will power.

Just by chance, I had to make a delivery there on Sunday — and there she was, making coffee! I went into the van and told myself it's now or never. I walked back inside through the back door and entered the kitchen area.

"I saw you making coffee on Tuesday," I asked her. "Do you like coffee?"

"Yes, Sharon replied, "how about you?"

"Yes, I like coffee, too," I said self-consciously. This small talk was heading nowhere, I thought. Who cares about coffee?

"I hear you like God," she said to me as I was still fumbling in my head for the right words.

"Well, I stopped drinking, and I'm going to A.A. meetings," I said to her.

"I just rededicated my life to Christ, and I live with my grandmother," Sharon said quickly. "Would you like to go to church with me sometime?"

I was stunned. As a Catholic, I was always told when never to attend another church. Ah, who cares? I said to myself. I have the chance to go with this beautiful girl. I'm going!

"Ah, yes, I would like to go with you," I replied. "What time should I pick you up?"

We arranged the time, and then I turned around and left the restaurant as fast as I could. I wanted to make sure she didn't change her mind while I was standing there.

"Well, I've got to go, so I'll see you on Sunday," I said to her, once again leaving quickly before she changed her mind.

Our first date was at Big Valley Grace Community Church. I picked Sharon up at her grandmother's house, and she introduced me to her grandmother. When we arrived at church, I was greeted by the friendliest people I had ever met. They extended their hands with smiles of love as we entered the doors.

I was with the most beautiful girl in the world, and she grabbed my arm as we walked forward and took a seat. This feels like family, I thought. Everyone had a smile. This is the way church should be, I told myself!

As I sat at the service, I began to realize that it was God who drew me to himself. I had been sober for ninety-three days and had been visited by God. My life was changing, and now this woman liked me. I realized that it was God who had led me through the troubles of my life.

I listened during the church service, as Pastor David preached,

"You must be born again," as it says in the Gospel of John: "Jesus said, I tell you the truth, no one can enter the kingdom of God unless he is born of water and the spirit. Flesh gives birth to flesh, but the spirit gives birth to spirit. You should not be surprise at my saying, 'You must be born again.'" (John 3:5)

He continued, "How can a person be born again? It is only by receiving Jesus Christ as God's remedy for our sins. He died on the cross for the sins of mankind so that we could have eternal life".

"God created you and loves you, but sin separates YOU from HIM," said the Pastor. "But God, in His great love and mercy, sent His only-begotten Son "Jesus" to die in your place on the cross. God offers salvation to every human being, and we are pardoned because of Jesus' death on the cross".

"To be saved, means to trust Chris, alone for salvation," he continued. "This happens when a person confesses to being a sinner, repents of it, and asks Jesus Christ to save them and take control of their life. Doing this isn't difficult, but it is by far the most important decision a person can ever make in his or her life."

Then Pastor David invited us to bow our heads, close our eyes, and pray with him.

"I want to give you an opportunity to change your life. Jesus said, 'I have come to give you life abundantly.' Jesus also said that 'if you confess me before men, I will confess you before my heavenly Father.'

"If you think God has been speaking to you about your own issues and would like to receive Jesus Christ for the forgiveness of your sins, then I am going to ask you to do something. Right where you are now, if God has been speaking to you and you are not sure if you have eternal life and would like to receive God's free gift, then just put up your hand."

My eyes were closed, and I put up my hand.

A couple of minutes later, as the choir sang "Come to the Cross," the pastor invited those of us who had raised our hands to come up to the altar.

I felt a tug on my heart. It was as if I knew the truth. I knew that God had touched my life. He had saved me in Vietnam countless times. Now, he was making all things new. I got up out of my seat with Sharon and I walked forward to where the Pastor stood.

He hugged me and then said, "Welcome home."

I was "born again." It was March 19, 1981.

"It is through repentance that you can be healed from sin," continued Pastor David. "Repentance releases people from the power of sin in their lives. Repentance brings healing and sets people free. Genuine repentance occurs when people confess their sins to God and ask for forgiveness.

"Sin is a self-inflicted wound to the soul," he taught. "God's remedy for sin is to bring it into the open through confession and repentance. When we come to God, we allow God to purify our hearts. The result is salvation and eternal life", he said, as we stood there.

I walked away from that church a new person. I felt born again, and the weight of sin had been removed from my life after I had placed my life and trust in God's son.

God had placed Sharon in my life to help me find Jesus. I began a new journey with God. I realized he had spared me through Vietnam. I had struggles with alcohol, sex, and sin all my life. That day I was set free from sin with the power of his forgiveness and love.

It took time for me to learn how to live a life with God and sobriety. I prayed every day and studied the Bible. I got involved in a support group called Alcoholics Victorious and made new sober friends.

Sharon and I were married in August 1982. We had a beautiful wedding. It was a perfect beginning and the best day of my life. I thought it would last a lifetime.

In 1983, we had our first son, Christian. A year and half years later we had another son, Matthew, and then a third son, Nicholas, another year later. Sharon gave me the most precious gifts of my life — my three children. I am so grateful to her for that.

Everything seemed to be going so beautifully for us both. I thought we had a good marriage. Somehow, though, I wasn't aware of my wife's disconnect from me. About the fourth year of our marriage, not long after the birth of Nicholas, it began.

I didn't understand, but felt there was nothing I could do or say to change the situation. So I made up my mind to focus my energies on developing my boys' character and their sports abilities. I poured everything into them.

It wasn't until years later that I realized I still needed help in recovering from my deficiencies. All those years of not getting help from my Post-Traumatic Stress Disorder didn't help our relationship. I often was cold, distant, and withdrawn at times. I had anxiety attacks from time to time. I don't think I ever got rid of the hurt and pain of Vietnam. I didn't know I needed help, possibly because I didn't want to admit failure.

I had a hard time learning to give and show love. I found it difficult to focus on one career. I found myself changing jobs frequently, only to become discontent with my choices trying to escape again to the easiest path.

CHAPTER 25: ON THE ROAD AGAIN – WILLIE NELSON

On January 25, 1995, my father died. The reign in the Mexican food industry of Art Campos, "The Tortilla King" of Central California, had ended. I sobbed uncontrollably for months after his death. I loved working for my father. I loved the person he was, and I respected him greatly. He was my hero and my role model.

He spent two weeks in a coma. Yet, I still didn't drink to soothe the pain. I knew alcohol was not a choice. It had ruined my life. I couldn't drink so I had to learn to deal with my grief. I did that through prayer and the friendship of my Christian friends.

I was thankful, though, for the dream and ambition he helped me achieve. My father was able to enjoy watching my sons play baseball before he died. Though he was very sick, he was able to come to the last game of the season. It was special because I knew this might be the last game he came to watch.

Matt was ten, and Christian was twelve years old at the time. They were playing on the same twelve-year-old baseball team. I was the assistant coach.

As the game progressed, the team fell behind. In the last inning, the team was losing 4-2. It was the last game of the season, and the winning team would advance to the championship game. The team needed a win.

In the sixth inning, the top of the order came to bat. The first batter reached base on an error, and the second batter grounded out. Next up was my son Matt. Matt got a base hit to right field and advanced the runner. The next batter popped out to second base. With two on and two out, and down by two runs, Christian came up to the plate.

On the first pitch he saw, Christian smacked the ball deep over the right-field fence. It would have been a game-winning home run if it had stayed fair, but it drifted foul. Eventually, the count went full, three balls and two strikes. The next pitch was low and might have been ball four, but Christian swung and hit the ball hard on the ground. It had good speed and slipped past the second baseman and into the outfield.

Christian was one of the fastest players in the league. Since we were down by two, scoring the two runners on base would only tie the game, and we would need Christian to score in order to win the game. Matt and the other runner crossed home plate easily as Christian rounded first base and headed on to second base.

Instead of holding up at second, Christian watched as the right fielder threw the ball toward the infield. Thinking he had a chance, Christian rounded second and sprinted on to third base. *He's not going to stop,* I kept thinking.

I was right. He wasn't even going to slide or stop at third! Nothing was going to stop him from scoring. Christian rounded third and headed for home. The shortstop received the throw from the right fielder, spun on his heels, and threw a strike to the catcher guarding home plate.

Christian slid into the catcher in a puff of dirt just as the ball arrived. "Safe!" shouted the umpire as Christian slid under the tag. The fans went wild! The whole team was screaming and jumping up and down. They had won the game and the right to advance into the championship series!

I looked over at my father in the bleachers. I could see tears of joy streaming down his face. Indeed, it was the last game he would ever watch. I will never forget to watch the joy on his face and tears in his eyes with happiness.

As the kids grew older and the years went by so did the disconnect with my wife Sharon. Maybe, she may felt my restlessness, as I struggled with many different jobs and my discontent.

So, just as the year began in 2001, she filed for divorce after nineteen years of marriage. My anxiety and depression hit me like a TON of bricks again. I was back down the dark lonely road again.

During those dark days all I could do was pray and read the Bible. I found some consolation in Isaiah: "Forget the former things do not dwell on the past, See I am doing a new thing! Now it springs up; do you not perceive it? I am making a way in the desert" (Is 43:18).

I was in a full state of anxiety and depression for the next several months. I went to the doctor and got some medication with the hopes of helping me lift my state of emotions. But, it didn't seem to help. He gave me depression pills. It was the first time I asked for medication.

In my loneliness and depression, I searched on the Internet for compassion and friendship on a dating site. Obviously, I couldn't go out to the bars to find women the way I did when I was younger. I didn't want to seem desperate. But, I was deeply hurt, and my depression was real.

So, we started a relationship. It made me feel good and lifted the depression for a while. I thought I had found someone who I seemed to be trustworthy, a woman named Candy, who lived in Oregon.

We would call each other on the phone and email each other daily. The relationship got very serious fast and before I knew it I was moving to Oregon. I left my job, my hometown and my kids. (THIS IS DEFINITELY NOT SOMETHING I WOULD SUGGEST TO DO. A person needs to stay still and work through their issues, especially when it comes to making any sudden changes).

But, I did. I moved to Oregon and was married a fourth time. I was divorced for one day and remarried the next. This is insanity!

I still believed that God would work things out for me, but I had to be patient. I found a church to worship in, which was important to me, and the support of believers who loved me.

My life had gone through so many changes. I hope others will heed my warning and not make the same mistakes. Try to work out your emotions, and get help with your loneliness. There are support groups like Divorce Care and Celebrate Recovery. There are programs that will help you, but you may have **to ask** for help first.

Yet, in my search for love and healing I reminded myself, that I had some unfinished business to do, that *with* Dyckes, Tiger, and me.

PART VIII: HEALING, HOPE AND RECOVERY

★ ★ ★ ★

CHAPTER 26: AMAZING GRACE – CHRIS TOMLIN

Dyckes and I had kept in contact with each other through letters over the years, but we had not seen each other in person since 1981. We both had lost track of Tiger after we returned home from Vietnam in 1969. We talked about Tiger in letters to each other over the years, but neither of us knew what happened.

After the divorce to Candy, my fourth wife, I moved to Baltimore, Maryland to live with my brother Roger and his wife Kay.

Several weeks later I contacted Dyckes to let him know my new whereabouts and that I was on the East Coast. It was then that he shared with me some good news: He had found a website dedicated to the 199th Light Infantry Brigade, which was nicknamed the "Red Catcher Warriors" (www.redcatcher. org). Through his contacts there, he had tracked down contact information for Tiger, who was living in his home state of Pennsylvania. Dyckes gave me Tiger's number.

I hadn't seen my comrade, since I left the 5th of the 12th on July 1, 1968, when I was transferred to the 4th of the 12th. That was a solemn day for the three of us. Tiger refused to talk to me, because he could not accept that I was leaving. I never had another chance to tell him how much his friendship meant to me.

I held on to Tiger's phone number for several weeks before I could get up the nerve to call him. One Saturday afternoon, I finally picked up the phone and dialed.

"I'm calling for Eric Tiger Yingst, the guy who served in Vietnam" I said.

"Who wants to know" he answered?

'My name is Stephen Campos; I served with him in Nam".

There was a hesitation, it seemed for a long time and then he said in, Army radio talk.

"Ah, is this Stone Pony" over? Really?

I was shocked. I forgot the radio talk we shared in the military and almost everything else deliberately.

"This is Tiger Zulu, what is your position, over"? asked Tiger.

His greeting broke down my fears about our friendship. It was as if not a moment had changed. It drew me back to our tight friendship with the 199th Light Infantry Brigade. It brought everything back to memory and I started to cry, so I held my breath.

Tiger told me he was the Senior Pastor at Armstrong Valley Bible Church in Halifax, Pennsylvania. He also invited me to attend an award ceremony at his church in November. He held a Vietnam celebration each November for the past several years. I agreed.

During the week before I left to meet with Tiger my emotions were on a roller coaster. I would be driving my car and would have to pull over, because I would start to cry. I was deeply touched by his friendship. I had never cared for someone like that before or ever could. In Vietnam death was hard to handle so we became close, in spirit.

The first week in November was a week at his church to honor

Vietnam veterans. The ceremony at Tiger's church would be my first award since I got out of the Army. I didn't want an award. I was just coming to see Tiger.

The day finally arrived. Kathy, my wife now, and I drove past Harrisburg toward Halifax. My anticipation grew as we rounded through the hills and countryside. Pennsylvania has a beautiful landscape with rolling hills. I can understand why the people of this state still believe in the patronage of the United States. There were flags everywhere we drove. Wow, I thought, there still is some patriotic loyalty and brotherhood in this country! It was awesome to see the American flags waving down the stretch of highways.

We finally made it to Tiger's church. I parked the car, gathered my things, and walked toward the church entrance. I had just made it to the doors when a woman greeted me. She extended her hand and said, "Hi, you must be Stephen." It was Tiger's wife, Joyce, the woman he had been dating before he went to Vietnam. She greeted me with a hug and smiled at me.

"Where is Tiger?" I said with anticipation. She pointed and directed me to go through the door on my right.

I rounded the corner wondering if I would recognize him or if he would recognize me. Finally, I saw him. He was all decked out in a blue full-dress Army uniform, medals and all. He looked the same, but older. He was tall and thin. His hair was receding and had a touch of hair dye, as did mine. But, he was in great shape, just like I remembered him.

"Ah, STONE PONY," Tiger said warmly, as he held out his arms. My emotions were racing. I never thought I would ever see him again. We hugged as if to never let go as he said, "Welcome home, Bro! I got to preach a sermon. Take a seat".

Kathy joined me as we took our seats. I felt like a sacred warrior returning from war. Tiger truly cared about me. He fought side by side with me to ensure I would make it home alive. He was my Vietnam buddy. He knew what we had to endure. He knew how I felt living in fear and in defeat. Yet, we had reason to feel proud. We had overcome the prejudice and the scorn we received when we returned home.

As the service began, I looked up from my seat and saw Tiger. Then he began the award ceremony.

"On this day, we are honoring Vietnam veterans," he said. "Today we are reading off a list of names of those in attendance who have served their country with distinction and valor. As I read your name, please stand."

As the names were read and each person stood, we rekindled our allegiance to the Army and to the United States of America. Then, it was my turn.

"Stephen P. Campos, Staff Sergeant, United States Army, 5th of the 12th, 199th Light Infantry, please stand up and come forward", said Tiger.

As I came forward to accept my award, Tiger invited me to say a few words. I was so emotional that all I could do was raise my hand in victory.

"To God be the glory. This is the first time I have seen Eric in forty years. We fought together in Vietnam. We were buddies. I never thought I would see him ever again. We made it." I BURST into tears and walked back to my seat.

At that moment, I felt that my life was worth all the pain I had been through these last forty years. I never would have found my lost buddy unless I had moved to Baltimore. This was a whole new beginning and healing for me.

After the service, Eric and I drove in my car to his house. Joyce and Kathy drove in his car. I enjoyed time our time together. It was a time of sharing our lives and getting to know each other again. There is a silence that we share together that no one else shares. It is the silence of war, death, fear, and a bond of brotherhood.

Tiger had some similar experiences as I did when he arrived home. His friends opposed the war. He wanted to share the truth with others, but was turned down again and again. But, he found someone who was trustworthy, Joyce. She was a huge influence that helped him to heal.

Joyce and Eric got married after he returned home, but he still had problems readjusting to society. The war had taken a toll on him as he was still living with the memories and fears of the war. I could see the pain in his face as he spoke.

Just before Kathy and I left Halifax, I suddenly remembered our vow to re-unit.

I asked Tiger, "Do you remember our covenant in the jungle, after our two combat buddies were killed?"

"You bet," he said.

And our covenant" I said. "That, if we got back to the world," you said, "we would reunite?"

"Roger that," he affirmed.

"Well, we need to get together and honor our vow," I said.

Tiger agreed. "On Memorial Day, we will meet together at the Wall."

He would arrange it during the reunion with our brigade. They had been meeting together since 1985. He would make the arrangements, if I could get Dyckes to attend with us.

It was hard to say goodbye to my Vietnam buddy after the hours we spent together. I didn't want to leave him again, but I knew we would be getting together again soon.

When, I got back to Baltimore I called Dyckes and told him about the meeting with Tiger. I also mentioned it was time to honor our vow. If he could attend, it would complete fulfill our destiny.

Later that week I contacted my hometown newspaper and the Harrisburg Herald to see if they would be interested on the story.

A month later I received a call from Jonathan Miller the Bee reporter. He asked me several questions and said he was going to do our story. It was time and America was ready to listen.

The following week I received a picture in the mail from Dyckes. It was a picture of the three of us together in Nam in 1968. Now, it has become our legacy to our story. On that picture Dyckes had written a verse from Scripture: "Greater love has no one than this, that he lay down his life for his friends" (John 15:13).

★ ★ ★ ★

CHAPTER 28: YOU RAISE
ME UP – JOSH GROBAN

On May 28, 2005, Eric "Tiger" Yingst and I waited at Dulles Airport in Washington, D.C., for James L. "Dyckes" Dyckhoff to arrive for our long-anticipated reunion. Eric's son, Eric, Jr., an infantry major in the Marine Corps, was with us as well.

I looked around at every person walking by and wondered if I would even recognize Dyckes. After all it had been twenty-five years!

Would he be heavy with a receding hairline? Would he have gray hair?

I called Dyckes on his cell phone and asked him where he was. He said, "I just got off the plane, and I am walking toward the baggage area." I looked toward Tiger and said, "Tiger and I are here waiting for you."

In our correspondence over the years, Dyckes and I never talked about our experiences in Vietnam. We always talked about our families. Dyckes had become a commercial fisherman a couple of years after he got back from Nam and had moved to the state of Washington. He would send me pictures of himself. He would tell me about his fishing trips in the Bering Sea. He would laugh at how dangerous it was to fish in Alaska. I would talk about my sons and how proud I was of them.

Dyckes, finally retired after twenty years in the dangerous

Alaskan fishing trade. He saved his money and bought 140 acres in eastern Oregon. He built a house by himself, piece by piece. He hauled in trucks across the John Day River, up a hill, and made a wood home from carved lumber. It took him five years to build his home, but he finally completed the project.

The home had no electricity, no phone, and no toilet. It was without most of the necessities of the normal world. Dyckes was different person than most. He lived like the mountain men did in the wilderness two hundred years ago. He hunted and fished for food, and he loved it! He knew how to survive. He loved danger and adventure. Yes, that was old Dyckes! He loved adventure and being alone and doing what he wanted to do.

I was the complete opposite. I hated being alone.

Dyckes was a person you could trust in combat. He would risk his life to save yours. He was my first choice in a fire-fight. He was someone who would lead you into safety. He would never leave you behind, and he would always back you up. He was a survivalist, aggressive and fearless. He always made the correct decision when it came to saving his men. Most men would freeze in tense situations.

"Lock and load!" he would call out with a smile on his face as he led his squad on ambush patrol. He would turn to me as he left the compound. "I'll be back one way or another!" he said jokingly. He always had a way of laughing off death. He was a rough, tough John Wayne type of personality, even though he stood only five feet, ten inches tall.

Finally, I saw Dyckes walking toward us. He looked about thirty pounds heavier than he was when he was in his twenties. His hair was thinning and looked like it needed to be cut. His moustache was bushy. He reminded me of the cartoon character Yosemite Sam! He had a big smile on his face. It was like he was stepping half on the air and half on the ground. He walked like he was always ready for action.

The three of just stood there looking at each other while Tiger's son took pictures. We couldn't believe it! We had made it out alive and intact! We hugged. We laughed and hugged some more.

How was your trip?" I asked.

"Long!" Dykes answered. He kept saying over and over, "Man, I can't believe it! We made it!"

"I drove from Oregon to Utah this morning to catch the airplane," he told us. "It took me six hours to get to the airport! I left my house at one o'clock this morning!"

"You're crazy!" I said back to him.

"Well, I was excited to get here!" Dyckes said with a snickering smile. "I couldn't sleep anyway."

We quickly left the airport and headed toward the hotel to get Dyckes checked in. Then, we took the bus to the Arlington National Cemetery, the National Archives, and the Smithsonian. We spent all day talking about Vietnam, our friendship, and the joy of being together again. The world seemed to stand still that day.

We were so excited that we stayed up talking all night. The next day was Memorial Day. It was the day we would meet the newspaper reporter and honor our dead combat brothers at "The Wall".

CHAPTER 28: UNITED WE STAND – TONY HILLER AND PETER SIMMONS

"The Wall". This was the place I have dreaded visiting, since it was first erected in 1982. I didn't want to be reminded of this war. I have tried to bury my emotions ever since I returned from Vietnam in 1969. It has taken me a long time to figure out why my life has turned out the way it has. I have come here to face my fears of this wall of stone, this Vietnam Veterans Memorial Wall, to bring to mind all that I have buried deep within me.

I find myself gasping for air as I fight back the tears. God only knows why I have come this far. I never planned to be here.

This wall represents many different things to many people. Each person has a different emotional reaction. To me, this wall represents the reality of a life, a person whom I knew, a person who once was and is now gone forever.

The reality of death is hard to accept. Yet, war is a reminder that life can be snuffed out in one nanosecond. It is a reminder that death awaits us all. I question, why does death have so much power over our lives?

This wall is filled with that reality. It's alive with memories and names of men and women who died for their country. It reminds me of my own war and the memories I hold within me about my combat experiences so long ago. And yet, when I reflect on my years in Vietnam, it seems only like yesterday.

This war has taken some men who were drafted and others who had enlisted. From all corners of the United States we came. We came from New York to California and from Texas to Maine. We were black, Indian, Italian, Mexican, Japanese, Chinese, German, Irish, English and every ethnic or national descent you could imagine.

We were called by our country, and we committed our lives into the care of the U.S. Army, Navy, Coast Guard, Marines, Air Force or National Guard. We all fought for the same thing, because our country needed us to defend against Communism and to FREE a people who wanted the same.

I didn't want to accept that my friends were here etched in stone on this cold wall, but there they are. I don't want to think about their deaths. I want to think about their lives and what they meant to me.

I guess I have been trying all these years to hide the fact that I served in this unpopular war. I hear some whispers and voices beyond the grave that say this war was senseless, that we couldn't win this war. That we should have never been in Vietnam.

I look in both directions to see if anyone notices me as I try to hold my breath before I BURST into a convulsion of tears. Everyone around me seems to be in their own world. Many of them have tears in their eyes. Most just walk and look in silence as they pass this ten-foot-high black stone wall. With my head down, my emotions overwhelm me.

The Vietnam Veterans Memorial Wall is set in the grassy park of Constitution Gardens. It is a tribute to those men and women who served in Vietnam. There are 58,249 men and women who were killed or remain missing from the war. The names are etched on black granite panels.

The wall has an eerie effect. It reflects light, such that as you look for a name, you see your own reflection looking back at you. I try not to look too deep or read the names as I walk past the black panels for fear my heart might crush. This is a place of sorrow, a path of seemingly endless rows of names.

This is a place I call "Holy Ground."

The wall seems to extend into eternity. It starts in chronological order, year by year, from the first killed to the last. Names still are added to the wall occasionally, whenever the remains of a soldier who was missing in action is found in Vietnam today. This war still goes on until every soldier is returned and accounted for.

As I walk down the path, I am on my own search for the names of my combat buddies. It is difficult searching for someone you know personally.

The first killed was David, and then Robert. They were my combat brothers and were killed in 1968, the first in my unit to die. We had only been in Vietnam for two weeks. Their names are written on these walls. They are my combat infantry buddies from the 199th Light Infantry Brigade, Charlie Company 5th of the 12th Infantry Division.

I remember David well. He was in my basic training unit at Fort Lewis, Washington. Both of us were in Advanced Infantry Training after just six weeks of basic training.

Robert was extremely well liked by everyone in our company. He was the company joker and was extremely smart. He also had a brilliant sense of humor. Robert was always clowning around, while David kept to himself more and was quiet.

Many Americans still believe this war was wrong. When we returned home, most people in America turned their back on us. They didn't seem to care about the sacrifices we combat veterans had to make in Vietnam. We had to endure combat. We had to endure the elements. Then we returned home to face our own countrymen and Politicians who told us Vietnam was a mistake.

Today, I will give honor to them my fallen comrades. **I WILL NOT** accept that my friends died in vain. There is a reason for everything. Their names are written on the **Masters list**.

As I stand here, I am still somewhat afraid to stir my memories of Vietnam, but I must. It is part of history now. It is time for me to face the demons that have haunted me since I returned home.

I believe many of my Vietnam combat buddies struggled with the same thing I did. I found it hard to trust people. This caused me to withdraw into my own world of self- destruction. I distanced myself and didn't care about the feelings of others. I used alcohol and marijuana after I returned home. It helped me escape temporally from my inner demons, but later contributed to enslaving me into bondage. The drinking caused me more emotional problems and I ended up hating myself. It altered my perception of reality and stole my self- worth.

It took me years to find recovery from my drinking problems. Then I had to learn to deal with another set of problems, my ego in order to stay sober.

The fact is the deaths of David and Robert and every soldier changed our counties future. I believe America is a stronger nation, because of their sacrifices.

The book is really about life, death and rebirth. I believe it is important to honor those who have sacrificed so that we may continue to enjoy our freedom.

So, here we are now. It has been thirty-seven years. It is time to say "Thank you for your sacrifices and Welcome home! Welcome home, Vietnam veterans!"

The next day, Sunday, we got up early. We hadn't slept all night anyway. The three of us had talked until six o'clock in the morning. At nine o'clock, we ate breakfast. Then we boarded the Metro to downtown Washington.

We wore our Army jungle fatigues along with our medals. We felt proud to wear our uniforms again. We walked all over Washington and then headed to the World War II Memorial.

Kathy, who is my wife now and my brother Roger, took several pictures.

We were on a mission and it was awaiting and still ahead of us. We walked slowly but deliberately. Five hundred feet ahead was the Wall. I gazed at my image in the reflecting pool in front of the Lincoln Memorial. I was standing close by the platform where "Forrest Gump" had looked out and told his story to thousands of people who had gathered to protest the war. I, too, was a part of this history.

As we approached the Vietnam Memorial, we were greeted by Jonathan, the reporter from the Bee. Jonathan introduced himself to us, and I introduced myself and the other guys.

"Hi, I'm Stephen," I said as I shook Jonathan's hand. "This is Dyckes, and this is Tiger."

"Nice to meet you," Jonathan said. "I'm going to be doing the story on you,"

Jonathan told us he was there to take pictures and would follow us around and take notes. Our story would be placed in the front pages of my hometown newspaper the following day, Memorial Day.

It made me feel proud that someone wanted to hear our story. Finally, I wanted others to know I had served.

We continued walking until we reached the statue of the three Vietnam soldiers etched in bronze. They were lifeless, of course, but they were as real to us as flesh and blood.

"How fitting it was to be standing next to statues of these three young soldiers" said Tiger. "When you look at their faces, you see the terror in their eyes. You see their youth and their bravery. Yet it seemed like *dejá vu*. Those three bronze soldiers could have been us, forty years ago, bonding in the jungles".

Dyckes said, "We were once young like those three soldiers standing in bronze. We wore the same fatigues and carried the same weapons. Our hearts were filled with fear and pride. We were well trained to kill the enemy. Now it was our turn to tell the truth, what really happened to us during our tour. The American public needs to understand our side".

"We were ready to tell our story", I said.

As we answered the questions of the reporter, people would approach us, curious about what was happening. The sun was beaming directly in our faces. It was if God was smiling on the three of us.

"There was an entire generation of people who lost their way over the protests of the Vietnam War, and there was another generation or two since who were too young to remember it and the questions they asked us are still being asked today. "Why were we in Vietnam, asked Jonathan?"

Tiger responded in anger" And our answer, now as then, was: "Because our government asked us to help a people, the Vietnamese people, to fight Communism." We fought while the rest of America said, "We want out!" So, who is right? Is there a right answer to Vietnam?

Dyckes responded in kind, "That is my point of view. I fought not only for my country, but for my comrades, and simply to stay alive. It was time to tell America that there were still a few who believe in the faith of our fathers": "One Nation, under God, indivisible, with liberty and justice for all." We Vietnam and war veterans have lived up to this higher calling".

I spoke, "We are happy we had made it out alive. It was only by the Grace of God that we are standing here today, especially after what we had to endure in Vietnam. Our brotherhood is a testimony that, God watched over our lives".

"It has taken many years for many of us to surrender to a higher calling. We were hardened from the face of war. Yet God in His great mercy found us and helped us realize the importance of His love. Without Christ's love and sacrifice we would be nothing. Our lives wouldn't make any sense" said Tiger.

Dyckles said, "We have come to set the record straight, to tell the truth about Vietnam. We had come to honor our vow and give honor to our brothers who fought beside us and who gave their lives for this cause."

"It's time", said Tiger. He motioned us to walk together as we searched for our deceased combat brothers.

It was an emotional and slow walk. We took our time to honor those who gave their lives. We kept searching for our friends' names among the 58,000-plus names of those who were killed in action.

"The Wall" is black, but it reflects your own image as you look at it. It is an eerie feeling: Your name is not on that Wall, and yet you become part of that Wall. You see your image, alive and well, as you stare at the names those who died alongside you — those who died for you. It makes you aware that you stand on "Holy Ground".

You can find the names several ways. There is a register at both ends of the memorial that contains the names of every man or woman who died and the year in which they were killed. There were pages and pages of names in alphabetical order. The names on the Wall appear according to the year of death.

"The Wall" puts it all in perspective. The majority of these 58,000-plus names belonged to young men nineteen to twenty-one years old. Most had families waiting back home for them to return. Some were married; some had children. Many were teenagers just out of high school or college. We came to "the Wall" to honor them. We owe them our lives. We owe them our thanks. They left us way too soon, but God needed them in his kingdom. They are treasures of the unspoken world. They are in a land now with no pain. We hope to see them again when we die.

We are thankful that we knew them. Our hearts go out to their parents and love ones who still feel their sorrow and have their own scares of disappointment. Death remains ahead for us who are in the land of the living. We will all have to pass the curse, and then we will be free. Their spirits remain in our memory.

Tiger said, "Their names should be close together. It was on the same day they were killed.

"I found them", said Dyckes. He turned and spoke to Jonathan.

"Two of our combat brothers, David and Robert, lost their lives first. We had only been in country for less than three weeks.

"I found Peter's name on the wall also, I said. Peter was killed around September 1968. He and I had been transferred together from the 5th of the 12th to the 4th of the 12th. He was the grenade launcher who inexplicably was asked to walk point and got killed during our incursion into Cambodia. I helped carry his body a mile over rugged territory and in the mud back to our command post.

Dyckes placed his fingers over the name of Robert. We spontaneously knelt as Dyckes ran his fingers over his name. Everything fell silent; you could almost hear your own heartbeat. Dyckes's fingers kept scrolling over each letter like he was reading Braille.

Jonathan broke the silence. "How are you feeling right now?"

"No one knows the truth about what happened. They have no concept was it was like," Dyckes said, his voice trembling. He put his arms over his face and began to weep. I stretched out my hands and placed it on his shoulder. "It's OK, Jim," I said. "It's OK, let it go."

Dyckes turned to me and said, "I can't help it! I just can't hold it back any longer!" Dyckes held back the tears. "It was odd," Dyckes said. "Just before Robert was killed, I took some pictures of him. I brought them with me today. I don't remember why I took those pictures that day, but here we are, and here is his name on the wall. He was my friend". Dyckes put his hands over his face and sobbed.

Silence consumed the area where we were kneeling. It seemed

to last forever as we recalled the men and what they meant. Each in his own way.

Tiger, whispered, "Let's stretch out our hands together and touch their names," Tiger suggested. The three of us knelt there, our fingers against the slate stone.

"This day will be remembered for eternity" professed Tiger.

Then, Dyckes reached in his pocket and pulled out a picture.

"I had this picture of Robert. I brought this all the way from Oregon".

Then, he placed the picture of Robert at the base of the Wall near his name.

It was his way of saying goodbye.

Next, we stood together and looked at each other, and then we hugged and smiled.

"I never dreamed this would be possible," I said to Tiger at one point. "It has been forty years, and I am standing here with the two people I trust the most with my life.

"I am honored to be your friend, and I am honored you feel the same way as I do." Stone Pony," said Tiger.

"Man, I wouldn't change a thing". If I had to do it all over again I would" said Dyckes.

"I feel like today we have been chosen to represent all Vietnam veterans who served in this unpopular war.

I spoke; "It's time to heal and let go of the demons of this war. We veterans can finally be proud to have served our country in a time of need. WE DON'T HAVE TO HIDE BEHIND THIS WALL ANY LONGER."

"I can say now WITH PRIDE. I am proud to be called an American. I am proud to have severed in the US Army and to be called a "Grunt" a soldier. For I am a Vietnam Veteran".

"My command is this: love each other as I have loved you. Greater love has no man than this, that he lay down his life for his friends." You are my friends if you do what I command. I

no longer call you servants, because a servant does not know his master's business. Instead, I have called you friends, for everything I learned from my Father I have made know to you. You did not choose me, but I chose you and appointed you to go and bear fruit-fruit that will last. Then the Father will give you whatever you ask in my name. Love one another." John 15:13

In loving memory of my best friend
And fellow combat brother.
Eric "Tiger" Yingst
1947- December 8, 2007

Our Reunion

The Wall

☆ ☆ ☆ ☆

IX: STEPS TO RECOVERY:

CHAPTER 30: ALL YOU NEED IS LOVE – THE BEATLES

Principles in Healing and Recovery

I want the reader to understand, that I am not a counselor, nor do I have a degree in counseling, nor am I educated in the field of Post-Traumatic Stress Disorder. I am not a doctor. I do not work in the Healthcare industry. I do not claim any responsibility that what you are about to read will be a cure for PTSD or other self-destructive habits..

What I do claim is that I was able to overcome my dysfunctions, addictions and anxiety through certain lessons that I put into practice through the years. These lessons have contributed to provide me and my love ones a better life and have helped me to live a life of sobriety.

I can tell you these principles I have practiced have given me peace, that has contributed to my happiness and sobriety.

I have written this guide with the hope that you too can find inner peace after experiencing PTSD and other self-destructive habits, with the hopes of you obtaining more productive and better quality of life.

What should I do if I have symptoms of PTSD?

PTSD symptoms usually start soon after the traumatic event. But for some people, they may not happen until months or years after the trauma. Symptoms may come and go over many years. So, you should keep track of your symptoms and talk to someone you trust about them.

If you have symptoms that last longer than 4 weeks, cause you great distress, or disrupt your work or home life, you probably have PTSD. You should seek professional help from a doctor or counselor.

Survival

You learned to survive in combat or your stressful situation and you will learn to survive in civilian life. There are many changes that will occur throughout your life. But, be of good courage. You can find help, but, for now you need to take ONE step at a time.

The things I've learned in my life I am passing on to you. I have been clean and sober since 1982. Staying sober has been a KEY factor in helping me deal with my PTSD and anxiety. I have found peace and serenity by ACCEPTING my circumstances and working through my issues.

STEPS TO RECOVERY- What I did to overcome addiction

WARNING---**DO NOT PROCASTINATE—OR** it will hinder your growth to recovery.

1. **START PRAYING TO GOD.**
   - When you first get up, set a time each morning alone, find a quiet place.

   ASK God to help you.
   - At the end of the day, before you go to bed **BE THANKFUL** for all things.
   - ASK **God for forgiveness**- for **yourself** and **for others.**
   - Be **KIND** TO OTHERS.
   - Treat others the way you want to be treated.

- Love one another, for LOVE covers a multitude of sins. 1Peter 4:8

2. READ, the bible, DAILY, start in Psalms.
- You must change your thinking, "Stinking Thinking", we call it.
- The bible WILL change your thinking, if you allow it.
- THINK about good things; that are lovely, holy, pure, acceptable, admirable, praise worthy, noble and right. Let your mind dwell (THINK) on these things.
- Be angry, but do not sin. Do not let the sun go down on your anger.
- Go to church. Find a place you feel the spirit of love surround you.
- FEED YOUR SPIRIT by listening to Christian music, DAY and NIGHT.

3. GET HELP- to overcome your addictions.
- You must make getting sober your NUMBER ONE PRIORITY or it will not let you heal.

Drinking or using WILL feed your anxiety and depression and anger. It will give you a victim mentality.

In order to be FREE you need to FEED your spirit.

- GO to your local V.A., attend meetings; Alcoholics Anonymous or Celebrate Recovery programs. The meetings will help!
- ATTEND 90 MEETINGS in 90 DAYS. WORK THE STEPS!
- ASK FOR HELP, find someone you can trust to help you

1. What are you doing to fill the void of friendship or the sense of belonging to a group? Are you hanging with the right group, person or the one's that seem to get you into trouble?

2. Do you feel alienated or want to withdraw from others or love ones? Do you feel you want to be left alone? Do you think no one understands your feelings? Do you avoid talk that makes you feel uncomfortable?

3. Do you get angry or irritated over simple things? Do you want your way most of the time? Are you stubborn? Do you feel not in control of your life? Do have a problem with mood swings?

4. Do you feel anxious, tired or depressed? Is it hard to concentrate on your job relationship or task at hand? Do you feel confused and want to do too many things at once?

These may be signs that you have PTSD or other issues. Now, WHAT can you do about it?

WHAT I DID WRONG

When, I first got home from war I wanted to forget about the things I had experienced. Many things that had happened had angered me DEEP inside.

I had seen things in combat, experienced death and decisions by our own military, as well as mistakes that caused people to lose their lives. I was angry about those things as well. But, I didn't say anything. I couldn't, because my job was to try to stay alive.

When I got home all I wanted to do was forget about all I had seen. I purposefully decided to just have fun and not deal with my issues. I was free from war and tribulation and nothing could stop me from experiencing life and having fun.

In public, I partied and drank with my friends and acted like nothing was wrong. But, when I was alone I was confused, withdrawn and in denial. Those that suffered were the ones closest to me who was my wife and family.

I mistreated my wife and abuse her and took out my frustration on her, until we finally separated for good. I continued to party with my friends and took drugs. I tried to fit in, but I felt like a square peg in a round hole.

And the cycle continued for another 14 years until I hit rock bottom. I went from job to job, relationship to relationship, only thinking about MY needs, because I wasn't sure what I wanted in life.

I had daily nightmares about my combat experiences when I returned home. It took a long time before those got fewer and fewer. But, the drinking and partying got worse, UNTIL, I almost killed myself.

I was addicted to alcohol, sex and had many dysfunctions. I drank daily and partied daily.

So, maybe you are not where I was YET, but you know you have a problem and aren't willing to admit. But, realize one thing; you picked up this book because you aren't happy with the way things are. Maybe you're struggling to find yourself. Maybe you have hurt the ones you love and didn't want to.

The reason just doesn't matter.

THE FIRST STEP TO HEALING- is to ADMIT that you have a problem. Once you admit you have a problem you are on the road to getting help and success.

FOUR SPIRITUAL LAWS
Just as there are physical laws that govern
the physical universe, so are there spiritual laws
that govern your relationship with God.

LAW 1
God loves you and offers a wonderful plan for your life.
God's Love
"God so loved the world that He gave His one and
only Son, that whoever believes in Him shall not
perish but have eternal life" (John 3:16, NIV).
God's Plan
[Christ speaking] "I came that they might have
life, and might have it abundantly" [that it might
be full and meaningful] (John 10:10).
Why is it that most people are not
experiencing that abundant life?
Because...

LAW 2
Man is sinful and separated from God.
Therefore, he cannot know and experience
God's love and plan for his life.
Man is Sinful
"All have sinned and fall short of the
glory of God" (Romans 3:23).
Man was created to have fellowship with God; but, because of
his own stubborn self-will, he chose to go his own independent
way and fellowship with God was broken.
This self-will, characterized by an attitude of active rebellion or
passive indifference, is an evidence of what the Bible calls sin.
Man Is Separated
"The wages of sin is death" [spiritual
separation from God] (Romans 6:23).

SIN separates us from God

This diagram illustrates that God is holy and man is sinful. A great gulf separates the two. The arrows illustrate that man is continually trying to reach God and the abundant life through his own efforts, such as a good life, philosophy, or religion
-but he inevitably fails.
The third law explains the only way to bridge this gulf...

LAW 3
Jesus Christ is God's only provision for man's sin. Through Him you can know and experience God's love and plan for your life.
He Died In Our Place
"God demonstrates His own love toward us, in that while we were yet sinners, Christ died for us" (Romans 5:8).
He Rose from the Dead
"Christ died for our sins... He was buried... He was raised on the third day, according to the Scriptures... He appeared to Peter, then to the twelve. After that He appeared to more than five hundred..." (1 Corinthians 15:3-6).
He Is the Only Way to God
"Jesus said to him, 'I am the way, and the truth, and the life; no one comes to the Father but through Me'" (John 14:6).
God has bridged the gap

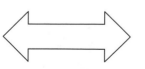

This diagram illustrates that God has bridged the gulf that separates us from Him by sending His Son, Jesus Christ, to die on the cross in our place to pay the penalty for our sins.
It is not enough just to know these three laws...

LAW 4
We must individually receive Jesus Christ as Savior and Lord; then we can know and experience God's love and plan for our lives.
We Must Receive Christ

"As many as received Him, to them He gave the right to become children of God, even to those who believe in His name" (John 1:12).

We Receive Christ Through Faith

"By grace you have been saved through faith; and that not of yourselves, it is the gift of God; not as result of works that no one should boast" (Ephesians 2:8,9).

When We Receive Christ, We Experience a New Birth
(Read John 3:1-8.)

We Receive Christ Through Personal Invitation

[Christ speaking] "Behold, I stand at the door and knock; if any one hears My voice and opens the door, I will come in to him" (Revelation 3:20). Receiving Christ involves turning to God from self (repentance) and trusting Christ to come into our lives to forgive our sins and to make us what He wants us to be. Just to agree **intellectually** that Jesus Christ is the Son of God and that He died on the cross for our sins is not enough. Nor is it enough to have an **emotional** experience. We receive Jesus Christ by **faith**, as an act of the **will**.

<u>There are TWO kinds of lives</u>:
Self-Directed Life
S-Self is on the throne

✝-Christ is outside the life

•-Interests are directed by self, often resulting in discord and frustration

Christ-Directed Life
✝-Christ is in the life and on the throne
S-Self is yielding to Christ,
resulting in harmony with God's plan
•-Interests are directed by Christ,
resulting in harmony with God's plan

Which circle best represents your life?
Which circle would you like to have represent your life?

The following explains how you can receive Christ:

You Can Receive Christ Right Now by Faith Through Prayer
(Prayer is talking with God)
God knows your heart and is not so concerned with your
words as He is with the attitude
of your heart. The following is a suggested prayer:
Lord Jesus, I need You. Thank You for dying on the cross
for my sins. I open the door of my life and receive You as my
Savior and Lord. Thank You for forgiving my sins and giving
me eternal life.
Take control of the throne of my life. Make me
the kind of person You want me to be.

Does this prayer express the desire of your heart? If it does, I
invite you to pray this
prayer right now, and Christ will come into your life,
as He promised and you WILL be Born Again.
Next, it is important to find a local church
that will help you grow spiritually.
READ, the bible daily, pray and BE SOBER minded.
Rid yourself of anything that makes you stumble.

Find a friend, you can trust and confess,
as you live a life of TRUTH.

If you need help, then get it. It may save your life and those who love you most.

Lastly, remember Jesus said " I am with you always, to the very end of the age." Matthew 28:20

EPILOG

LOVE CAN HELP THE HEALING PROCESS
The healing I found after being reunited with my combat buddies helped me to be able to accept my role WITH PRIDE in this unpopular war. It also opened my eyes and heart to reach out the other veterans that need help. I learned many things about what "NOT" to do, by trying to deal with PTSD on my own. I don't want other veterans to make the same mistakes. I ENCOURAGE YOU TO GET HELP NOW.

I was fortunate to get help through God's intervention, going back to church and working on my issues to overcome my addictions. I also got help from my local Veterans Administration. They care and have programs to help veterans and their families.

I work "daily" on staying sober by my "one day at a time attitude" and attend recovery programs like Alcoholics Anonymous and Celebrate Recovery. I am currently involved with "The Road to Recovery Fellowship" in Glendale, Arizona. I work the steps!

I found LOVE in GOD- through accepting Christ, my church, with my Christian friends and in my relationship with my wife Kathy. She has encouraged me to write this book. Her love for me as been my strength and a God send.

In December 2007 I received a phone call about my best

friend Eric Tiger Yingst. He died of an apparent heart attack. It crushed my heart to let him go. He continued to honor veterans until the day he died. He leaves behind a wife Joyce, a son Eric Jr., a daughter Rachel and five grandchildren. He will be forever missed.

I still keep in touch with Dyckes who lives in Eastern Oregon. He is retired and hunts and fishes a lot now. He is not married and has a son Eli who is 12 years old. We continue to communicate by email and phone. He will always remain my best friend. He sends me information about the Vietnam War from time to time.

I live in phoenix, Arizona and am still sober! I do book signings and speaking engagements with churches and other civil organizations. I am involved with veteran's support groups and attend events. For more information you can email me at spc@a-bout-face.com or visit www.a-bout-face.com.

★ ★ ★ ★

So, how did our military stand up against the North Vietnamese?

The Hanoi Government revealed on April 4 1995 that the true civilian casualties of the Vietnam War were 2 million in the North, and 2 million in the South. Military casualties were 1.1 million killed and 600,000 wounded in 21 years of war. These figures were deliberately falsified during the war by the North Vietnamese Communists to avoid demoralizing the population.

THE END

THE WHITE HOUSE
WASHINGTON

April 23, 2010

SSG Stephen Paul Campos, USA, (Ret)

Glendale, Arizona 85302

Dear Sergeant Campos:

I would like to extend my deepest thanks for your wonderful gift.

Your thoughtfulness and generosity are much appreciated, and I am honored to serve as your President. As we work to address the great challenges of our time, I hope you will continue to stay active and involved.

Thank you for your service and sacrifice.

Sincerely,

Printed in the United States
By Bookmasters